Sex on Earth as It Is in Heaven

Sex on Earth as It Is in Heaven

A Christian Eschatology of Desire

PATRICIA BEATTIE JUNG

SUNY PRESS

Cover image from iStockphoto.

Published by State University of New York Press, Albany

Printed in the United States of America

For information, contact State University of New York Press, Albany, NY
www.sunypress.edu

Production, Diane Ganeles
Marketing, Michael Campochiaro

Library of Congress Cataloging-in-Publication Data

Names: Jung, Patricia Beattie, author.
Title: Sex on earth as it is in heaven : a Christian eschatology of desire / Patricia Beattie Jung.
Description: Albany, NY : State University of New York, 2017. | Includes bibliographical references and index.
Identifiers: LCCN 2016031463 (print) | LCCN 2016048535 (ebook) | ISBN 9781438463810 (hardcover : alk. paper) | ISBN 978-1-4384-6382-7 (pbk.: alk. paper) | ISBN 9781438463834 (e-book)
Subjects: LCSH: Future life—Catholic Church. | Resurrection. | Sex—Religious aspects—Catholic Church. | Desire—Religious aspects—Catholic Church.
Classification: LCC BT903 .J85 2017 (print) | LCC BT903 (ebook) | DDC 236/.2—dc23
LC record available at https://lccn.loc.gov/2016031463

10 9 8 7 6 5 4 3 2 1

Contents

Acknowledgments

This argument was several years in the making. It was interrupted by the development and publication of other books and research projects, as well as by a major change in my teaching context. It is an understatement to say that it lost momentum more than once. Thus, it is with truly heartfelt gratitude at this happy juncture that I acknowledge the ongoing support of many colleagues who encouraged me to continue working on the manuscript. Special among these good-humored promoters of "sex in heaven" were Aana Marie Vigen, Angela Sims, and Mary Jo Iozzio. I would also like to acknowledge the support of Harold Washington, who while serving as vice president for academic affairs and dean at Saint Paul School of Theology, supported my request for a semester-long research leave in the spring of 2014, during which I was nearly able to finish drafting this book. I would also like to thank the Reverend Joy Simpson and the Reverend Dr. Melissa Browning. Their service as my graduate research assistants while I was researching this text proved invaluable. Dr. Browning also graciously agreed to help me copyedit the manuscript in its final stages. Several colleagues read and gave me much-needed feedback on various portions of the manuscript. They include Drs. James L. Bailey, Young Ho Chun, Richard Deibert, Arland Jacobson,

Israel Kamudzandu, Elizabeth Leeper, Brian J. Matz, Darryl Stephens, and Edward Vacek. I am deeply indebted to the support of two editors at SUNY Press: the late Nancy Ellegate, who steadily encouraged me as I revised the manuscript, and Beth Bouloukos, who shepherded the manuscript through to production and marketing.

This book is both dedicated to and inspired by my beloved husband, colleague, and friend, the Reverend Dr. L. Shannon Jung, with whom I have enjoyed sex on earth for well over four decades and with whom I hope to celebrate life in the world to come.

Introduction

Thinking Eschatologically about Sexuality

At the end of his volume *Surprised by Hope: Rethinking Heaven, the Resurrection and the Mission of the Church*, N. T. Wright concludes that "people who believe in the resurrection, in God making a whole new world in which everything will be set right, are unstoppably motivated to work for that new world in the present."[1] Christian convictions about life in this new creation impact Christian approaches to the transformation of life on earth here and now. Jesus taught the disciples to pray: "your will be done, *on earth as in heaven*" (Matthew 6:10; emphasis added).[2] Our call as Christians includes the call to transform the world in light of our convictions about this new creation. I argue here that this includes a call to transform and cultivate our sexuality.

This book defends the notion that there might well be sex—by which I mean sexual desire and delight as well as gender—in heaven in a healed and transfigured sense. Thus the Christian mission on earth includes a call to form our sexual lives in light of those eschatological convictions. In contrast, the church has taught for the most part that there will be no experience of sexual desire or delight in heaven, though saints might be gendered as male or female. This book critically examines the rationales for the traditional view that sexual desire will not be transfigured and concludes they do not make good theological sense. This book explores the reasons for associating sexual desire and delight only with those other dimensions of life (such as disease, defect, diminishment, and death) that we hope to leave behind in the fullness of risen life. I find those arguments wanting. Why conclude this good of creation will have no enduring and glorious future? The purpose of this book is to outline a cogent, theologically well-grounded, alternative to the traditional perspective on sex in heaven in Western Christianity. I then trace the import of two of its ethical implications for our perspective(s) about sex on earth.

This work joins a growing chorus of theological voices raised in the construction of a new theology of erotic, including sexual, desire.[3] We claim that however warped our experience of sexual desire might now be—and certainly within the desire one can vividly encounter the depth of sin's embodiment—sexual desire can be healed and transfigured so as to bear glorious witness to God. When we groan for the redemption of our bodies, we are groaning in part for the transformation, not erasure, of our experiences of sexual desire. I invite the reader to look afresh at sexual desire, to look at it with "Easter eyes," and to consider the possibility that the eschatological hope in our bodily resurrection might well entail the eventual perfection *on earth as it is in heaven* of our sexual desires.

SEX IN HEAVEN?

Theologians have for centuries imagined heaven as completely bereft of sexual desire and activity. Traditionally, most theologians—Augustine and Thomas Aquinas among them—speculate that we will remain distinctly male or female in risen life, but they retain little place for other aspects of sexuality in heaven. They argue that in risen life while some transformed experience of gender difference may abide, sexual attraction and joy will be "left behind." Though not quite a conviction that has been held "always, everywhere, and by everybody," the conclusion that there will be no sexual desire and delight in heaven enjoys nearly such unanimity.

The purpose of this book is to examine that conclusion critically and to develop a new theology of sexual desire that explores how it is being healed and transformed here as it might well be in the life of the world to come. If sexual activity is one of the most decisive ways humans draw near to each other, "quite physically, quite literally," as theologian David Jensen puts it," then it might well be a key way we draw near to, commune with, and make room for one another in glory.[4] The traditional view denies (except with regard to gender) that God intends to heal and restore this way of relating to each other. But several contemporary theologians have begun to suggest that our sexual desire, as James Alison notes—just like the rest of nature—is "capable of being gradually transformed and ordered by grace so that we are brought to flourishing starting from where we are."[5]

It might be helpful at this early juncture to differentiate my argument from some others. I will not be wrestling seriously with any Mormon-like efforts to make the restoration of nuclear or extended forms of marriage and family life central to eternal life. In fact, my own view is that a considerable portion of the Jesus tradition is almost radically anti-family or anti-clan. With one notable exception to the contrary discussed in chapter 4, I think there are numerous Jesus sayings that reflect a view of earthly conjugal and blood ties that would seem countercultural, certainly in many patriarchal societies.

Arland Jacobson is one of many New Testament scholars who suggest Jesus may have demanded that his followers abandon their families.[6] While he does not think Jesus was a kind of proto-monk, Jacobson suggests that very early on—maybe even already during Jesus's ministry—His followers formed fictive families. This could explain why salutations like "brother" and "sister" emerged in the early church, and why some testified that God alone should be called "father" (Matthew 23:9). Jesus called for a radical trust in the graciousness of God, a trust he wanted to be both experienced and demonstrated by himself and his followers, who were to be completely dependent on "strangers," not on their immediate or even extended families, for sustenance. Jesus's presumed singleness is best understood in this context. Within this perspective, Jesus's celibacy is not a rejection of sexual desire or delight but rather a desire to embody radical dependence on God and the communion of saints for life itself.

My own view is more qualified. I think it is clear that Jesus asked all his followers to see themselves as "related" in his new Kin-dom.[7] He asked some, but by no means all, of his followers to leave their families of origin and even their marriages for the sake of the gospel. But the scriptures also testify to Jesus having been formed within a traditional Jewish family structure. They bear witness to his mother Mary's pivotal role in launching Jesus's public ministry at a wedding feast at Cana and her faithful discipleship even unto the foot of the cross.[8] Such "special relationships" held dear on earth will surely not pass away. Yet, we may find risen life opens us to an ever-deepening communion with an ever-widening circle of dear ones. All persons are shaped (for good and ill) by their natal origins, the family and community in which they were raised, and then too by the covenants (communal, marital, or parental) most forge in adulthood. We can only speculate about whether marriages, families, and religious communities (as socially constructed through marital promises, blood ties and religious vows, and so forth) will abide as social institutions for eternity (though I suspect not). I do believe however that all that is good about them will be preserved, just as all that is evil will be purged.

Defining Sexual Desire

Sexual desire is a visceral attraction to and longing for the specific delicious pleasures and exquisite delights associated with sexual, including genital, touch. It is that feeling, that energy and excitement, elicited by what turns us on.[9] Sexual desire is evoked by what we experience as "hot." It can be ignited by smells, tastes, sights, sounds, movements, and our sensuous imaginations. For my purposes I suggest we focus on sexual desire's relationship to erotic touch in general and to genital touch in particular.[10] I want to focus my discussion on the times when our erogenous zones are stimulated and engorged with blood and we experience sexual desire.[11] I acknowledge (and will discuss in more detail in chapter 6) that human sexual desire is psychologically, socially, and culturally constructed and that this affects and constrains the drives imposed by human biology.

Sexual desire denotes not only our delicious capacity for pleasure but also, in turn, our desire's capacity to and interest in arousing similarly passionate feelings in others.[12] We not only want; we want to be wanted in return. Consider touch: when I touch I am automatically, inescapably touched (back in return). Desire itself is reflexive in this same way. Thus it is constitutively intersubjective. This is why sexual desire must be defined as interpersonal; it is automatically both self and other referential. This is why our sexual desires render us so vulnerable. In its fullness there is about sexual desire and delight a reciprocity that—much like dancing or making music together—requires responsiveness and mutual adjustment to one's partner. Both sexual desire and pleasure intensify when the body catches this mutual rhythm and spontaneously takes over. Like playing jazz together, there is no one set way to engage sexual desires and activities.

This focus on sexual desire does not deny that there are other emotional and intellectual ways we might be drawn into one another's arms. In her wonderful book *Erotic Attunement: Parenthood and the Ethics of Sensuality between Unequals*, theological ethicist Cristina H. L. Traina defines eroticism as our longing for connection or intimacy with the world on multiple levels, sometimes but not always including sexual attraction.[13] Sexual desire is conceived most properly as a subset of erotic desire. Though obviously erotic, all longing for companionship is not sexual.[14] Eros is an energy that draws us toward what we experience as beautiful. It encompasses many different types of desire, including sexual desire. Sexual desire is that which excites a person and alerts him or her to the beauty of the other and to the pleasures of sexual activity, arousal, and ecstatic orgasm, which include of course sensual pleasures as well as the pleasure of being a sexual delight to, of being sexually pleasing to, another.

Eschatological Convictions and Christian Ethics

Eschatology refers most generally to the study of "last things," and in Christian theology, this category has included a variety of subjects: from the last seven words of Christ during his crucifixion to "predictions" about the Parousia, or the coming of Christ from heaven for the Final Judgment at the end of the world. In this text eschatology refers to reflections on that for which we hope in light of the "already but not yet" resurrection destiny God has promised us.

Traditionally Christians interpreted the life, death, and resurrection of Jesus Christ and the outpouring of the Spirit that followed shortly thereafter as the first fruits—the inauguration—of this promised Kin-dom of God. According to this tradition, all those identified with Jesus Christ—all Christian disciples—will share fully in this final destiny, of which Christ's own resurrection was a foretaste. In and through their encounters with the Risen Christ, the early disciples recognized both (1) that they had *already* experienced this new creation, and (2) that this new Reign was *not yet* fully realized. Thus, they continued to pray—as Jesus had taught them—"your will be done, on earth as in heaven."

Within a few generations, however, the hope for the imminent establishment of this new heaven and new earth began to fade for some believers. Their hope began *not* to be associated with the glorious transformation of this world. For some their hope was not for this world's redemption but only for release from the body and escape from this earthly life into the next life, conceived of as a transcendent, purely spiritual realm. In this kind of heavenly place, the faithful soul would finally rest with God in peace. At the same time, other Christians remained adamant in their belief that God's promise included an earthier renewal. By the middle of the second century of the Common Era, these Christians had codified their belief in "the resurrection of the body and life everlasting" in what has become known as the Apostles' Creed. Indeed, it is the development and discussion of this creedal claim that constitutes one of the richest ecumenical sources for material about early Christian insight into what theologian James B. Nelson first labeled "body theology."[15]

It would be a mistake to associate attention to the ethical implications of our eschatological beliefs only with the early church. The explication of such ethical implications is commonplace throughout Christian history across all denominations. While this is not a volume devoted to the rehearsal of that entire story, let me sketch a bit of it. Since I cite in the next chapter several Roman Catholic sources, consider here the perspectives of John Calvin, the Wesley brothers, and Dietrich Bonhoeffer as a sampler of such thinking in a Protestant key.

Reformed scholar Raymond Kemp Anderson has argued compellingly that John Calvin believed meditation on our promised future life together in Christ was necessary to Christian ethical reflection. Calvin believed that this orientation to the fullness of our transformation in relationship to one another in Christ had broad moral implications, including its commendation of the joyful use of the world and its goods. Anderson suggests additionally that attention on the part of men to their future permanent partnership with women in the communion of saints with God clearly brought late twentieth-century biblical scholars (like Robin Scroggs in his groundbreaking work on "Paul and the Eschatological Women")[16] to reassess the status and roles of women in the church on earth. He suggests further that "erotic feelings will not have the same disruptive force if my actions are tempered by regard for the everlasting, mutually respectful friendships" that will characterize the life of the world to come."[17] Divorcing couples may find solace in the prospect of being able to relate to each other in peace in the life to come.

In his book *Anticipating Heaven Below: Optimism of Grace from Wesley to the Pentecostals*, United Methodist church historian Hal Knight notes that "heaven below" was a term used by Charles Wesley in his hymns to describe the present sanctifying impact of knowing Jesus and his love. Though he did not use this term, John Wesley had "his own eschatologically-charged language: 'the beginning of heaven,' 'walking in eternity,' and 'tasting the powers of the world to come,'" to describe what

Knight labels his "inaugurated eschatology."[18] Though not yet come in fullness, the Wesley brothers understood the Reign of God to be already breaking into life here and now. Since salvation included the redemption of our bodies, both brothers not only anticipated miraculous healings through prayer, but they also considered the promotion of health and healing through medicine a properly theological, pastoral concern.

Likewise, Christopher Morse notes in his book *The Difference Heaven Makes: Rehearing the Gospel as News* that Dietrich Bonhoeffer rooted his worldly ethics of responsibility in the already at-handedness of heaven on earth.[19] For him there were imperatives embedded in the declarative proclamations of the gospel. For Bonhoeffer, reflection on heaven did not induce passivity or hope for "pie in the sky," but rather such hope yielded courageous ethical responses to what God was already doing in the current situation.

THINKING ESCHATOLOGICALLY ABOUT SEXUAL ETHICS

While it is most certainly true that intuitions about what is of value in our experience of sexual desire and delight will inform eschatological speculations about their future, the primary focus in this book will be on the implications of convictions about the resurrection destiny of sexual desire and delight for Christian sexual ethics here and now. What does it mean for Christian sexual ethics today if sexual desire and delight are reconceived as part of the life of the world to come? How is this new life breaking into our life here and now? Liberation theologian Nestor Miguez calls this "anticipatory ethics," that is, the practice of living in today's world (as much as possible) by the standards of our hope.[20] While doing so, we echo the call: "conduct yourselves as worthy of the God who calls you into his kingdom and glory" (1 Thessalonians 2:12).

The aim of this book is to explore carefully the connections between Christian convictions about the ultimate destiny of sexual desire and delight and Christian norms about sexual activity here and now. In the end—as my title suggests—my aim is to think about *sex on earth as it is in heaven* . To get there, however, we must first think carefully about what it is exactly that Christians hope for, as well as consider seriously whether sexual desire and delight have any place there.

A fine essay by David Cloutier entitled "Composing Love Songs for the Kingdom of God? Creation and Eschatology in Catholic Sexual Ethics" encouraged me to think more systematically along this line.[21] Here Cloutier demonstrates compellingly that in the last fifty years some Catholic ethicists have begun to shift away from a more traditional way of thinking about marriage as only a means to holiness or as merely an instrumental good of creation. They have begun instead, he argues, to view elements of marriage (and implicitly dimensions of sexuality beyond gender) as goods in themselves. They have begun to see them as goods having an eschatological future and a capacity to be realizations (however partial) of life in the New Jerusalem.

My aim in this volume is to contribute to that shift by addressing commonly held arguments against such speculations and deconstructing their theological underpinnings. As Cloutier himself concedes, many theologians do not hold that any dimensions of sexuality (at least beyond gender) have an eschatological future. He quotes John Paul II in this regard, who is quite explicit: marriage "belongs exclusively to this age. Marriage and procreation do not constitute, on the other hand, the eschatological future of man [*sic*]."[22] Others argue that all sexual attractions, as well as one's gender and familial identities (as husbands or daughters, and so forth) will be left on this side of the pearly gates. Though they might not agree on anything else, and have quite different reasons for thinking such, both conservative theologian William W. Orr and feminist theologian Elizabeth Stuart have concluded that resurrection will move us not only beyond our sexual desires but beyond our gendered identities.[23]

To propose that our hope should include more, that we should engage what Andrea Bieler and Luise Schottroff call our "eschatological imagination" in this new way, could be misinterpreted as escapist.[24] Of course, in some instances Christian eschatological thought had a tendency toward precisely this sort of otherworldliness and it produced just such neglectful acceptance of injustice in the status quo. On other occasions it was used to justify radicalism and violence. Such dualistic, otherworldly thinking is precisely why many feminist theologians initially eschewed eschatological thinking.[25] But my aim is decidedly not to escape this world in favor of another, purely spiritual life without bodies.[26] On the contrary when properly engaged, the eschatological imagination generates a "critical otherworldliness" that can disrupt our routine acceptance of "empty stomachs" and reverse our complicity within deadly systems.[26] In regard to sexual ethics, the exercise of our eschatological imagination hopefully will disrupt much that makes our sexual lives "empty."

Many contemporary arguments about sexual ethics (including my own) have revolved around the doctrine of Creation. They have stressed the goodness of the body, erotic desire in general and sexual desire in particular. They have affirmed that shared (sexual) pleasure can be bonding, and injustices suffered by the beloved become part of the lover's agenda because of that bond. Rita Nakashima Brock and Carter Heyward—both heirs of Audre Lorde's insights—have rightly celebrated the capacity of *eros* to nurture bonds of love and energy for the work of justice.[27] Such insights into the connection between erotic desire and compassion enabled Wendy Farley to connect desire with the experience of wanting to do justice.[28] These are legitimate and important points to emphasize in contemporary Christian sexual ethics, especially since they were often neglected in the past.

However, it is equally important to attend to the systemic, social and personal forms of sin that infect our experiences of *eros*, including our experiences of God's good gift of sexual desire. Since sexuality has often been, and still remains, a locus of oppression, injustice, slavery, betrayal and shame, it is not helpful to proclaim its gracious goodness in ways that do not take these realities seriously. Unqualified enthusiasm for sexual desire can prove harmful, particularly to those who are vulnerable among us.[29] Romantic notions of innocent sexuality offer us only "a precarious and false security," according to Geoffrey

Rees, who proposes that sexual ethics should begin with a confession of the sinfulness of all sexuality.[30]

Christian eschatological beliefs about the resurrection of the body with their "already but not yet" format provide this more realistic framework for analyzing sexuality. Although we may *already* taste of its goodness and grace here on earth, we know all too well that our body, including our sexuality, is *not yet* glorious! This is one way that Christian convictions about the "life of the world to come" contribute to the Good News that the church has to share with the world about human sexuality.

This book will also provide a deeper theological foundation for the cultivation of sexual desire and delight. I was pleasantly surprised to find chastity defined in terms of the cultivation of desire by theologian John Anthony McGuckin. He writes: "In an Orthodox marriage the chastity of the couple is the manner in which their sexual powers are constantly nurtured in reference to one another, and for the purpose of maintaining the flame of mutual interest and delight across the years of living together."[31] But because chastity connotes for most people a repressive and suspicious attitude toward sexual desire per se, which I do not endorse, I am most likely to speak of sexual virtue rather than chastity in this volume. However, it is worth noting here that traditionally all Christians—whether single, married, or vowed celibates—were understood to be called to live chaste (that is, sexually virtuous) lives. The specific shape such sexual virtue took depended upon one's sexual vocation. Married couples were to practice fidelity, vowed religious celibacy, and so forth.

All Christians will profit from thinking about human sexuality and sexual ethics in light of our Christian hopes about the resurrection of the body and the life of the world to come. I am not arguing that this is the only appropriate starting point for reflection on sexuality, or that it is the best. My wager is far more modest: because this is a perspective that has been neglected, I believe that attention to it might provide us with a fresh and more realistic approach to Christian sexual ethics.

Others have recently made similar wagers, most notably William Stacey Johnson, Margaret D. Kamitsuka, and David

H. Jensen. They are all making contributions to a new theology of desire. Johnson in his fine text *A Time to Embrace: Same-Gender Relationships in Religion, Law and Politics* offers his readers a theological reassessment of seven different perspectives on homoeroticism held by contemporary Christians.[32] He notes that at bottom these different perspectives reflect various degrees of emphasis on one or another theological doctrine. He sorts these arguments about gay sexuality in reference to the Christian doctrines of creation, of reconciliation in Christ, and of redemption in the Spirit. While my own project will not be typological in character, I do take it to be axiomatic (as did Johnson) that our vision of God's intended future for our sexual desire should provide Christians with a roadmap for how desire ought to be cultivated and embodied here and now. And like Johnson, I seek to avoid any false separation between what God is doing as Creator and what God is doing as Redeemer and Sanctifier.

In her anthology *The Embrace of Eros: Bodies, Desires, and Sexuality in Christianity*, Margaret D. Kamitsuka has collected several essays that touch upon eschatological views of sexuality, but her own contribution—entitled "Sex in Heaven? Eschatological Eros and the Resurrection of the Body"—is most notable because it focuses directly on the question.[33] Here Kamitsuka reviews brief arguments by Beth Jones, Ronald Long, and Elizabeth Stuart on the questions of sex and gender in heaven. Unlike those whom she reviews, Kamitsuka carefully distinguishes sexual differences from rigid gender roles and desire from lust or clinging. Thus she is able to conclude that in glory we will delight in transformed experiences of sexual differences and desire.

In *God, Desire, and a Theology of Human Sexuality*, David H. Jensen addresses some of the theological issues foundational to my question about whether a transformed experience of genital sexual desire might be part of the life of the world to come. But in the end he falls short of making this claim himself. Straddling the explicit rejection of this conclusion by Stanley Grenz in *Sexual Ethics: An Evangelical Perspective* and its "whispered" assertion by Kamitsuka in the previously cited work, Jensen prefers instead simply "to leave the question open."[34] In contrast I intend in this book to mount an explicit, systematic argument in support of precisely such a possibility. Of course, I too must leave the question ultimately "open." All eschatological "conclusions"—whether they deny or affirm the presence of sexual desire and delight in heaven—are in the end imaginative speculations. But my intention in this volume is to identify many of the biblical and theological reasons why its affirmation might well not only be plausible but deeply congruent with other theological convictions.

AN OUTLINE OF THE ARGUMENT

The bulk of this book—found in part 1—focuses on Christian speculations about "Sex in Heaven." Part 2 examines a couple of the implications of those convictions for "Sex on Earth." In part 1 the first chapter opens with a comparative review of popular ideas about death and the hereafter. The nature of bodily resurrection is described, and some of the problems with conceptions of risen life that leave the body behind are identified. The existential foundations for this temptation are traced through the ambivalence of Christian teachings about the body back to the ambiguity of our experience of embodiment itself. The chapter concludes by showing some of the problems with traditional speculations that deny that there will be sex (beyond gender) in heaven.

The next two chapters address the biblical witness concerning the resurrection of the body in general and then resurrection and sex in particular. Biblical testimony about whether, and in what sense, risen life will be bodily is the focus of chapter 2. Here I review Jewish and Hellenistic ideas about death and the afterlife because they constitute the background for the New Testament. In chapter 3 the focus shifts to the question of whether risen bodies might be not only gendered but also sexual in some transfigured sense. It will pay special attention to gospel stories about the empty tomb, the appearances of the Risen Christ, and the relevant teachings and sayings of Jesus.

Chapter 4 begins with a sampling of the competing views in early Christian antiquity about the so-called "general" resurrection of the bodies of all and, particularly, of competing views about the question of sex in heaven. Augustine, Bishop of Hippo, taught in the context of this nearly chaotic struggle to define orthodoxy and orthopraxis. Because of its defining character for theology in the Latin West, especially in relation to Christian sexual ethics, this chapter traces and evaluates the development of Augustine's theological anthropology and eschatological thought in regard to sexuality. Part 1 concludes with a fifth chapter that is a speculative exercise in the eschatological (re)imagination of sex in heaven. This attempt to establish the plausibility of sex in heaven is framed by the construction of a new theology of desire, both human and divine.

In part 2 the focus shifts from sex in heaven to sex on earth. Chapter 6 discusses sexual desire in greater detail and explores what sexual desire must be like, if sexual transformation is to prove a tenable hypothesis. It will examine facts about the biological constraints on sexual desire and also the cultural construction of sexual desire with an eye to the question of whether, and to what degree, sexual feelings can be reformed. An ethical analysis of the morality of sexual feelings and their implications for our very limited, and yet quite real, capacity to transform our experiences of sexual desire will be explored.

Chapter 7 briefly addresses one cluster of related ethical questions in light of this revised eschatological vision. If there will be sex in heaven, how should we respond to the loss of desire on earth? Should we cultivate as well as curtail sexual desire and delight? In this chapter I explain why the nurture of sexual desire may be an important moral task for some of those who experience no/low sexual desire. I conclude by offering an expanded conception of sexual virtue, one that denotes practices that strengthen and intensify, that nurture, sexual desire, as well as disciplines that curtail its lustful expression.

This book concludes with a discussion of what it might mean concretely to nurture sexual desire for love. Much of chapter 8 focuses on the potential of sexual desire to be cultivated in ways that fuel love making. Important caveats about sexual pleasure—about why it must be shared, if it is to prove to be love making, and why sexual pleasure by itself doesn't really satisfy desire—are also laid out here. The chapter ends with a close look at internet pornography and an extended account of why its consumption is a poor strategy to employ, if one is seeking to embody *sex on earth as it is in heaven*.

PART 1

Sex in Heaven

CHAPTER 1

General Resurrection of the Body

Our question about whether people might enjoy sex in heaven—that is, enjoy some sanctified experience of sexual desire and delight—presumes that risen life will be in a significant (though of course transformed) sense embodied. It presumes belief in what is technically known as the general resurrection of the body. To state the obvious, if you do not believe in bodily resurrection, then this query about sex in heaven makes no sense. Furthermore, if your resurrection hope is eviscerated—so "spiritualized," as to be unrecognizable as hope in the bodily resurrection of the whole self—then the answer to the question of whether there might be sex in heaven would be "obviously not!"

To dive deeper into this conversation, I begin with a delineation of the notion of the general resurrection of the body and also briefly examine contemporary Christian views of death and the hereafter. In the second half of this chapter, I trace the roots of such dualistic ideas back to Christianity's ambivalence about human embodiment. I argue that hope in the resurrection of the body is a faithful response to the truly ambiguous nature of our experience of embodiment. I detail the considerable theological support that such resurrection hope enjoys and close the chapter with a brief word about the weak spots in speculations that deny sex in heaven.

THE NATURE OF BODILY RESURRECTION

Beliefs about bodily resurrection have been and are conceptualized in many and various ways. Nevertheless, there is a broad consensus among those that affirm the notion of bodily resurrection that it must express both continuity and discontinuity with embodiment as we know it here and now. Some accounts of bodily resurrection are distorted because they overemphasize the likelihood of discontinuity with life on earth as we know it. In such a framework new life cannot embody a gracious process of sanctification. From such a viewpoint, creation is annihilated. Other accounts of bodily resurrection are distorted because they stress too much of a continuity between this world and the next. At best, resurrection is merely a restoration of creation or a recapitulation of paradise, as the original blessing is imagined to have been. At worst, it is merely imagined to be the resuscitation of life as we know it. Neither of these perspectives adequately expresses Christian claims about glorification, if you believe in the resurrection of the body.

Like the body of the Risen Christ, the transfigured body must be recognizable in some sense as a personal, healed body. And yet, again like Christ's, this glorified body must be enhanced beyond recognition, even beyond our imagination! Such glorification differs dramatically from resuscitation. Though miraculously brought back to this life, Jesus's friend, Lazarus, was not resurrected to new life in this transfigured sense (John 11:1–43). Lazarus, like others who were resuscitated, would eventually die (again). Like the rest of the faithful departed, he too awaits the resurrection of the dead.

To believe in the general resurrection of the body is to believe that the embodied, historical identity of a faithful person is not destroyed by death. In some meaningful sense, recognizable individuals will be raised up and transformed into newly sanctified psychosomatic wholes. Why believe this? Why believe in the resurrection of the body? This will be discussed in even greater detail in chapters 2 and 3, but here let me sketch some of the important theological and anthropological foundations for such a conviction.

Resurrection of the body makes sense once the body is recognized as central to who we are. People are embodied; we do not merely have or possess bodies. It is important to recognize that human beings are constituted by their bodies. Our embodiment differentiates and distinguishes us as individually unique, while it simultaneously unites us together in the human family and with the rest of creation. For these reasons, a truly personal notion of salvation must include the redemption and sanctification of our bodies in all their particularity. Because it is integral to personhood, the body must be integral to resurrection.

Additionally, it is embodiment—along with all the desires and feelings that spring from it—that makes possible all our social interactions, including our friendships and loves, only some of which are sexual. For this reason, though deeply personal, it follows that risen sanctified embodied persons will not have private, isolated experiences of God. Our corporeality connects us to the rest of creation. Hence, it follows that we enjoy the Presence of God in the company of all the angels and saints, indeed in the midst of all that is. Risen life is communal cosmic life.

For many Christians hope in the resurrection of the dead is joined with hope for the resurrection of the body, since we do not merely have bodies but rather are embodied people. If we are raised up, then we are raised as psychosomatic wholes. And because we are embodied, we are not only socially bound up with and raised in community with other people on earth, but we are so tied to all other creatures, to the earth, indeed to the cosmos in its entirety. As the Bible testifies, all that is—even the trees—will clap their hands in glory!

CONTEMPORARY CHRISTIAN VIEWS OF DEATH AND THE HEREAFTER

The vision of the general resurrection previously sketched indicates some of what it means to believe in the resurrection of the body and the life of the world to come. Even among those who hold this to be true, there has never been unanimity about precisely how and/or when the faithful departed will experience this bodily resurrection. Today there are three primary conceptions of death and afterlife prevalent among Christians. Some believe people "sleep" between death and the Second Coming of Christ. Others believe that the souls of the dearly departed exist in an "intermediate state" between death and the fullness of risen life. Still others believe that at the very moment of death the faithful are brought—as if into another dimension—into the new creation. Let us consider each of these imaginative accounts of the hereafter in turn.

Peaceful Slumber in the Dust until Christ Comes Again

Some early Christians presumed that there would be only a brief interim between their individual deaths and the general resurrection that would accompany the Second Coming of Christ to earth. A number of scholars believe this was probably the shape resurrection hope took among the earliest Christians.[1] Because persons were understood to be psychosomatic wholes, what happened to the body was presumed to happen to the soul. So when the person died, both the body and soul died. The person disintegrated. When the faithful spoke of their beloved departed as simply "sleeping" or "resting" in the dust, this was just a polite, euphemistic way of saying that the person in his or her entirety had died. The dead simply "rest" in the dirt until the end of time, when with the return of Christ, the general resurrection will take place.

Even though they believed the Parousia to be imminent, we know from biblical testimony their faith wavered and doubts arose about the resurrection of the body. Consider the Christian community at Thessaloniki. Paul felt it necessary to encourage them not to grieve for their dearly departed, at least not like their neighbors who had no hope: "Brothers and sisters, we do not want you to be uninformed about those who sleep in death, so that you do not grieve like the rest of humankind, who have no hope" (1 Thessalonians 4:13). Paul assures them that at the time of the Second Coming of Christ, "God will bring with Jesus those who have fallen asleep in him" (1 Thessalonians 4:14b) and the faithful on earth will be swept up to meet them all. Like most among the first few generations of Christians, they expected the return of Christ—and with His return their own bodily resurrection into a world fully transformed into the Reign of God—to be imminent. Even so, Paul recognized that Christians must encourage one another in resurrection hope.

Contemporary Ash Wednesday liturgies still remind Christians: "Remember thou art dust and to dust thou shalt return." And many today have experiences that resonate with the notion that the departed simply await bodily resurrection in the grave as Christ Himself did. Some who hold this view take solace in the fact that the dead await their awakening at the End Time to the glories of risen life peacefully unaware, even of their own death. Others find this to be a vision—however hopeful in the long run—that offers little immediate solace to those who mourn the bodily corruption of their loved ones.

Soul Abides in an Intermediate State

During the course of Christian history, considerable eschatological speculation turned on the question of whether something else—other than returning to dust while awaiting the Second Coming—might happen between the moment of death and the End Time at which the Reign of God would be fully realized. As the decades turned into centuries, the early hope for the imminent return of the Risen Christ began to wane. At first only the Christian hope for the imminent establishment of God's Reign on earth faded. Eventually, however, especially as views of the nature of the person changed, some began to see the body and soul as divided by death.[2] Under Hellenistic influences, many came to believe that a person's soul could "live on" after the body died. The notion that there could be such a division between body and spirit and the idea that the soul is immortal in this sense are Greek, not Jewish, in origin. Though the soul came to be viewed as immortal by some, the Christian hope in resurrection of the body remained important because the body remained an essential component of the person. In her remarkable study of *The Resurrection of the Body in Western Christianity, 200–1336*, Caroline Walker Bynum concludes that the idea of bodily continuity after death showed remarkable persistence through the late Middle Ages.[3]

Eventually, the hope for the coming Reign of God became too distant to be of much comfort. As the centuries passed, for some Christians the hope for this new creation was forsaken altogether. Their hope shifted largely toward the vision of a purely spiritual home, where the souls of the faithful departed were thought at last to rest in peace eternally.

Not all Christians followed this path. Many rejected this trajectory away from hope in a general bodily resurrection of the body and a new creation. Because of a tendency of some versions of this perspective to supplant hope in a new heaven and new earth, accounts of this intermediate state are still contested. Why? As Wright so aptly puts the matter, salvation is not just about the future but concerns the present. It is about "what God does through as well as in and for us."[4] It is the "this world" focus of our future hope that enables us to be hopeful here and now. If risen life does not incorporate our bodies, does not include the transformation of all that is into a new heaven and new earth, then as St. Paul declared long ago ultimately our labor—what happens here and now on earth—doesn't really matter much.

The idea that following death the soul could await with God the general resurrection of the body and final judgment associated with the Second Coming of Christ does not necessarily undercut the notion that ultimately a new heaven and new earth will be established. Much depends on how the idea that there is such an intermediate state is interpreted. Additionally, though some reject as unbiblical this notion of an interim or preliminary stage to resurrected life, others contend this idea has considerable biblical warrant.[5] For example, the evangelist Luke depicts the Crucified Jesus as promising the so-called Good Thief, "Amen, I say to you, today you will be with me in Paradise" (Luke 23:43). Not surprisingly, this passage is frequently cited as evidence in debates among Christians about the existence of human souls in a heavenly realm prior to the general resurrection. When coupled with the body/soul dualism that characterized some Greek philosophies, this viewpoint became popular among many Christians and acquired considerable weight in the tradition.[6]

Many Christians have lives of faith colored by a lively sense of the presence here and now not only of the Risen Christ but also of the Communion of Saints with whom as "through a glass darkly" they already pray and worship.[7] For these believers (myself included) the promise of the resurrection of the body and the promise of our transfiguration in a new heaven and a new earth is not only that for which one personally hopes. It is a sense of communion of whose proleptic reality one may catch a glimpse through the grace of God.

Resurrection at the Moment of Death

More recently a third idea about death and the afterlife has emerged among some Christians. Many Protestants and Catholics alike have come to link resurrection of the body with the moment of individual death itself.[8] In this view, death functions as a kind of passage into another dimension, into a radically transfigured, fully New Heaven and Earth. Clearly this conception of the Christian hope in resurrection aims to solve the problem of the utter coldness of the grave in which the faithful departed "rests." But many object to this way of thinking. Opponents echo criticisms first raised by the deutero-Pauline author of Second Timothy: "Avoid profane, idle talk, for such people will become more and more godless, and their teaching will spread like gangrene. Among them are Hymenaeus and Philetus, who have deviated from the truth by saying that (the) resurrection has already taken place and are upsetting the faith of some" (2 Timothy 2:16–18). They argue that this notion threatens to eviscerate the concept of bodily resurrection.

Consider the reaction of then Joseph Cardinal Ratzinger—who later became Pope Benedict XVI—to this notion of resurrection. He argued that to suggest that "resurrection" happens immediately at the moment of our personal death actually "undermines the resurrection, because a resurrection which concerns neither matter nor the concrete historical world is no resurrection at all."[9] This idea does not cohere with several other important theological considerations as well. For example, it conflicts with the contemporary understandings of the person operative at the Second Vatican Council: "The human person, though made of body and soul, is a unity."[10] Likewise, it is unclear how one's personal relationship to the world could be fully integrated and healed prior to the completion of history and the transformation of the world.

In sum, the nature of risen life has been the subject of intense ongoing debate among Christians because what it means exactly to believe in the resurrection of the dead isn't at all self-evident. But there is some agreement that belief in the resurrection of the body implies that the whole person, body and soul—albeit in a transformed, glorified state—is destined for new life. This vision of a new creation implies both discontinuity and continuity. It entails the belief both that life as we know it now will pass away and a belief in new life to come. Among contemporary Christians there are different views of when this will occur. As we have seen, some believe it happens: (1) when Christ comes again, (2) following an intermediate state, or (3) at the moment of death itself.

In the next five chapters I will examine in considerable detail the contours this debate took early in church history. What I want to underscore here is simply that there remain deep divisions among Christians today about exactly what it means to believe in the resurrection. As we shall see in the next section, some have come to deny altogether the bodily character of risen life.

SURVIVING DEATH AS A SPIRIT

Many Christians currently do not believe in a general bodily resurrection at all. In 2007 roughly 80 percent of the adult U.S. population self-identified as Christian, but only about 74 percent of those who identified as Christian believe in any sort of afterlife.[11] In her book *Heaven: Our Enduring Fascination with the Afterlife*, Lisa Miller reported that a 1997 *Time*/CNN poll showed only 26 percent of the U.S. population believed they would have bodies in heaven.[12] It appears that many Christians believe that people do not really die. Instead they believe that in essence the person is a spirit and that in the afterlife the essence of the person exists independently of his or her body, not just for an interim or intermediate period but for eternity. From this perspective, people are just pilgrims on earth, "just passing through," and the earth itself will be "left behind." It follows that ultimately neither bodily life nor this material world matter much.

I contend in contrast that authentic Christian faith neither denies, nor does it bow before, the threat of personal obliteration posed by suffering and death. Christianity does not proclaim salvation from this world, from human community and relationships, or from embodiment. Instead Christian faith testifies to salvation from sin and death, promising healing and salvation in a new creation. Encounters with the Risen Christ invite believers to face their own deaths and the loss of their loved ones, with enduring hope for abundant life in a new heaven and new earth. Jesus himself names this hope as central to the work of redemption: "I came so that they might have life and have it more abundantly" (John 10:10b).

Neither scripture nor tradition can be easily interpreted as supportive of a purely spiritual notion of resurrection. Certainly, the scriptures are clear that only God should be considered immortal in this sense.

> I charge (you) before God, who gives life to all things, and before Christ Jesus, who gave testimony under Pontius Pilate for the noble confession, to keep the commandment without stain or reproach until the appearance of our Lord Jesus Christ that the blessed and only ruler will make manifest at the proper time, the King of kings and Lord of lords, *who alone has immortality*, who dwells in unapproachable light, and whom no human being has seen or can see. To him be honor and eternal power. Amen. (1 Timothy 6:13–16; emphasis mine)

The very notion of a disembodied soul finds only minimal support in the New Testament. The few times the term "soul" is used in the scriptures, it connotes the whole person, not a disembodied spirit.

The same holds true for Christian tradition. It does not easily support the notion of a purely spiritual resurrection. Early Christian burial traditions were an important sign of belief in the resurrection of the body. Until relatively recently, cremation was not generally practiced by Christians. For example, cremation was expressly forbidden by the Roman Catholic Church until 1963 and remains officially discouraged in that denomination even now.[13] Why? The reasons are largely symbolic and date back to ancient times. The church seeks to bear a public tangible witness to its convictions about the resurrection of the body through its teachings about burial practices.

In the ancient Mediterranean world, many first-century Greeks and Romans had no hope: "When you're dead, you're dead." Period. End of story. One of their most common memorial inscriptions can be translated: "I was, I am not, I care not." Even those among them who believed in some type of "afterlife" believed in the immortality only of the soul.[14] So, they normally just cremated their dead. In contrast, early Christians insisted upon internment whenever possible. Indeed, the word "cemetery" comes from a Latin term that literally means "sleeping places," because they wanted Christian gravesites to signify physically their resurrection faith. While Christians never questioned God's power to raise bodily everyone, including those intentionally cremated, those burned as martyrs or burned by accident, they nevertheless found through burial a way "to practice" their distinctive Christian belief in the resurrection of the body. The church preferred the internment of intact corpses in part because inhumation was thought to bear a more effective witness to the Christian anticipation of the resurrection of the body.[15]

Any conception of afterlife that leaves the body behind is problematic.[16] Christians must think carefully about the implications of their belief in the bodily resurrection of Christ. If the Reign of God was inaugurated in the Risen Christ, then salvation concerns whole human beings, not just souls. Indeed, redemption is about the entire material cosmos. Along with many Christians I have concluded that resurrection faith is not compatible with the idea of the eternal "survival" of only the spiritual aspects (of only the soul or spirit) of a person, even if glorified. But while rejecting such a view of the hereafter, it is critical to grapple with why it appeals to people and to trace its deep roots in the mixed messages Christianity has sent across the ages about the body. To that task, let us now turn.

CHRISTIAN AMBIVALENCE ABOUT THE BODY

Let us examine the Christian ambivalence about the body and all its desires, sexual and otherwise, as well as its deep roots in the ambiguity of embodiment itself. An exploration of this ambiguity will prove foundational to the explication of the full meaning of the Christian hope in the resurrection of the body. I posit that hope in the resurrection of the body is the Christian "answer" to the questions posed by the ambiguities of the body. It is an alternative to the dualisms that suggest it is best to leave the body behind.

Christianity sends mixed, though not contradictory, messages to the world about the human body in general and human sexuality in particular, and not coincidentally, of course, about the entire material universe as well.[17] Sometimes, Christians celebrate human embodiment, and even sexuality, as sacramental, that is, as a dimension of reality that enables God's Presence and grace to be made tangibly manifest in the world. Such claims have deep roots in Christian understandings of creation and redemption. At other times, Christians denigrate the body, and sexuality, treating it with suspicion and loathing. Such claims have deep roots in Christian understandings of sin and "the Fall." While it is important to highlight the tradition-specific theological roots of these beliefs, it is also important to illumine the way ambivalence about the body and sexuality coheres with the ordinary human experience of the ambiguity of sexuality and the body itself.

Despite this conflicted heritage, it can be said without question that Christianity celebrates the body as good.

Sanctification of the body, along with the sensual desires and the visceral emotions that stem from it, is expressed in a variety of ways. For example, Christians celebrate the goodness of beauty.[18] Through the ages, especially in its Roman Catholic and Orthodox expressions, the church—while careful to avoid any idolatrous objectification of the Divine—has at the same time encouraged a vivid life of faith through religious icons, stained-glass windows, tapestries, paintings, vestments, and sculpture. One can find a celebration of the transcendent power of erotic love in icons of Mary's parents, Joachim and Anna, and likewise in icons of St. Peter and St. Fevronia, a holy couple commonly regarded as the patrons of marriage and family life among Orthodox Christians. Many Christians facilitate the worship of God through the composition, performance, and appreciation of sacred music and dance as well. Through these arts the church invites everyone to savor creation in all its beauty.

In addition, the church sponsors a great many festivals in which the life of Jesus Christ and the feast days of Mary and the saints are joyfully celebrated with abundant food and drink, song and dance, as well as communal processions. Marriage is viewed as a sacrament—a means of grace wherein people may encounter God—by Orthodox and Roman Catholic Christians, and arguably at least as "sacramental" by many Protestant Christians.[19]

The Christian affirmation of the body also finds expression in various corporeal works of mercy. Traditionally seven in number, these practices recognize and address the bodily needs of persons. They include feeding the hungry, giving drink to the thirsty, clothing the naked, visiting the imprisoned, sheltering the homeless, caring for the sick, and burying the dead. Though these good works are commended to all the faithful, historically many Christian religious orders have devoted their apostolate to one or more, such as the care of the homeless, orphaned, and the sick. Many of these religious communities have built and staffed hospices for the dying. Even today the Catholic Worker Movement and the Salvation Army are renowned for the hospitality they offer to strangers, pilgrims, and drifters alike.

Despite grievous instances of abuse by church leaders across all the denominations, the church as an institution has long been committed to welcoming and nurturing children. Parents in desperate situations still choose to abandon their children near the entrances of cloisters, or on the steps of nearby churches, because Christians have been from the beginning, and still are, well known for the way they welcome and nurture girls and boys alike. Catholic and Protestant mission stations traditionally include medical, dental, and educational personnel, as well as evangelists. The New Testament makes it clear: from the very beginning of their ministry the apostles understood themselves to have been commissioned to preach, teach, and practice the corporeal works of mercy, especially healing the sick.[20]

Christians are far from indifferent to bodily matters. From the earliest days of the church, faithfulness has included a call to offer one's body, as Paul proclaimed so well, "as a living sacrifice, holy and pleasing to God, your spiritual worship" (Romans 12:1). The body alone can tangibly symbolize to the world this wholehearted response to God. Like Jesus who is reported to have proclaimed this before him (John 2: 21), Paul likened the body to a temple of God. He wrote to the Christians at Corinth: "The body, however, is . . . for the Lord, and the Lord is for the body; . . . Do you not know that your bodies are members of Christ? . . . Do you not know that your body is a temple of the holy Spirit within you, whom you have from God, and that you are not your own?" (1 Corinthians 6: 13, 15, 19). Reverence for the human body includes taking care of one's own physical needs, as well as being concerned about the bodily needs and sufferings of others.

Minimally, this entailed the prohibition of suicide, which was judged an offense against God, neighbor, and self. It also entails *prima facie* the obligation to care for one's physical health through proper exercise and diet, as well as through the pursuit of ordinary medical treatments like wellness checkups.[21] Such connections between faith and bodily self-care are part of Christian tradition and practice today. Though the casual observer might not notice the difference, for Christians, honoring the body is part of how one honors God.[22] Bodily self-care does not find a driving rationale only in the pursuit of exercised-induced release of endorphins or in concern for keeping up appearances. For many the bodily capacity to enjoy food, drink, sex, beauty, and exercise is celebrated as a gracious gift of God.[23]

Perhaps no contemporary theologian gave clearer voice to the Christian view of the sacramental character of the world than the late Flemish Dominican Edward Schillebeeckx, O.P. His final message delivered in 2008 to his theological colleagues at Leuven is reported to have been: "Extra mundum nulla salus!" This translates: "There is no salvation outside the world." Mary Catherine Hilkert, O.P., a master of his work, writes that Schillebeeckx "helped readers grasp the core sacramental insight disclosed by the Incarnation. The mystery of God is to be encountered in human life and creation."[24]

And yet, from the earliest days of the Jesus movement, disciples recognized the need to discipline the body and the affections that spring from it. The body and its emotions were recognized as a significant source of temptation, if not a primary locus of evil.[25] Paul noted in his letter to the church at Corinth that he struggled to train his body: "No, I drive my body and train it, for fear that, after having preached to others, I myself should be disqualified" (1 Corinthians 9:27). The point of such discipline is to restrain or strengthen one's immediate, "spontaneous," visceral responses (or lack thereof), so that the believer is inclined toward right action. Christians believe that the virtuous life is a consequence of gracious habits of the heart.

However pleasurable, gluttony, drunkenness, sloth, and lust are matters of serious sin for Christians because they incarnate vicious ways of "enjoying" bodily life. They are vices that hold the heart prisoner. They also deprive others of what they need. Vices take from and exploit others. The body and its desires are always about us, never just about me. Christians recognize that the reckless gratification of bodily desires can prove addictive to themselves and harmful to others. Thus, Christians have traditionally tried to develop virtuous responses to these bodily desires.

The Christian endorsement of bodily disciplines is not rooted in an idolatrous glorification of physical fitness, youth, or otherwise attractive "perfect" bodies. For Christians, fasting is not the same as going on a diet, at least not one undertaken for cosmetic purposes. The purpose of fasting is to (re)educate and properly nurture our bodily desires, so we might bear an incarnate witness to Christ. To fast is parallel to and has the same characteristics as prayer. Indeed, for Christians it is a nonverbal form of prayer.

Several biblical passages testify to the way our passions can lead us astray. And yet, when the entire Christian canon is taken seriously, faithful scriptural interpretation cannot support an overridingly negative view of the material world. Exhortations to bodily self-denial, even sacrifice, may be more frequent in Christian tradition than are declarations of the body's gracious potential. But the latter are a vivid part of Christianity. The body is both celebrated as good and suspected as dangerous. So, where did this ambivalence about embodiment come from? Susan A. Ross in her fine book *Extravagant Affections: A Feminist Sacramental Theology*, argues convincingly that these mixed messages about the body can be traced back to the ambiguity of the body itself.[26]

THE AMBIGUITY OF THE BODY AND RESURRECTION HOPE

Embodiment is the basis for all personal thought and action, as well as the foundation of our life together. The body facilitates our relationships with each other and energizes our individual connections with the world. Our interdependence with each other—for both survival and love—is the bodily basis of our vulnerability to each other. This same body that sustains us is also the gateway whereby we experience alienation, diminishment, disease, disintegration, death, and decay. This is why we may feel ambivalent about our bodily experiences.

One need not be Christian to recognize the truth in Jesus's lament that quite often "the spirit is willing, but the flesh is weak" (Matthew 26:41). Paul gives further voice to this experience of our divided state in his letter to the Romans: "But I see in my members another principle at war with the law of my mind, taking me captive to the law of sin that dwells in my members. Miserable one that I am! Who will deliver me from this mortal body?" (Romans 7:23–24). Some exegetes speculate that Paul might have been referring here specifically to a personal difficulty he had either with an addiction, serious illness, impairment, or disability. We will never know exactly to what he was referring. Whatever it was, though, this experience typified for him the human condition. Our bodies can both empower and debilitate us. Sometimes we experience our bodies as noncompliant, to say the least!

The body can be more than a source of human vulnerability and risk. Our bodies can be a locus of human sin and of suffering. The point here is not to foster loathing for the body but rather to encourage our "facing into" the truth about its brokenness. The ambivalent language about the body within Christianity attests to the human experience of the body's fundamental ambiguity. Earlier I noted that sometimes it seems like we simply *are* embodied. But it is important to add here that at other times it seems like we just *have* a body.

On the one hand, we often experience ourselves as a psychosomatic unity. It is a fact—and not one accidental to the heart of our existence—that we are corporeal creatures. This sense of wholeness, our psychosomatic unity, is evidenced in a variety of ways. It is evident in our language when we say, "I am hungry" instead of "my body is hungry." The human capacity to make love through sexual activity expresses precisely this sort of personal, psychosomatic integrity. More negatively, we recognize in the threat death poses the risk that "I will die." Our incarnate personal selves will dissolve. Or again, the fact that we recognize assault as a crime against persons, rather than merely their (bodily) property or possessions, reflects the profound degree to which we experience ourselves as embodied.[27]

On the other hand, it sometimes seems more natural to say that we have a body rather than that we are embodied. Certain kinds of experiences—of illnesses, injuries, pain, and death—confirm our alienation from and discomfort with the "otherness" of our body. Frequently, we do not identify with the syndromes that plague us. People resist (and perhaps rightly so) being reduced to the diseases they suffer. We say, "I have ocular histoplasmosis" or "I have a cold."[28]

We are connected to each other and to the world by our bodies.[29] Yet, the very embodiment that helps us to make these interpersonal connections is also, sometimes simultaneously, a source of our vulnerability to individual disintegration and interpersonal alienation. In other words, the body is the source of our capacity, power, and energy to negotiate the world, and it is frequently a source of our frailty, frustration, and fault. Visceral emotions—like rage, lust, and despair—can reverberate through the body, inclining us toward vicious choices. Other affections—like courage, hope, righteous anger, compassion, and joy—can reverberate through the body, inclining us toward virtuous choices. However limited, the human body is what enables us to connect with the world and people around us. Through the body we encounter not only goodness, beauty, and grace but also finitude and the mystery of evil. For this reason, when Christians testify to their resurrection hope—to the promise of personal, communal, and indeed cosmic salvation in Christ—I am arguing we must include a witness to the promised transformation of the body.

THEOLOGICAL SUPPORT FOR HOPE IN RESURRECTION OF THE BODY

Hope for human bodily resurrection not only offers a cogent response to the everyday experience of the ambiguity of bodily existence. It also coheres with many other, deeply traditional, theological tenets of Christian faith. An outline of the various convictions that frame the Christian hope in the resurrection of the body follows. Because there is a stark contrast between this well-supported theological anthropology and the view that the prospects for sex in heaven are dim, it is important to underscore the dramatic way this traditional speculation departs from its larger Christian framework.

The Christian hope for the sanctification of the body has roots not only in the admittedly ambiguous, anthropological realities of bodily existence but also in several convictions about God. Beliefs about the goodness of the Creator, the Incarnation of God, the bodily glorification of the Risen Christ, and the ongoing real Presence of Christ through the Spirit in the church constitute some of the theological foundations for Christian convictions about the sanctification of human embodiment.

Christian convictions about the goodness of the Creator ground Christian celebrations of the goodness of the created world. Christianity sees bodily life, like the universe and all therein, as a good and gracious gift. Delight in the life of the senses, along with the enjoyment of friendship, beauty, and good health, are all understood by Christians to be precious gifts from the Creator. It is important to understand that the "abundant life" already (but not yet fully) coming toward us from God is that risen life toward which God is drawing us. As Christopher Morse puts it, "heaven" is at hand but not in hand.[30]

All are invited to enjoy life with gratitude and gladness.[31] Many Christians see "nature" as being designed for perfection. Commenting on the "this-worldly" immanence of "heaven," in her recent book *Heaven: Our Enduring Fascination with the Afterlife*, religion journalist Lisa Miller quotes J. D. Salinger's comment from Zooey to Franny: "Jesus knew—*knew*—that we're carrying the Kingdom of Heaven around with us, inside . . ."[32]

Another important justification for celebrating the goodness of the physical world in general and human embodiment in particular is the Christian belief that in Jesus of Nazareth, God became incarnate and the Risen Christ through the Spirit continues to inhabit the world. Arguably the central tenet of the Christian faith, belief in the Incarnation of God is certainly among those convictions that distinguish Christianity from Judaism and Islam. As testified to in the New Testament: "And the Word became flesh and made his dwelling among us, and we saw his glory, the glory as of the Father's only Son, full of grace and truth" (John 1:14). As Christians see it, when God became human, the holiness of the universe, and all therein, was decisively revealed.

At some junctures the New Testament seems quite clear about this. Consider this passage from the letter to the Hebrews about Jesus.

> Now since the children share in blood and flesh, he likewise shared in them, that through death he might destroy the one who has the power of death, that is, the devil, and free those who through fear of death had been subject to slavery all their life. Surely he did not help angels but rather the descendants of Abraham; *therefore, he had to become like his brothers in every way*, that he might be a merciful and faithful high priest before God to expiate the sins of the people. Because he himself was tested through what he suffered, he is able to help those who are being tested. (Hebrews 2:14–18; emphasis mine)

However, the degree to which, and perhaps even whether, this promise incorporates the human body has been a matter of considerable controversy among Christians.[33] But as one early church father put it, "That which was not assumed is not healed; it is what is united to his divinity that is saved."[34] Because of this unity of the divine and human natures in the incarnate person Jesus Christ, our world and our bodies will *not* be left behind. This doctrine conflicts with the idea that we are on a journey to a better "purely spiritual" place. On the contrary, God embraced all that is through the Incarnation and inaugurated a new creation in the Risen Christ.

Christians believe in the resurrection of Jesus Christ. We believe that the mortal, fully human historical person known as Jesus of Nazareth truly died. But He was not destroyed by death. Instead, in the Risen Christ, God established on earth a new creation. Though this ontologically new life in the Spirit will not be evidenced in its fullness until the end of time, it has been inaugurated already in the glorified body of the Risen Christ. The individual Christian's hope for abundant life has its foundation in their communion—here and now—with the Risen Christ, whose glorious resurrection is understood to be "the first fruit" of the life-giving Spirit of God. Hence the model for the general resurrection of all the saints is the Risen Christ.

It is the person's relatedness to God through Christ that is the way into this new reality. But this connection to God is not understood to be private. Though deeply personal, our relationship to God is not solitary. As Christians we are baptized into Christ's Body, the church, so salvation is basically communal in character. Resurrection is and will be both corporeal and corporate. The shared etiology of these terms is not accidental!

This is precisely the significance of belief in the *bodily* resurrection of Jesus Christ. Revealed in the bodily resurrection of Christ is our own transformed bodily future with one another in God. Indeed, Christians believe this cosmic ontological transformation was begun in the Risen Christ. Nothing in the doctrine of the Ascension of the Risen Christ negates or renders temporary the ongoing truth of this central confession. God is with us still; we have not been abandoned. Yet we await the establishment of this new creation in its fullness when Christ comes again.

Though ascended into heaven, the Risen Christ remains present to humanity and the world through the work of the Holy Spirit. It is difficult to identify a single Christian perspective on the nature of this gracious Presence. Indeed, it could well be argued that denominational divisions among Christians are rooted fundamentally in disagreements about the precise nature of Christ's ongoing Presence in the world. However, most Christians believe that Christ is present as Word of God, whenever that Word is rightly preached. Many also believe Christ is really present in the church, indeed, wherever two or three gather to pray in Christ's name. God continues to become human—to take on flesh—amid the People of God. Indeed, the one, holy, catholic, and apostolic church is believed by many creedal Christians to be the Body of Christ. Some believe in the Real Presence of Christ in the Eucharist. Here God's passionate and self-giving love is made tangible in the transformation into the Body and Blood of Christ of the bread, wine, and gathered community by and through the power of the Holy Spirit.

DECONSTRUCTING DENIALS OF SEX IN HEAVEN

Whether you are inclined to hope for a transfigured experience of sexual desire and delight in heaven or not, what precisely will characterize risen life is in both instances a matter of speculation and eschatological imagination. But there is considerable consensus within the Christian tradition that in the life to come persons will be identifiable, whole (that is, raised in their entirety) and immortal.[35] And yet for the most part theologians have taught that those who are glorified will experience no sexual desire or delight in heaven. Suffice it to say here that while one can find considerable support for belief in the general resurrection of the body, there is little support within the Christian tradition for the notion that this will include the healing and glorious transfiguration of our sexual desire and delight.[36]

This denial crosses denominational barriers. Pope Saint John Paul II felt free to assert without significant argumentation that marriage (and by implication genital conjugal activity) is a sign of God's saving power in the redemptive order and it does *not* "pertain to the eschatological reality of the future world."[37] Similarly, evangelical theologian Stanley Grenz asserted that in heaven "human sexuality will no longer be expressed in genital sexual acts, and the sexually based drive toward bonding will no longer be expressed through male-female coupling," right after conceding that "Jesus does not explicitly declare that sexuality will be absent, only that marriage will no longer be practiced."[38]

The consequence of this pattern of denial is that the predominant message about sexuality sent by Christianity over the centuries was and in some instances still is this: the best sex on earth is no sex. While it has always been the case that only a relatively few Christians choose not to marry for religious reasons, even today vowed celibacy is taught to be by both Roman Catholic and Orthodox Christians markedly superior to a conjugal way of life. (Though Orthodoxy permits a married priesthood, celibacy is still required of bishops.) Historically, sexual abstinence (especially virginity) became so idealized over the course of church history that the church proclaimed with notable consistency that the best form of sexual activity, even in marriage, was no sexual activity at all.

While it is true that Protestants eventually broke with this idealization of celibacy, this change in practice at least initially did not reflect a change in theory about what was morally ideal. Reformers may have abandoned the practice because they thought counsel toward celibacy to be unrealistic, and hence unwise, for most people. We cannot be certain of their motives in full but we do know that they did not disclaim as mistaken the idealization of virginity. We shall return to this issue in much more detail later in this volume.

Over the centuries most theologians argued that if such abstinence was not individually a realistic personal lifestyle, then sexual activity should be "contained" in marriage. Many taught as well that sexual activity in marriage should be minimized to whatever extent possible. Though not discussed, it would follow that if or when desire withers, its loss should be accepted, if not celebrated. It comes as no surprise that sexual desire and delight have no place in most eschatological speculations about risen life.[39]

While I disagree with his conclusions, it is to his credit that in his text *The Rest of Life: Rest, Play, Eating, Studying, Sex from a Kingdom Perspective*, Ben Witherington III develops an extended explanation of why there will be no sexual intercourse among "Kingdom dwellers."[40] Here Witherington argues that there is a difference between eternal and temporary goods, the latter of which includes the sexual desire to engage in coitus. As he sees it, in this life on earth, the primary purpose of genital activity is (1) species propagation. Its secondary purposes are twofold: sexual activity should (2) enhance conjugal bonding and (3) make pleasurable the fulfillment of the Creator's mandates "to multiply" and fulfill one's marital duties. Though each is a blessing, these three goods of sexual activity will no longer be needed in the life of the world to come.

From my perspective Witherington's reasoning begs the question. He argues that since there will be no death, there will be no need to propagate. But why assume that the survival of the species (or the establishment of a sort of "immortality" through heirs) is the only reason for creating new life? Similarly, Witherington concludes spouses will no longer need to bond sexually in the life of the world to come because "in a sense it will be like we are all married to each other in the Kingdom [*sic*], the communion or *koinonia* will be so grand."[41] Why presume this new, transfigured form of a conjugal-like way of relating will not be sexual? That begs the question. He argues that in risen life sexual pleasures will be superseded by something even more wonderful. Again, why assume that this something more will not be sexual in some transfigured sense?

Witherington concludes that a celibate "singleness for the Lord" is the clearest sign here and now of the eschatological age because everyone needs to sit lightly with things that will be passing away. These include for Witherington not only opportunities for sexual relations but also opportunities for work, rest, play, eating, and study. Otherwise, we risk making what is "less than God the object of our ultimate concern."[42] All the faithful ought to practice detachment so as to make greater room in our lives for what will be everlasting—"the union and communion with God in Christ and his people."[43] But for the same reasons should not celibates sit lightly with concern for themselves, their vows, and their religious communities? Could that vocation not also prove to be idolatrous? And will not celibacy be just as surely transfigured in the life to come?

Witherington notes that for those who are married the conviction that there will be no sex in heaven means recognizing that less sex, even no sex, "doesn't mean there can't still be love and intimacy," despite what Viagra commercials imply to the contrary.[44] This is most certainly true but not necessarily for the reasons put forward by Witherington. After all, it is not self-evident that sexual desire is at best a temporal blessing that will pass away in the long run.

Admittedly both the risk of turning a sexual partnership into an idol (which is what seems to worry Witherington) and the ambiguity of sexual desire (discussed earlier in this chapter) offer some support for concluding that there might not be sex in heaven. But the central purpose of this volume is to argue against such a conclusion, by refuting the biblical and traditional rationales frequently offered in support of it and by constructively detailing the rationales supportive of its alternative. The next three chapters take up the task of systematically reinterpreting through "Easter eyes" the scriptures and traditions key to the denial of sex of heaven. To that task let us now turn.

CHAPTER 2

The New Testament about the General Resurrection of the Body

Here I explore key elements of the biblical witness about bodily resurrection, especially in the New Testament. As I pointed out in chapter 1, if there is no hope for bodily resurrection, then there could be no affirmative speculations about gender, sexual desire and delight, and/or genital activity in the life to come. We cannot explore the biblical witness about the latter, more particular claims, until the biblical foundation for the former, more general hope is established. Differences among the relevant texts themselves, as well as among their interpretations, complicate this analysis. The theological tensions within Christianity about what characterizes risen life, especially about the general resurrection of the body, have their roots in the New Testament. It must be admitted from the start that there is no consensus among biblical theologians about what should be said about the "historical" character of the narratives about the empty tomb, the appearances of the Risen Lord and/or their ontological implications.

Christian eschatological thought emerged in the ancient Mediterranean world, where—as in our world today—there were many competing views about death and the afterlife. When interpreting the biblical witness about resurrection, it is especially important to understand the Jewish and Hellenistic traditions in regard to these matters. These perspectives provide important background information against which the New Testament witness to bodily resurrection stands out. In addition to reviewing key ideas within these two contexts, in this chapter I will provide a brief overview of the exegetical debate about how best to interpret the claim to the resurrection of the body in the Pauline corpus and the gospels.

JEWISH BACKGROUND

Within Jewish thought there were, and still are, many views of death and of the afterlife. According to one of its oldest traditions a natural, nonviolent death at the close of a long and fruitful life is the inevitable, enviable, and the completely natural end of a good life. Death was not seen as a consequence of, or even associated with, sin.[1] Whatever occurred after death was for most ancient Hebrew people largely unimportant. At most, one hoped at the end of one's life to be laid to rest in the earth, near the bones of one's ancestors.[2]

For the most part, ancient Israelites believed that life simply ended with death.[3] There was no promise of afterlife, no hope for or even the notion of personal immortality of any sort. This is why having children, particularly sons, to inherit and carry on their father's legacy here on earth became so important. This is why infertility was viewed as such a tragedy. Of course, ancestors were to be honored, but the focus in ancient Israel was largely on life in this world, in the here and now. Israel's hope was for, and much of its prophetic literature pointed (and still points) to, the eventual establishment of God's Reign on this earth.

> Lo, I am about to create new heavens and a new earth; the things of the past shall not be remembered or come to mind. Instead, there shall always be rejoicing and happiness in what I create; for I create Jerusalem to be a joy and its people to be a delight; I will rejoice in Jerusalem and exult in my people. No longer shall the sound

> of weeping be heard there, or the sound of crying; no longer shall there be in it an infant who lives but a few days, or an old man who does not round out his full lifetime; he dies a mere youth who reaches but a hundred years, and he who fails of a hundred shall be thought accursed. They shall live in the houses they build, and eat the fruit of the vineyards they plant; they shall not build houses for others to live in, or plant for others to eat. As the years of a tree, so the years of my people; and my chosen ones shall long enjoy the produce of their hands. They shall not toil in vain, nor beget children for sudden destruction; for a race blessed by the LORD are they and their offspring. Before they call, I will answer; while they are yet speaking, I will hearken to them. The wolf and the lamb shall graze alike, and the lion shall eat hay like the ox (but the serpent's food shall be dust). None shall hurt or destroy on all my holy mountain, says the LORD. (Isaiah 65:17–25)

Since ancient times, generation after generation of faithful Jews have looked for this promised Reign of God on earth, have wrestled with their personal disappointment, and yet have continued to hope for this better future for their descendants on earth.

There is not much hope for a personal life after death evidenced in ancient Israel, at least not until the second century BCE.[4] But there is some mention in the Hebrew scriptures of all the dead—with a few notable exceptions like Enoch and Elijah—"existing" in a shadowy netherworld called Sheol. Here the restless spirits of those who died young, died without heirs, died violently, and/or who had displeased God, are reported to have an ongoing, if ethereal, existence of sorts.[5] But in Sheol the dead are described as neither punished nor rewarded; they generally know no pleasure or pain, no community nor even any relationship to God. (Of course, though Yahweh is described as not being there, even Sheol is never described as beyond the sovereign power of God.)

Whatever this notion represented among the people of ancient Israel, Sheol was certainly not ongoing life in any meaningful sense. Similarly, while there are dramatic stories of healing the dead in the Elijah-Elisha narratives found in the Hebrew Bible, these are basically accounts of the dead being restored to ordinary life. Resuscitation, however, is not equivalent to resurrection to transformed life. For all these reasons, many reviewers of Jewish thought on death and "the afterlife" conclude that the Hebrew Bible evidences little hope for either immortality or resurrected life.

Such a conclusion, however, might not express adequately the complexity of Hebrew thought on this matter. In his book *Eschatology: Death and Eternal Life*, Ratzinger argues against such a conclusion. He suggests instead that there was actually significant variation, perhaps even development, in Jewish thought on this matter. He argues that resurrection hope found at least indirect expression in important biblical texts. Indeed, he hypothesizes that "the indestructibility of communion with God, and therewith our eternal life, follows in strictly theo-*logical* terms from Israel's concept of God." It is indeed an understatement to admit, as Ratzinger himself did, that there is "no little objection at the historical level" to such a theo-*logical* claim. Nevertheless, he argues that in at least a few Hebrew texts the hope that life will prove to be stronger than death is expressed.[6]

For example, though dead and buried, the Hebrew Bible envisions the Suffering Servant as being not only vindicated but also eventually brought into the light himself.

> A grave was assigned him among the wicked and a burial place with evildoers, though he had done no wrong nor spoken any falsehood. (But the LORD was pleased to crush him in infirmity.) If he gives his life as an offering for sin, he shall see his descendants in a long life, and the will of the LORD shall be accomplished through him. Because of his affliction he shall see the light in fullness of days; through his suffering, my servant shall justify many, and their guilt he shall bear. Therefore I will give him his portion among the great, and he shall divide the spoils with the mighty, because he surrendered himself to death and was counted among the wicked; and he

> shall take away the sins of many, and win pardon for their offenses. (Isaiah 53:9–12)

Similarly, at key junctures the psalmists declare that God will not leave the faithful "among the dead or allow your godly one to rot in the grave." Instead, the psalmist sings: "Therefore my heart is glad, my soul rejoices; my body also dwells secure, for you [God] will not abandon my soul to Sheol, nor let your devout one see the pit. You will show me the path to life, abounding joy in your [God's] presence, the delights at your right hand forever" (Psalm 16:9–11; interpolations mine).[7]

Israel's longstanding hope for its eventual restoration as a great nation could also be interpreted as an undercurrent—deep in the people's psyche—that oriented them toward the prospect of a glorious future.[8] Though not widely accepted, it is interesting to note that Ratzinger's hypothesis has found at least a qualified advocate in the recent work of a prominent Jewish scholar. In *Resurrection and the Restoration of Israel: The Ultimate Victory of the God of Life*, Jon D. Levinson concludes that a belief that at the end of history God will resurrect the dead and restore them to full bodily existence eventually became central to Rabbinic Judaism.[9]

But it was the emergence during the Second Temple period of hope for the full vindication of the righteous that proved to be the most important foundation for belief in a general resurrection among some Jews by the time of the Common Era. Explicitly apocalyptic visions about what might happen at the end of time began to appear around the second century BCE in Israel.[10] About this time there emerged a clear Hebrew voice expressing the hope that ultimately the wicked would be punished and the righteous restored to a transformed body and an ideal life. It seemed that many of this era thought that martyrdom for a just cause merited precisely this more personal, individual honor. The solace that accompanied being laid to rest near one's ancestors, with its appeal to extended family and tribal values, simply wasn't enough.

Many biblical scholars today believe that at the time of its compilation the book of Daniel is a chronology of current events, only thinly disguised as prophecy from preceding centuries. Compiled by many authors over several years during the period of the Maccabean Revolt (that is, during the second century BCE), it contains the only explicit reference to resurrection (generally accepted as such) within the Hebrew Bible. In this text the prophet Daniel is portrayed as encouraging the faithful to trust in the following promise: "Many of those who sleep in the dust of the earth shall awake; some shall live forever, others shall be an everlasting horror and disgrace. But the wise shall shine brightly like the splendor of the firmament, and those who lead the many to justice shall be like the stars forever" (Daniel 12:2–3).

John J. Collins notes in his commentary that this brief text does not specify resurrected life as embodied (as does, for example, 2 Maccabees 7:11 considered later), nor does it suggest an event universal in scope. Instead it focuses on "many."[11] Still, even if astral in character, Daniel's vision of what is to come at the end of the world proved to be of great importance in the development of Christian eschatological thought.

Written in *Koine* Greek probably by a Pharisee in Alexandria around 128 BC, 2 Maccabees is a revisionist history of the events recounted in the first seven chapters of 1 Maccabees with the addition of elements from the Pharisaic tradition. The story narrated in 2 Maccabees 7 is the gruesome tale of a heroic Jewish mother and her seven sons, who all choose torture and death rather than violate the purity laws of their faith. They did so—the text makes clear—in the hope of future vindication and bodily resurrection.

At the point of death he said: "You accursed fiend, you are depriving us of this present life, but the King of the world will raise us up to live again forever. It is for his laws that we are dying." After him the third suffered their cruel sport. He put out his tongue at once when told to do so, and bravely held out his hands, as he spoke these noble words: "It was from Heaven that I received these; for the sake of his laws I disdain them; from him I hope to receive them again." Even the king and his attendants marveled at the young man's courage, because he regarded his sufferings as nothing. After he had died, they tortured and maltreated the fourth brother in the same way. When he was near death, he said, "It is my choice to die at the hands of men with the God-given hope of being restored to life by him; but for you, there will be no resurrection to life." (2 Maccabees 7: 9–14)

Though its canonical status is a matter of ongoing debate,[12] this testimony makes it clear that the Pharisees held beliefs—probably of various kinds—about resurrection. One can find ideas of resurrection in some of the Dead Sea Scrolls as well. It can be accurately concluded that, by this time, ideas about resurrection, though probably not uniform, were fairly widespread.

By the first century of the Common Era, the idea of a general resurrection of the body at the end of time was at least familiar to some within Judaism. This Pharisaic idea was far from universally accepted. Many Jews of this era—among them the Sadducees—were deeply skeptical of the notion of a general resurrection of the body. There is no precedent among the Jews of Jesus's era—even among the Pharisees—for the notion that any single person, however heroic, would be bodily resurrected before the end of the world.

HELLENISTIC BACKGROUND

Alongside those within Judaism, there were many other traditions about death and the afterlife during the first century CE in the ancient Mediterranean world. Alexander the Great had annexed Jerusalem and its environs into his empire around 333 BCE. Even though he had left it alone to govern itself, Hellenistic culture permeated the atmosphere throughout the Mediterranean world. Greek and Jewish traditions intermingled. Several Greek ideas proved to be important in the early development of Christian thought regarding the resurrection of the body.[13] Certainly, the Greek emphasis on personal accomplishments challenged the traditional Jewish emphasis on honoring the past and serving the present and future generations of the extended family and tribe.

Greek philosophical thought clearly exposed the Jews of the Common Era to a different, more individual notion of immortality.[14] A prime example of this perspective can be found in

Plato's *Timaeus* written around 360 BCE. This philosophical treatise (written in the form of a speech) is about the human soul's journey into material embodiment and the world and its subsequent moral struggle to escape this incarnate existence and return to an eternal life in its "native star" in the heavens. According to Plato, the rational soul has no desire for the body (its "prison") or for life on the earth, but it rather seeks to enjoy a purely spiritual, eternal life. Many prominent Jews during the first century of the Common Era—among them Philo—incorporated such Greek notions about the immortality of the soul into their thinking.

At the opening of the Common Era, variations on such dualism were not the only, or even necessarily the most important, ways Hellenism shaped early Christian thought. Included within traditional Greek religious myths and rituals, and depicted in its art and literature, were profoundly influential stories of important, heroic mortals who died and were then resurrected. Some of these were tales of mere resuscitation; others were narratives of resurrection. For example, according to Greek tradition, even prior to his divination, Asclepius, who became the god of healing, brought the newly dead back to life. In these instances, those so healed returned to normal life and eventually died (again). They were not portrayed as having been rendered immortal or otherwise transfigured. Other stories, however, involved tales of resurrection into eternal life. Achilles, for example, was a popular hero around whom a cult evolved on Leuce Island. He was portrayed as having died and been resurrected, becoming immortal, and hence as disappearing from ordinary life.[15]

These older Greek traditions about heroic figures in which immortality is linked with an incorruptible transformed body were familiar to most people in the ancient Mediterranean world. These figures participated in both the human and divine realm. In all of these Greek religious stories of resurrection, however, there is clear continuity between the body that had recently died and the one raised up and made incorruptible. It was *de rigueur* that all wounds and warts present at the time of death become eternal! An account of the Risen Christ appearing with stigmata would make perfect sense to the Hellenistic mind. Claims about the resurrection of a heroic leader like Jesus would probably not have offended most Greeks listening to the Good News.

It was the claim of a *general* resurrection of the *bodies* of the dead that would have seemed outlandish.[16] Undoubtedly, this struck the Athenian imagination as absurd. Such a reaction was reported in Acts: "When they heard about resurrection of the dead, some began to scoff, but others said, 'We should like to hear you [Paul] on this some other time'" (Acts 17:32; interpolation mine). And as shall be delineated in detail in the analysis of 1 Corinthians 15 later in this chapter, surely it evoked much skepticism in Corinth. There was no precedent in either Greek philosophy or mythology for the claim that the bodies of ordinary disciples that had turned to dust, had been burned to ashes, or had been devoured and digested by wild beasts could then be raised up. In Greek mythology, most of humanity is eternally lost through death. There is simply no precedent whatsoever for belief in something like the general bodily resurrection of the dead in Hellenistic thought.

THE NEW TESTAMENT AND RESURRECTION: AN OVERVIEW

In Jewish thought there was little precedent for the idea of a heroic individual being physically raised from the dead prior to a time of general bodily resurrection.[17] In Greek thought, there was no whisper of a general bodily resurrection. Individually divinized exceptions simply proved the rule of human mortality in Greek thought. And yet, it is precisely beliefs in both the Risen Christ and a general bodily resurrection that became central to—and distinctive of—Christianity in the opening centuries of the Common Era.

The New Testament makes it clear that Paul proclaimed both the Risen Lord and preached the general resurrection of the dead everywhere he went. Both claims were central to his account of the Good News, whether his pulpit was in Athens or Jerusalem.[18] He proclaimed them in nearly every letter he penned (or that has been attributed to him).[19] In this chapter I will focus on Paul's treatment of these fundamental beliefs as expressed at length in 1 Corinthians 15. The seed metaphor expressed therein is widely recognized to be the oldest Christian metaphor for the resurrection of the body.

Within decades, the four evangelists also produced written testimony about this distinctive feature of Christianity through their diverse stories about the empty tomb and Christ's resurrection appearances. Because I am particularly interested in the bodily character of the risen life to come, and because the Risen Christ is identified by Paul as the first fruits of this great harvest, what little is revealed about this new bodily life must come from these early accounts. We will attend to them carefully in the next chapter.[20] At several junctures the gospels also portray Jesus as teaching the general resurrection of the dead in ways that accord more with the thinking of the Pharisees than the Sadducees.[21] However, Jesus is portrayed in these passages as saying little that was new, given his Jewish upbringing, except of course to declare that he would be vindicated "on the third day." Still, in chapter 3 I will also attend to the record of the arguments Jesus had with those (like the Sadducees) who found such a notion unbelievable. This is of certain import since the dispute at that time speaks to the very heart of the matter under scrutiny in this book.[22]

In his analysis of the early Christian testimony about resurrection, biblical scholar N. T. Wright identifies several ways in which it modified its Jewish antecedents. Four of these points seem particularly noteworthy to me. First, beginning with the distinctively Christian witness, the idea of resurrection is split into a two-phase event. Paul is especially clear on this point. Everyone's eschatological future begins with the Risen Christ, whose personal resurrection inaugurated and is the foundation for our current experience of the in-breaking of the Kin-dom of God. Belief in a general resurrection has its foundation in that decisive event.

Second, in the New Testament Jesus is not portrayed as having been turned into a heavenly light through resurrection (as was suggested in the book of Daniel). Instead, the New Testament portrays the Risen Christ as radically transformed by God and, yet, still recognizable as their beloved Teacher who was crucified, dead, and buried. In the stories of the empty tomb and resurrection appearances, the Risen Christ is portrayed as having a body that is normal in some ways,[3] and not so normal in other ways.[24] At times Jesus was mistaken for an ordinary gardener; he was touchable, touched, and asked to be touched. He asked that his disciples not cling to him. He was portrayed as cooking, sharing food, and eating. He was recognizable as Jesus of Nazareth. At other times, however, the Risen Christ is portrayed as having a body that is not normal. He was not always recognized. At these junctures he is portrayed as able to enter locked rooms and suddenly disappear. He ascended into heaven.

According to Wright early Christian testimony about resurrection modified its Jewish antecedents in a third way. The promise of resurrection was expanded beyond a hope for the glorious restoration of Israel's sovereignty. The promise was expanded to include the transformation of all humankind, indeed the renewal of all the cosmos.[25] Fourth, this promised new creation is proclaimed as both gift and task; present-day disciples are called to teach, preach, and heal in light of their destiny in this new heaven and new earth.

What triggered the production of such dramatically different expectations about the life of the world to come? Many Christians would certainly answer: "The events we celebrate at Easter." While one should not be naïve about the complexities that characterize the relationship between history and truth, it is not necessary to conclude that narratives that have been fabricated through human experience and language are therefore false or not historical. While skepticism about the resurrection is as old as the hope it promises, faith abounds as well.

There is undoubtedly some truth in the conclusion reached by Alan F. Segal at the close of his analysis in *Life after Death*, when he notes that a vision of the afterlife—in heaven or on earth, as souls or bodies, after death or at the end of time—mirrors "the values of the society that produced it."[26] He cautions, therefore, that they frequently "benefit a particular social class." One can certainly demonstrate how eschatological visions of "pie in the sky" have functioned as an "opiate of the people" (to use Marx's language) and thereby served to "quiet" the underclass. But one can also demonstrate with certainty how these same visions have functioned to embolden resistance to injustice and liberate martyrs on the margins of society.

What Segal fails to see is that one can recognize the all too partial and distorted nature of all human, socially constructed testimonies, and recognize the perspectival nature of the experiences they give voice to, without precluding the possibility that these traditions, however contextual and limited, have in fact developed in response to unique historical events. Of course, no one can prove (scientifically) that the tomb was really empty, or that the women (or their "brothers") were not hallucinating or that they had not encountered a mere ghost. But as Wright indicates, the ability to repeat an event has never been what makes it historically plausible or even intelligible. History as a discipline aims to study and propose plausible (in terms of the canons of reason) yet admittedly imaginative and inevitably perspectival (re)constructions precisely of what is not repeatable.

1 CORINTHIANS 15

During the time Paul was writing to the church in Corinth, that congregation was experiencing serious doubts about Christ's resurrection. There is currently considerable debate among biblical commentators about how to characterize the misunderstanding(s) among the Christians at Corinth at that time. What was the confusion Paul was trying to clear up? Did the new converts at Corinth come to doubt (so soon after their conversion) the resurrection of Jesus of Nazareth? Were they denying the possibility of their own postmortem existence? How so? Were they confused about when to anticipate the so-called general resurrection? Did they deny the bodily nature of this promise? What was the precise problem Paul sought to address?

Paul begins this chapter (1 Corinthians 15:1–8) by referring to what seems to have been an early creedal formula accepted in the early church.

> Now I am reminding you, brothers [*sic*], of the gospel I preached to you, which you indeed received and in which you also stand. Through it you are also being saved, if you hold fast to the word I preached to you, unless you believed in vain. For I handed on to you as of first importance what I also received: that Christ died for our sins in accordance with the scriptures; that he was buried; that he was raised on the third day in accordance with the scriptures; that he appeared to Kephas, then to the Twelve. After that, he appeared to more than five hundred brothers [*sic*] at once, most of whom are still living, though some have fallen asleep. After that he appeared to James, then to all the apostles. Last of all, as to one born abnormally, he appeared to me. (1 Corinthians 15:1–8)

He starts with the church's accepted confession of faith. Most biblical scholars do not believe that the resurrection of Jesus Christ was widely disputed in Corinth. Nevertheless, Raymond F. Collins's position on this matter seems the most nuanced to me.[27] He notes that even if it was not an issue of widespread debate in Corinth, nor a direct concern of Paul's in this letter, the reality of the resurrection of Christ may have been contested by at least a few Corinthians. Why else, argues Collins, would Paul have devoted so much attention to the matter, rehearsing as he does the early Christian proclamation (in the Greek *kerygma*) about the Risen Christ and citing six different witnesses to it?[28] Collins says the review of these many appearances of the Risen Christ to a significant number of different people serves at least two purposes. It establishes that Paul's encounter on the road to Damascus was not merely a subjective hallucination, and also that this (divine) exaltation (in the Greek *egegertai*) of Jesus of Nazareth "has legs," that is, that indeed Christ lives!

Nevertheless, even if it was denied by a few, belief in the resurrection of Christ appears not to have been widely contested within the early Christian community at Corinth. So the question arises: if this was not the primary issue Paul sought to address in his letter, to what debate might he have been responding?[29] Paul wants to demonstrate why it is mistaken to claim that "there is no resurrection of the dead" (1 Corinthians 15:12) as some in Corinth were doing. While the resurrection of Christ was not widely disputed, the idea of a general bodily resurrection could well have been hotly contested. Many biblical scholars believe the corporate and corporeal implications of Christ's resurrection were disputed.[30] A significant number of the Corinthian converts were struggling with the notion that they too would eventually be raised bodily from the dead.[31] Here Paul is linking the raising of all the faithful with the raising of Jesus, naming His resurrection as "first fruits" that anticipate and initiate this final resurrection.

The fledging church at Corinth was divided over the question of whether they, like Christ, would eventually be raised bodily from the dead. What we now refer to as the general resurrection of the dead was deeply contested in Corinth.[32] But at least some Corinthian Christians did not doubt that they too would be raised on the last day.[33]

As a Pharisaic Jew, Paul believed in life after death and had long held that God's ultimate salvific act would entail the bodily resurrection of the dead. Indeed, he came to see that his earlier Pharisaic hope was reinforced by his encounter with the Risen Christ.[34] Apart from this conviction, he thought faith in Christ pathetic and labor for Christ in vain.

> But if Christ is preached as raised from the dead, how can some among you say there is no resurrection of the dead? If there is no resurrection of the dead, then neither has Christ been raised. And if Christ has not been raised, then empty (too) is our preaching; empty, too, your faith. Then we are also false witnesses to God, because we testified against God that he raised Christ, whom he did not raise if in fact the dead are not raised. For if the dead are not raised, neither has Christ been raised, and if Christ has not been raised, your faith is vain; you are still in your sins. Then those who have fallen asleep in Christ have perished. If for this life only we have hoped in Christ, we are the most pitiable people of all. . . . Moreover, why are we endangering

> ourselves all the time? Every day I face death; I swear it by the pride in you (brothers) [*sic*] that I have in Christ Jesus our Lord. If at Ephesus I fought with beasts, so to speak, what benefit was it to me? If the dead are not raised: "Let us eat and drink, for tomorrow we die." (1 Corinthians 15:12–19, 30–32)

Paul's response to the problem raised by the Corinthians was Christ's resurrection. It was for him simply the "first fruits" of God's harvest, and as such, it was a glorious herald of the destiny all Christian disciples would share as Christ's brothers and sisters.[35]

> But now Christ has been raised from the dead, the first fruits of those who have fallen asleep. For since death came through a human being, the resurrection of the dead came also through a human being. For just as in Adam all die, so too in Christ shall all be brought to life, but each one in proper order: Christ the first fruits; then, at his coming, those who belong to Christ . . . (1 Corinthians 15:20–23)

As Paul conceived of God's plan, Christ's resurrection inaugurated the fulfillment of the Kin-dom of God.[36] When the time is right, this will include—"each in its own turn"—the "general" resurrection of the dead and the Second Coming of Christ.[37] This—the general resurrection of our bodies—is at the heart of the gospel for Paul. In fact, for Paul, the whole cosmos groans for its recreation in this new heaven and new earth.[38]

Evidently, however, this testimony remained controversial. Consider the explicit condemnation of those who denied the promise of a general bodily resurrection by the deutero-Pauline author in the second letter to Timothy. This epistle is thought to have been written considerably after Paul's death, sometime in the early second century, and perhaps addressed to communities quite different from those of Paul's era. Nevertheless, while we cannot be certain of precisely what was being condemned—were these early teachers "spiritualizing" the resurrection? or were they proclaiming a too fully "realized" eschatology?—the potential widespread appeal of their erroneous teachings was thought to pose a clear and present danger to the faith community (see 2 Timothy 2:16–18). And yet, doubts about this claim should not surprise us. This glorious vision of embodiment challenges the profoundly ambiguous experience of the body we have here and now. Indeed, it is a vision of embodiment difficult for most of us even to imagine, let alone upon which to place our hope.

Paul insisted that this general resurrection of the dead included the resurrection of the body. But he recognized this was an idea difficult to grasp, as well as easy to doubt. Giving voice to questions raised by those who would doubt the promise of bodily resurrection, Paul writes: "But someone may say, "How are the dead raised? With what kind of body will they come back?" (1 Corinthians 15:35). Paul contended that this corporate and collective (cosmic even!) resurrection would be a mysterious event that would happen "in an instant, in the blink of an eye, at the last trumpet" (1 Corinthians 15:52a). Questions about this mysterious event, such as would the dead be raised with perfect bodies? would they be naked or clothed? focused especially on the form of our newly transformed, resurrected bodies. They were not unique to Corinth. They had long been commonplace in Jewish apocalyptic thought. Familiar though these questions were to him, Paul doesn't speculate very much about such details.

Generally, Paul thought it foolish to speculate too much in this regard because at this time "we shall be changed" (1 Corinthians 15:52). After all, it is a radical, barely imaginable transformation. But Paul excluded some hypotheses.

> And what you sow is not the body that is to be but a bare kernel of wheat, perhaps, or of some other kind; but God gives it a body as he chooses, and to each of the seeds its own body. . . . So also is the resurrection of the dead. It is sown corruptible; it is raised incorruptible. It is sown dishonorable; it is raised glorious. It is sown weak; it is raised powerful. It is sown a natural body; it is raised a spiritual body. If there is a natural body, there is also a spiritual one. (1 Corinthians 15:37–38, 42–44)

Resurrection is not mere resuscitation. Rather, Paul testified to the resurrection of an imperishable body:

> This I declare, brothers [*sic*]: flesh and blood cannot inherit the kingdom of God, nor does corruption inherit incorruption. Behold, I tell you a mystery. We shall not all fall asleep, but we will all be changed, in an instant, in the blink of an eye, at the last trumpet. For the trumpet will sound, the dead will be raised incorruptible, and we shall be changed. For that which is corruptible must clothe itself with incorruptibility, and that which is mortal must clothe itself with immortality. And when this which is corruptible clothes itself with incorruptibility and this which is mortal clothes itself with immortality, then the word that is written shall come about: "Death is swallowed up in victory. Where, O death, is your victory? Where, O death, is your sting?" The sting of death is sin, and the power of sin is the law. But thanks be to God who gives us the victory through our Lord Jesus Christ. (1 Corinthians 15:50–57)

In fact, the adjectives Paul used to describe this glorious body were multiple: "So also is the resurrection of the dead. It is sown corruptible; it is raised incorruptible. It is sown dishonorable; it is raised glorious. It is sown weak; it is raised powerful. It is sown a natural body; it is raised a spiritual body. If there is a natural body, there is also a spiritual one" (1 Corinthians 15: 42–44). In addition to being transformed and imperishable, he proclaimed that the risen bodies of the faithful united to Christ would be mysteriously glorious, powerful, and spiritual.

CONTEMPORARY INTERPRETATIONS

Just exactly what Paul meant by this seed metaphor and this notion of a "spiritual body" has been debated for eons. We shall consider some of these patristic and early medieval reflections at more length in chapter 4. Segal's word study suggests that what is commonly translated "natural body" (Greek *soma psychikon*) could be more precisely translated "ensouled-body." It might well also be translated as the "living creature" described in Genesis 2:7, since the Septuagint translation of Genesis 2:7 has the words "and the human being (*anthropos*) became a living psyche (*psychēn*)." The first Adam who was created from ground (*adamah*) becomes a "living psyche" by God breathing into the clay body. Such an expression would have been easily understood by Greek members of his audience familiar with Platonic thought. However, Paul's notion of a "spiritual body" (Greek *soma pneumatikon*) would have undoubtedly struck his audience as a contradiction in terms. Segal suggests it was an expression completely out of the ordinary. Perhaps Paul understood that only an expression bearing such "contradictory" connotations could adequately point to such a transformed yet recognizable body.[39]

Many modern interpretations of "spiritual body" (Greek *psychikon soma*) are quite misleading in my opinion because they suggest the risen life will lack physicality. But as Wright points out, in Greek *ikos* (often translated as spiritual in the phrase "spiritual body") refers to the power or energy that animates a body, not to the substances from which it is made. This would mean that Paul was trying to say that while our present corruptible bodies are animated by the Creator's soul force, in the life to come our glorious risen bodies will enjoy the energizing power of the new creation, God's *pneuma* or Spirit. So it might best be translated as "Spirit-animated body" (and here, think of God's Spirit) rather than the "Psyche-animated body." Paul is saying that in risen life the faithful share in the reality of Christ as the "new Adam," not the "first Adam." For this reason, I prefer the translation of this verse provided in the *New Jerusalem Bible*: "When it is sown it embodies the soul, when it is raised it embodies the spirit" (1 Corinthians 15:44).

Many of us today, perhaps not unlike the Corinthians before us, seem to be uncomfortable with, if not embarrassed by, the notion of the resurrection of the body. At the very least, Paul's vivid language about the "rising of the corpses" (Greek *anastasis nekron*) strike some as more than a little creepy at least at first. One need only recall scenes from Michael Jackson's video *Thriller* to sense why some today might find the claim embarrassing. Unsettlingly as this may be, however, it should not prompt us to doubt the bodily nature of this new life.

The struggle to discern the nature of the life to come continues today. Some still contend that all that Paul meant by "spiritual body" was simply that a purely spiritual self would be raised. For example, William Barclay concludes that what Paul "really meant was that man's [*sic*] personality would survive."[40] Other biblical theologians, however, such as Richard B. Hays, N. T. Wright, Dale E. Martin, and J. Richard Middleton[41]—and I stand within this camp—argue, in contrast, that the resurrection for Paul involves a Spirit-ruled body, perfectly refitted for risen life. Otherwise, claims to cosmic resurrection (with all its physicality) fall flat. The Christian hope is that the whole of the created order, including our bodies, will be given a new existence by the Spirit of God.

It cannot be denied that Paul's seed analogy connotes very little continuity between earthly and glorious bodies. It implies tremendous transformation. There is a great deal of discontinuity between what is sown and what springs to new life, between what is perishable, dishonorable, weak, and natural on the one hand, and what will be the imperishable, glorious, powerful, and spiritual on the other. For Paul, grace is not only unmerited, forensic justification; it is radically transformative as well. He understood that the change implied by the general bodily resurrection of the dead is so great that the very prospect of such cosmic sanctification could unnerve the human imagination. In the end we must all allow Paul's words of assurance to the Corinthians to comfort us. God will provide appropriate bodies for all! It is time to tackle the question whether such glorified bodies will be sexual.

CHAPTER 3

The New Testament about Sex in Heaven

Might there be sex (gender and/or sexual desire and delight) in heaven? The Bible does not speak directly to this, but theologians make arguments on both sides of the question based in part on their interpretations of what scriptures seem to imply about it. Consider as representative of this debate arguments from Daniel J. Louw and Laura A. Smit.

Louw believes the following passage from the Pauline corpus grounds his claim that there will be sex in heaven.

> "Everything is lawful for me," [say the Corinthians, interpolation mine] but not everything is beneficial. "Everything is lawful for me," but I will not let myself be dominated by anything. "Food for the stomach and the stomach for food," but God will do away with both the one and the other. The body, however, is not for immorality, but for the Lord, and the Lord is for the body; God raised the Lord and will also raise us by his power. Do you not know that your bodies are members of Christ? Shall I then take Christ's members and make them the members of a prostitute? Of course not! [Or] do you not know that anyone who joins himself

> to a prostitute becomes one body with her? For "the two," it says, "will become one flesh." But whoever is joined to the Lord becomes one spirit with him. Avoid immorality. Every other sin a person commits is outside the body, but the immoral person sins against his own body. Do you not know that your body is a temple of the holy Spirit within you, whom you have from God, and that you are not your own? For you have been purchased at a price. Therefore, glorify God in your body. (1 Corinthians 6:12–20)

Louw points out that Paul is claiming here that those who have been baptized into Christ become part of a new reality. Through baptism they have been given what theologians call a new ontological being in Christ. This new reality is both already but not yet fully realized in them. So, Louw argues, Paul's exhortations to the Corinthians about sexual morality invite them (and us!) to ever more fully embody this new life in Christ. Because this new life is both an already present reality and our not yet fully realized destiny, it is both a gift and a moral calling. We ought to avoid all manner of bodily intemperance, including sexual immorality, precisely because now that we are "in Christ" our task on earth is to embody God's Spirit.

Louw notes that Paul is quite explicit in this passage: the body—including our sexuality—is united with the Lord. Thus, when we are fully "in Christ" we will fully—including sexually—embody God's Spirit. Thus, he concludes, there will be sex in heaven! Far from left behind, our sexuality will be enlivened by God's Spirit. This "already but not yet" eschatological destiny is the reason why faithful disciples even in their sexual lifestyles and habits during this interim between the present and End Times ought to display the fruits of life in the Spirit. These include love, joy, peace, forbearance, kindness, goodness, faithfulness, gentleness, and self-control (see Galatians 5:22–23).[1]

In contrast, consider the argument mounted by Laura A. Smit. Her reading of scripture is quite different from Louw's. Smit claims there will be no place for marriage and no need or place for sex in God's new creation. While the human capacity for love will be wondrously expanded in heaven in ways that "make our current experiences of sexual intimacy seem pale and uninteresting," Smit argues we will no longer need to embody the presence of God to one another. Since that is the purpose of sex, there will be no sex in heaven!

She too bases her argument on Paul's first letter to the Corinthians, but her focus is on Paul's preference for singleness as expressed later in that same epistle.

> Do not deprive each other, except perhaps by mutual consent for a time, to be free for prayer, but then return to one another, so that Satan may not tempt you through your lack of self-control. This I say by way of concession, however, not as a command. Indeed, I wish everyone to be as I am, but each has a particular gift from God, one of one kind and one of another. Now to the unmarried and to widows, I say: it is a good thing for them to remain as they are, as I do, but if they cannot exercise self-control they should marry, for it is better to marry than to be on fire. (1 Corinthians 7:5–9)

Smit emphasizes Paul's claim that the only good reason to marry is as a concession to overwhelming sexual temptation.[2] She interprets Paul as arguing people should remain single because the "End Time" is near and because particular commitments (to spouses and children) distract people from God and the needs of the wider community. For Smit, since both sex and marriage will be transcended in the life to come, their place in discipleship here and now is quite limited.[3] Far from what typifies the selfish "swinging singles" life of some today, the Christian vision of singleness, as Smit describes it, is a call to serve community. Unlike the intimate family relationships built up around marriage, this call into community will not become obsolete in heaven.

For Smit a celibate form of singleness is the default (or *prima facie* preferred) sexual lifestyle for Christians. This means that those Christians who wish to marry need to justify that choice. They must have some overwhelming reason for doing so. Like Paul, Smit suggests that many experience their sexual desire as overwhelming. Apart from this experience of "burning with passion," that is, of experiencing sexual desire as beyond probable self-control, Smit considers what else might meet the required burden of proof. At this juncture she departs a bit from Paul's reasoning. Smit recognizes that while the current age is passing away, still the End Time may not be imminent. Additionally, unlike Paul, she does not assume marriage and family will always distract disciples from God and the wider community.[4] So, Smit concludes Christians here and now should decide whether to remain single or marry, based on a careful assessment of which way of living will enable them to be most faithful this side of the pearly gates. Nevertheless, she remains adamant that neither sex nor marriage will have a future in the life of the world to come.

Two quite different sets of theological assumptions frame both the selection and interpretation of these biblical texts. Smit treats both human sexuality (at least as experienced in sexual desire and delight) and marriage as fixed orders of creation. In contrast, Louw views human sexuality and marriage as far more fluid. For him, they belong both to the order of creation and (like all that is subject to transformation) to the order of redemption.[5] This is why, he reasons, wedding imagery dominates both Jesus's and Paul's witness about the coming Kin-dom of God.[6]

In contemporary debates about whether there will be sex in heaven, questions like these frequently arise. How should we understand Jesus's remark that we will be "like angels" in the life to come? How should we interpret His assertion that in heaven people will "neither marry nor be given in marriage?" What should we make of Paul's preference for celibacy? What is the meaning of Jesus's singleness? This chapter will give special attention to competing interpretations of the texts often associated with these questions. Since for Paul resurrection results in a Spirit-ruled body, perfectly refitted for risen life, I will conclude this chapter by discussing what this promised transformation of the body might mean for our sexuality.

The tensions about sexuality just within First Corinthians, along with the theological tensions represented by Louw's and Smit's competing interpretations of Paul's outlook, suggest at the very least that we would do well to keep our speculations modest about the eschatological destiny of sexuality. For this reason, Richard B. Hays reminds us: "No one can predict the final shape and texture of the mature plant from the seed. God is the one who chooses what sort of body to give. . . . We must wait for the harvest to find out."[7] Even so, Hays himself draws our attention to Paul's claim that "just as we have borne the image of the earthly one, we shall also bear the image of the heavenly one (1 Corinthians 15:49). Hays suggests that as Paul saw it, in Christ's resurrection we get a glimpse of our own. Once raised, we can expect to bear fully the likeness of Christ! We can know a little something about this mystery based on what we know about the glorious body of the Risen Christ. What kind of body will those who are brothers and sisters in Christ enjoy fully in the life of the world to come? Paul's answer: a body similar to that of the Risen Lord.

As discussed in the previous chapter, Paul's letters include much earlier confessions about the risen Jesus (for example, Romans 8:11), and what is thought to be its earliest creedal formulation (1 Corinthians 15:1–11), but they do not say much about the nature of the Risen Christ. For clues about that, we turn to the gospels. They were composed more or less one generation after Paul wrote his letters. These later narratives say more in various ways. The gospels offer us several sources of insight into the nature of risen life. Within these narratives one finds the stories of the empty tomb and of the appearances of the Risen Christ, as well as the teachings of Jesus during his public ministry about resurrection.

EMPTY TOMB AND APPEARANCE STORIES

In the gospel of Mark, we are told that some women—Mary Magdalene and Mary the mother of James and Salome—walked out of the city of Jerusalem to the tomb where the corpse of their leader, teacher, and friend, Jesus of Nazareth, had been laid to rest. Their plan was to anoint his corpse with spices. They found the stone blocking the entrance to the cave already rolled back and the tomb empty. A young man dressed in a white robe tells them: "'Do not be amazed! You seek Jesus of Nazareth, the crucified. He has been raised; he is not here. Behold the place where they laid him.' But go and tell his disciples and Peter, 'He is going before you to Galilee; there you will see him, as he told you'" (Mark 16:6b–7). In the most ancient version of this gospel that we have, the story ends with the women leaving the empty tomb in terror and saying nothing.[8]

The Markan account of the empty tomb has parallels in the other gospels.[9] These narratives about the empty tomb aim to challenge doubts about the bodily resurrection of Jesus. Such testimony stands over against those—both in the first century and now—who might interpret the stories of the appearances of the Risen Christ as purely spiritual encounters. It refutes those who might have been or are now inclined to dismiss such talk as mere "ghost stories," hero worship, hysterics, or expressions of grief. As Daniel A. Smith notes, there is a continuity between the empty tomb and the appearance stories in the canonical gospels that naturally links the body that was buried to the embodied form that appears.[10]

The account of the Apostle Thomas's encounter with the Risen Christ in the gospel of John emphasizes the transformed and miraculous nature of Jesus's glorious body. Christ came to them through closed doors! At the same time the display of the wounds on his hands and side demonstrates the ongoing, wondrous physicality of His resurrected body (John 20:24–29). In Luke's anthology of post-resurrection stories, the Risen Christ himself is portrayed as directly addressing the doubts about the bodily nature of his resurrection.

> Then he said to them, "Why are you troubled? And why do questions arise in your hearts? Look at my hands and my feet, that it is I myself. Touch me and see, because a ghost does not have flesh and bones as you can see I have." And as he said this, he showed them his hands and his feet. While they were still incredulous for joy and were amazed, he asked them, "Have you anything here to eat?" They gave him a piece of baked fish; he took it and ate it in front of them. (Luke 24:38–43)

All the evangelists are notably assertive about people *seeing* the Risen Jesus and recognizing him in a "bodily" existence. His eating with them (in the gospel of Luke) and showing "wounds" to Thomas (in the gospel of John) probably are meant to counter an easy kind of spiritualizing of encounters with the Risen Jesus. Though radically transformed and glorious in nature, this new existence of Jesus as the Risen Lord affirms the eschatological redemption of all creation, including our bodily existence.

TEACHINGS OF JESUS ON MARRIAGE

One of the most often cited biblical texts in the debate about whether there will be sex in heaven is a teaching ascribed to Jesus: "When they rise from the dead, they neither marry nor are given in marriage, but they are like the angels in heaven" (Mark 12:25). The broad context for this saying is the debate within Judaism about resurrection. As detailed in the opening section of the previous chapter, belief in the general resurrection of the body (at least for an interim period of Final Judgment) was central to the Pharisaic form of Judaism that emerged during the late Second Temple period. While Jesus clearly sought to reform this movement, he affirmed this particular Pharisaic teaching.[11] In contrast, the Sadducees and Essenes adamantly denied the notion that there would be a general resurrection of dead at the end time.

This debate within Judaism occasioned an argument during Jesus's earthly ministry about the nature of risen life. This argument between Jesus and a few Sadducees is the context for the previously quoted saying. Let us consider the Markan version of this exchange first.

> Some Sadducees, who say there is no resurrection, came to him and put this question to him, saying, "Teacher, Moses wrote for us, 'If someone's brother dies, leaving a wife but no child, his brother must take the wife and raise up descendants for his brother.' Now there were seven brothers. The first married a woman and

> died, leaving no descendants. So the second married her and died, leaving no descendants, and the third likewise. And the seven left no descendants. Last of all the woman also died. At the resurrection [when they arise] whose wife will she be? For all seven had been married to her." Jesus said to them, "Are you not misled because you do not know the scriptures or the power of God? When they rise from the dead, they neither marry nor are given in marriage, but they are like the angels in heaven. As for the dead being raised, have you not read in the Book of Moses, in the passage about the bush, how God told him, 'I am the God of Abraham, [the] God of Isaac, and [the] God of Jacob'? He is not God of the dead but of the living. You are greatly misled." (Mark 12:18–27)

The "case" under discussion stems from the ancient practice known as Levirate marriage.[12] According to Jewish law (see Deuteronomy 25:5–6, for example) it was the right and duty of a widow's brother-in-law to marry her and raise offspring, so as to provide some security and protection for the widow, preserve the deceased's name and memory (and family line), and to keep his property in the family. The Sadducees presumed that Jesus thought risen life would not differ in significant ways from earthly life as we know it now. They probably conflated the idea of resurrection with experiences of resuscitation or revivification, and so the question arose: to which of the seven brothers would the widow be married in the life to come?

In his reply to this question, Jesus teaches that scriptural testimony about hope in the resurrection can be found in the Torah itself (Exodus 3:6, 15–16) and that belief in resurrection rests on trust in the power of God. In their commentary on *The Gospel of Mark*, John R. Donahue and the late Daniel J. Harrington help us understand Jesus's reply. They note that according to Josephus, a first-century Jewish historian, the Sadducees were "men of the highest standing," though they had only limited popular influence. Theirs was an aristocratic, conservative style of priestly leadership. A strong belief in life after death—like that espoused by some of the Pharisees—was still something of a comparative novelty in the Judaism of Jesus's day.[13] The Sadducees did not accept what were in their day "modern" apocalyptic ideas about resurrection, angels, and demons. They accepted only the Torah—the first five books of the Christian Old Testament—as scripture, which is why Jesus took pains to trace resurrection back to it.

And what of Jesus's remark that their God is the God of the living? In his introduction to and commentary on this section of Mark, Joel Marcus notes that the Marcan Jesus speaks of resurrection life as if it had in some real sense already begun. God is still the God of living patriarchs. In some sense, those who have died or been martyred are not really dead![14] And yet, as M. Eugene Boring notes in his commentary, this is not yet the fullness of resurrection, which is future both to Exodus 3 and Mark 12.[15] He suggests further that the talk of angels in Mark at this point was a way of saying that the martyrs are not lost, but rather hidden from the living, like angels in heaven. So, it may well be that the Marcan community believed that at death the righteous would in some sense be taken immediately into God's presence, but that bodily resurrection was part of God's eschatological redemption of history in which God's justice would prevail and God's Kin-dom would come.[16]

The Marcan Jesus further proclaims: "when they rise from the dead, they neither marry nor are given in marriage, but they are like the angels in heaven" (Mark 12:25). This has been interpreted in several different ways. Some conclude that Jesus is here teaching that there will be no sex in heaven. This leads others to argue further that this means—at least ideally—that there should be no sex on earth. Still others conclude both such judgments to be premature at best. Colleen MacDannell and Bernhard Lang in their book *Heaven: A History* offer what I consider a popular version of the "no sex in heaven" interpretation.[17] They distinguish Jesus's perspective from both the Sadducean denial of risen life and from the apocalyptic expectation that the righteous would live blissful lives in a divine kingdom on earth, enjoying married life and progeny for a millennium. In their interpretation of the exchange, Jesus clearly puts marital relationships (and by implication parental, sibling, and family relationships of all sorts as well) outside the framework for the life to come. MacDannell and Lang conclude that in heaven, all human and ecological interrelationship will simply disintegrate *coram Deo* (before God). As will be evident shortly, however, others argue that the theocentrism proper to risen life may simply center all other relationships in God, simultaneously strengthening and relativizing them in relation to God, the Center in Whom we live.

Like MacDannell and Lang, biblical scholar Joel Marcus concludes his interpretation of this portion of Mark by arguing that this text suggests humans will be celibate in risen life. Glorious bodies may be gendered, as he interprets the Bible, but they will certainly not enjoy sexual desire and/or delight. He notes that while in the Old Testament and Jewish literature angels are routinely described as gendered (usually male) and as capable of sexual desire and activity, the latter is associated only with evil, which of course has no place in heaven.[18] For nearly one thousand years, this lustful, sexual activity "across species" (that is, between angels and humans) was associated with the origin of evil, until the story of "the Fall" in Genesis 3 eclipsed it as the etiology of evil after the Babylonian captivity. But as Marcus points out, at many junctures in the scriptures (for example, Jude 6) such lustful activity is associated with "fallen" angels and is interpreted as the primal sin.[19]

On the face of it, Luke's account of Jesus's encounter with the Sadducees seems not only to reinforce this line of interpretation, but to press beyond it. Does Jesus teach that ideally there should be no sex on earth either? Consider the passage in Luke that "parallels" this Marcan text.

> Jesus said to them, "The children of this age marry and are given in marriage; but those who are deemed worthy to attain to the coming age and to the resurrection of the dead neither marry nor are given in marriage. They can no longer die, for they are like angels; and they are the children of God because they are the ones who will rise. That the dead will rise even Moses made known in the passage about the bush, when he called 'Lord' the God of Abraham, the God of Isaac, and the

> God of Jacob; and he is not God of the dead, but of the living, for to him all are alive." (Luke 20:34–38)[20]

In the course of Christian history, this version of the exchange between Jesus and the Sadducees has been and is still interpreted by many to mean that those best able to witness here and now to our eschatological future are virgins, vowed celibates, and/or spouses who practice mutually agreed upon celibacy within marriage.[21]

Tradition teaches that John the Baptist, Jesus, and Paul were all single at the time of their public ministries. This is sometimes cited as evidence supportive of this line of reasoning.[22] In the final chapter of his book on *Sexuality and the Jesus Tradition*, William Loader speaks to the question of the eschatological meaning of the presumed single status of Jesus, John the Baptist, and Paul (along with the positive images in the New Testament of the celibacy of Mary and Anna). He concludes that all three viewed their celibacy (which can only be presumed in the case of Jesus and John) as a preferred (but not required) lifestyle, because it best embodied their vision of the future Kin-dom of God. Celibacy, as Loader interprets the New Testament, was tied to the hope for the life to come.

Dale C. Allison goes even farther down this interpretative path. While he recognizes that most biblical scholars today do not believe Jesus was an ascetic, he argues against that contemporary consensus in his book *Jesus of Nazareth: Millenarian Prophet*. In regard to worldly standards of success (symbolized by *mammon*) and in regard to sexual activity, Allison contends Jesus practiced detachment and rigorous self-denial. Allison claims Jesus exited from the course of ordinary life and invited his disciples to do likewise. He argues Jesus was an ascetic in regard to money and sex, though not food and drink. His sexual asceticism was intended as a sign of judgment and a solemn call to repentance. Allison interprets Jesus's celibacy as a proleptic recovery of the celibacy Adam practiced prior to the Fall. As is often typical of those who reach this conclusion, Allison contends that sexual activity occurred only after sin entered the world.[23]

Again, this line of interpretation seems to be reinforced by other biblical passages. For example, as was mentioned earlier, Paul expressed a similar preference for celibacy. He thinks that while marriage is an acceptable "remedy" for those who burn with desire, sexual activity within marriage is at best just a concession to the threats posed by sexual temptations. Paul seems to see marriage per se as troublesome (1 Corinthians 7: 28). If possible, marriage should be avoided (1 Corinthians 7:6–7, 38) because such sexual relationships distract disciples' devotion from God and divide their interests (1 Corinthians 7:8, 32–35).[24]

This way of interpreting these texts contributes significantly to the ongoing moral idealization of virginity and celibacy on earth. It also pits particular, deep friendships and intimate spousal/family bonds against faithful discipleship. It has had a tremendous impact on the history of Christian sexual ethics. But I believe it is mistaken. The evidence for this reading is not as strong as it first appears. There may well be good reasons to imagine sex in heaven!

First, consider how qualified Paul's preference for celibacy is. Paul clearly distinguishes what he describes as the Lord's teachings about divorce and remarriage from his own preference regarding celibacy. In his letter to the Corinthians he repeatedly notes in this regard, "I say . . . " Still, he presents his views as having some authority, in his words as trustworthy and Spirit-filled, at least as much as those of the Corinthians with whom he is arguing: "Now in regard to virgins: I have no commandment from the Lord, but I give my opinion as one who by the Lord's mercy is trustworthy. . . . She [a widow] is more blessed, though, in my opinion, if she remains as she is, and I think that I too have the Spirit of God" (1 Corinthians 7:25, 40; interpolation mine). Paul is quite clear: his preference for virginity and celibacy is his best judgment, not a command from the Lord.

Second, Paul's preference for the single life could not have been very strong, since some of his rationale for this preference simply reflects his opinion that it would be best if everyone were simply to remain "as they were." Believers should stay married, unmarried, uncircumcised, engaged, even enslaved (if an opportunity for release does not present itself), and so on, given his probable (though now in hindsight clearly mistaken) presumption that the world as he then knew it would be "passing away soon." In this light, given the political and economic role of patriarchal marriage in the ancient Mediterranean world, Paul's statement of preference may well reflect (at least in part) a concern to establish the dignity and value of the single life, in a social context that routinely condemned the single life as neglectful of one's family duties and treasonous to the empire.

It is also significant that Paul viewed marriage as an acceptable calling for Christians. Even though Paul viewed his own "singleness" as a gift of God (literally, a *charisma*), it is clear that he did not expect it to be the gift given everyone in the congregation (1 Corinthians 7:7). And though in Paul's view marriage brings trouble (1 Corinthians 7:13), Paul describes the call into marriage as a gift from God like celibacy (1 Corinthians 7:7).

Although we can be certain of Paul's unmarried status at least at the time of his ministry, we cannot be as certain of the marital status of John the Baptist or Jesus, though most accept the traditions that they too were single. Still, there is no biblical testimony to their status as single. Furthermore, there is no record of John the Baptist's call to repentance including a call to or preference for virginity or celibacy. Similarly, Jesus does not state a preference for this sexual lifestyle. He notes only that some may be given and choose to accept a call to become a eunuch for the sake of the kingdom.

Jesus's singleness is often treated as a sign of his asexuality, or at least as an indication that his experience of sexual desire was negligible. Nothing in the Bible confirms this view and much contradicts it. Consider what the author of the epistle to the Hebrews has to say about the full humanity of Jesus.

> Surely he did not help angels but rather the descendants of Abraham; therefore, he had to become like his brothers [*sic*] in every way, that he might be a merciful and faithful high priest before God to expiate the sins of the people. Because he himself was tested through what he

> suffered, he is able to help those who are being tested. . . . For we do not have a high priest who is unable to sympathize with our weaknesses, but one who has similarly been tested in every way, yet without sin. (Hebrews 2:16–18; 4:15)

A careful reading of Genesis 2 contradicts the conclusion that the experience of sexual desire per se is shameful. Thus it is reasonable to presume this passage from Hebrews to mean that Jesus of Nazareth must not only have been complete in all his parts,[25] but also that he knew firsthand sexual desire and may even have experienced sexual temptations. Even those (like Smit) who conclude there will be no sex in heaven recognize this to be true: "All healthy adult human beings feel sexual desire, including Paul and, yes, even Jesus."[26]

What then is to be made about the gospel's silence about whether Jesus was ever stirred by sexual desire, sexually tempted, or sexually active? Apart from an account of his circumcision in the gospel of Luke, the Bible is mute about Jesus's sexuality.[27] Surely this is the source of the tendency toward Docetism—toward believing heretically that Jesus is not really human—within the faith, especially since the scriptures are explicit about his experience of things like hunger, thirst, exhaustion, death, and the like. And yet, as Lewis B. Smedes concludes, Jesus's choice not to marry may simply confirm that one can be a fully sexual human being without entering into a genital sexual relationship.[28]

What about the Marcan and Lukan passages that testify to the absence of weddings in heaven? Do they confirm without qualification that there will be no sex in heaven? Loader himself takes note of the logic that may have undergirded them. They may presume that the sole function of marriage (and sexual activity) is procreation; and that the sole function of procreation is in turn presumed to be the achievement of a certain sort of "immortality" through progeny. Given these assumptions, since there is no threat of death in heaven, it would make sense to see both marriage and procreation as without value to life in Christ, both in heaven and at least for some on earth. But since few Christians today would view these premises as sound, it is not at all clear what this text might mean today.

Indeed, the Lukan passage reads as if that community envisioned heaven as a kind of restored Paradise or order of creation, rather than the transformed, new creation testified to elsewhere in the Bible. Interestingly, Loader notes that heaven may have been envisioned by these early Christians as a holy place or temple. If that were the case, they would have wanted to distinguish their religion from any sort of Hellenistic fertility cults involving sexual activity before deities. The Jewish Holiness Code had clearly forbidden sexual activity in such locations because of its association with idolatry. This did not mean that sexual activity was not thought to be holy. Consider the Jewish custom of encouraging spouses to keep the Sabbath holy through sexual activity.

TEACHINGS OF JESUS ON EUNUCHS AND CELIBACY

Let us attend in closer detail to what Jesus had to say about eunuchs as reported in the gospel of Matthew.[29] Jesus's teaching against remarriage following divorce, and the apparent dismay it engendered among his disciples, is the context for this passage.

> [His] disciples said to him, "If that is the case of a man with his wife, it is better not to marry." He answered, "Not all can accept [this] word, but only those to whom that is granted. Some are incapable of marriage because they were born so; some, because they were made so by others; some, because they have renounced marriage for the sake of the kingdom of heaven. Whoever can accept this ought to accept it." (Matthew 19:10–12)

Certainly, at first this teaching was (mis)taken by some to be an endorsement for voluntary literal castration. As late as 325 CE, ritual castration was a practice widespread enough among some Christians to require its explicit condemnation at the Council of Nicaea. The idealized, ascetic forms of celibacy that came to be associated with its more traditional allegorical, rather than literal, interpretation were centuries in the making.[30]

Some modern interpreters speculate that here Jesus may have been responding to a taunt about his status as unmarried. Many read the text suggesting that celibacy, if not virginity, was idealized by Jesus here. The problem with such an interpretation is that it doesn't fit the historical facts. Eunuchs were associated with the gender characteristics and roles of both males and females. In the ancient Mediterranean world, eunuchs were generally not viewed as celibate or virginal. Rather eunuchs were seen as passive (that is, "mounted") sexual partners, who like females and slaves, both male and female, could (and did) give sexual pleasure through fellatio, cunnilingus, and manual sexual activity. They clearly had at best an ambivalent social status because they were a third type of person, outside of the ordered, heterosexist binary that was considered normative. They certainly symbolized masculine vulnerability to the loss of patriarchal social standing and privilege.

Far from ascetic, the sexual lifestyle of most eunuchs was presumed to be morally dubious by some and held in suspicion by many. Though not capable of reproduction, and usually not of coitus, eunuchs were nevertheless viewed as "highly sexed," if not promiscuous. Postpubescent castration made some eunuchs difficult to identify as such. Some powerful women viewed eunuchs as ideal lovers and/or marriage partners precisely because such unions would relieve them of the prospect of childbearing with its attendant risks.[31]

Two features of the text are noteworthy. First, nothing in Jesus's teaching suggests eunuchs required healing of any sort. Certainly, their gender transgressive behavior—their rejection of roles typically associated with masculinity—posed no apparent problem for Jesus. And second, nothing in this passage itself suggests that voluntary eunuchism, either physical or ascetic, is preferred over marriage.

Those who believe there will be no sex in heaven do not address well the tension between this conclusion—that the life for which disciples in the Jesus movement hoped was celibate—and the absence of an explicit biblical assertion of it.

Additionally, they do not adequately explain—if sex is left behind—why celibacy was not required of all. Why was marriage permitted to early Christians, indeed affirmed as a gift even by Paul,[32] who recognized that in some marriages a pagan spouse might be sanctified, that is, converted through the spouse's grace-filled witness to God? Why did Jesus rehearse the Hebrew conviction that "one flesh" experiences are part of the of the Creator's good design? "He said in reply, 'Have you not read that from the beginning the Creator "made them male and female"' and said, 'For this reason a man shall leave his father and mother and be joined to his wife, and the two shall become one flesh'?" (Matthew 19:4–5). Why was marriage celebrated by Jesus at Cana (John 2:1–11)?[33] How could salvation have been linked as explicitly as it was to childbearing in 1 Timothy 2:15? As even William Loader concludes, throughout the New Testament there is "a strong affirmation of sexual relations."[34]

For those both in the first century and now who associate marriage with domestic and sexual abuse, Jesus's apparent dismissal of the institution they associate with violence and oppression may well come as good news. And yet, for those who associate marriage with emotionally intimate relationships, companionship, erotic desire, and sexual delight, its absence in the resurrection seems almost unthinkable.[35] Consider a contrasting line of interpretation represented here by Joel B. Green and others.[36] Green suggests that the language in Luke about our being as angels does not point toward celibacy. But rather, it testifies to the notion that though humans will not become immortal in risen life (an attribute belonging to God alone), neither will they suffer diminishment and die. Hence, in a manner like unto angels, people in risen life will have no need for the familial legacy or the financial support associated with *levirate* marriage. Green argues that what is at stake in this exchange are two competing notions of life after death: (1) the hope for risen life in communion with God and one's brothers and sisters in Christ as proclaimed by Jesus versus (2) a notion of "continuity" maintained through countless progeny as produced in a heavenly, fertile marriages.[37]

Additional commentators argue that Jesus's talk in Mark 12:25 about angels is purely figurative (like Paul's talk of seeds in 1 Corinthians 15). They conclude that this comparison with angels should not be read as a literal description of the risen life to come.[38] Several good reasons support this way of reading the text. In the first place, Jesus is making a claim about his own teaching authority as an interpreter of Scripture and the power of God. His primary aim is not to offer an account of risen life. Second, insofar as the latter is addressed, Jesus is emphasizing what risen life will not be like. It will not be a continuation of life as we know it. Resurrection is not resuscitation. Many preoccupations of sexual life as they knew it—such as the orderly transfer of property, the protection of widows, and the propagation of the species—will disappear in the life to come. Certainly at least some (patriarchal? abusive?), if not all, forms of marriage will not continue, but that does not necessarily mean that in the life to come we will be asexual, nor does it mean that sex in glory will not be steadfast.

This line of interpretation is reinforced by the context in which another parallel version of this encounter between Jesus and the Sadducees is found.[39] In the gospel of Matthew, the story of this exchange is surrounded by vivid portrayals of risen life as great sensuous wedding banquets,[40] which make its interpretation as an ascetic endorsement of celibacy seem problematic. These sensuous, highly relational images of our risen life to come found in Matthew are expanded into geopolitical, indeed ecological, images of God's Kin-dom in the book of Revelation. Here the City of God is described in a vision rife with conjugal imagery.

> Then I saw a new heaven and a new earth. The former heaven and the former earth had passed away, and the sea was no more. I also saw the holy city, a new Jerusalem, coming down out of heaven from God, prepared as a bride adorned for her husband. I heard a loud voice from the throne saying, "Behold, God's dwelling is with the human race. He will dwell with them and they will be his people and God himself will always be with them [as their God]. He will wipe every tear from their eyes, and there shall be no more death or mourning, wailing

> or pain, [for] the old order has passed away." (Revelation 21:1–4)

Whether labeled the "Kingdom of Heaven" (as is predominantly the case in Matthew) or the "Kingdom of God," or "holy city" (as it is here), it is important to note that this "new creation" is portrayed as coming with authority from, but not as existing elsewhere in, a "heavenly" realm.

Yet precisely such confusion has been and is widespread. Many Christians simply equate the promise of resurrected life with the promise of a spiritual paradise in heaven after death, with "pie in the sky, by and by," rather than with a gloriously transformed "new creation" here in a new heaven and new earth. Wright suggests that what the world is waiting for will be both continuous and discontinuous with life as we know it now. People will not go to heaven, but rather the City of God will come down to earth. The new life of communion with others and God that we already taste in the best of sexual relationships (and religious communities and friendships) will burst forth fully in the life to come!

Jesus is nowhere in the Bible reported to have said that those who are raised from the dead would become angels. Rather the gospel writers indicate the faithful are destined to be like (in Mark and Matthew) or equal to (in Luke) angels. How so? In what sense? Jesus's retorts are difficult to understand. Certainly, the Sadducees were insincere in their query. It was well known then that they thought the idea of the bodily resurrection ridiculous. In addition, they seem to have misunderstood the notion. To believe in the resurrection is not to believe that life as we know it will continue, as it had before death. To reiterate: resurrection is not bodily resuscitation.

CONCLUSION

The precise meaning of these specific texts is not at all "plain" or self-evident. It is not implausible to conclude that they imply there will be no sex in heaven, as suggested by Joel Marcus and

Dale C. Allison. Such a conclusion is not completely incompatible with biblical claims about both human sexuality and risen life. But I do not think this is the best of all the plausible interpretations. It does not complement and reinforce all these testimonies. It will not vivify our hope in the body's glorious resurrection. Consider the merits of the following summary interpretation.

On the one hand, human beings in risen life will be like angels in that they will no longer face death, and, therefore, they will have no need to establish their security or a sense of personal continuity through heirs.[41] Insofar as this is what marriage might still mean to some, it is important to reiterate that "in heaven neither will they marry nor be given in marriage." And undoubtedly there are many additional ways in which marriage as we know it will be no more.

On the other hand, while Jesus explicitly associates eunuchs—those who most vividly transgress the rigid gender binary associated with heterosexism and patriarchy—with the Kin-dom of God, he does not explicitly reject males or females per se. (That a baptismal formula quoted by Paul in Galatians 3:28 was interpreted by some church fathers to mean that gender would be left behind will be addressed in the next chapter.) Nor does Jesus's teaching necessarily mean that other expressions of gender will be excluded from the life to come.

Furthermore, Jesus is not reported as saying specifically that there will be no sexual desire or no sexual delight in this new creation. Nor is he reported as saying that already established marriages will not (in some transformed sense) be recognized. Indeed, some Christians argue that bonds created under God's authority on earth are indissoluble, even in heaven.[42] Jesus is only reported to have indicated marriages (of at least some, if not all, types) will not be contracted.[43] Even if marriage as it was known early in the Common Era, or as we know it today, will be no more, this does not necessarily mean that steadfast forms of emotional intimacy, companionship, and sexual desire and delight will be excluded from the life to come.

And yet, while many contemporary theologians believe the continuation of gender to be plausible, many continue to exclude sexual delight and delight from heaven. One of the most thoughtful of these theologians, Dennis P. Hollinger, offers three reasons for why he reached this conclusion.[44] In the first place, notes Hollinger, to affirm God's gift of sexuality as only finite and temporal does not undermine its earthly goodness and beauty. Secondly, that there will be no sex in heaven reminds us that sexual relationships will never be finally satisfying. Third, our need for relationship will be fully, indeed extravagantly, satisfied by our communion with God and with others in heaven.

In contrast, other theologians—such as Lewis B. Smedes, J. Harold Ellens, and Richard B. Hays, whose thinking on this matter I commend later—believe holy, bodily pleasures could characterize our life to come. Furthermore, they suggest that those in sacramental partnerships on occasion even now may taste of such graces. Sexuality may not be annihilated, but rather "newly clothed." They conclude the redemption of sexuality will entail more than its forgiveness. The relational and creative ends for which sexuality is designed will be gloriously fulfilled and sanctified. This vision of the great communion with God and each other that is to come—far from increasing the risk that sex will be idolized—constantly upholds our earthly passions to this holy standard. Of course, all needs will be fulfilled in heaven, but the attraction toward and energy nurtured by what is beautiful and good that is sexual desire stems not from a lack but rather is a creative impulse both to know—really know—the other and to be known, in mutual gladness and delight.

Despite the several specific sexual behaviors condemned in the Bible, it is crucial to remember that the Bible in general broadly endorses human sexuality. For example, it is clear from the record of Jesus's teachings on divorce found in Matthew 19:1–6 and its parallel in Mark 10:6–8—with their references to the creation accounts found in Genesis 1:27 and 2:24—that the gospels portray Jesus as affirming "one flesh" unions. Such sexual "couplings" are attributed in Genesis to the ongoing providential work of God among us. This is the same God who is drawing us into eternal life! As Smedes notes: "if sexuality is what God gave us to reflect his own [Trinitarian love] life, it would be strange indeed if he de-sexed us as our reward in heaven. And if sexuality is forever, we are doubly assured of its goodness on earth."[45]

J. Harold Ellens suggests in his book *Sex in the Bible: A New Consideration* that given the transformation of some of the experiences of human finitude, perhaps Jesus meant that in the resurrection this widow could enjoy steadfast, fully attentive, genuinely loving sexual partnerships with all seven of these brothers. Could our possessiveness and vulnerability to neglect and betrayal that make sexual exclusivity so necessary here and now on earth be healed and transformed? Ellens suggests exclusivity might not be requisite in heaven. He suggests that perhaps risen life "is a setting of holy promiscuity, where we shall enjoy total union with everyone who really delights us."[46]

Such a suggestion undoubtedly proves shocking to many. We may have had such dehumanizing experiences of sexuality that the very notion that polyamory could be in any sense holy is scandalous. For many people claiming any kind of sexuality to be holy is not only profoundly countercultural, but sacrilegious. Richard B. Hays notes that many Christians today, like some before them in Corinth, find it hard to believe that our weak, flawed, mortal bodies are so beloved by God that God will not leave them behind or annihilate them. It is difficult to really trust that our bodies—including our sexual desires—will not be abolished, but instead will be healed and sanctified for the glory of God. Indeed, some theologians argue that the Bible says everything human was made with an orientation toward what is to come. All of creation is interpreted as summoned *ad imaginem Dei*, that is, *toward* its holy, sanctified future.

As Paul wrote elsewhere: "He [Christ] will change our lowly body to conform with his glorified body by the power that enables him also to bring all things into subjection to himself" (Philippians 3:21; interpolation mine). "The resurrection of the dead," Hays writes, "is necessary in order to hold creation and redemption together."[47] Otherwise God would simply be abandoning the bodies He has created. This anticipated enhancement is the theological reason why what we do here on earth with our bodies matters so much.[48] In fact, Hays argues that according to Paul, "underneath all the dismaying problems of the Corinthians lay one massive theological fallacy: they denied the resurrection of the dead."[49] This theological denial was the origin of many, subsequent moral confusions. Our task as disciples of Christ on earth—like theirs was—is to make of our bodily selves a prayerful witness to the transformation, not destruction, that is God's plan for our world and absolutely everything created good therein.

CHAPTER 4

Augustine and Other Early Christians on Sex in Heaven

Most Christian theologians presume that sexual desire and delight, along with reproductive capacity, will disappear in the new heaven and new earth. As is quite evident by now, I think this speculative trajectory mistaken, but an important, first step in faithfully developing any tradition is to wrestle with it. So, this chapter consists of a careful, if brief, review of what many Christian theologians in antiquity, particularly Augustine, had to say about the bodily nature of the general resurrection overall, and about the prospects for sex in heaven in particular. We begin with a consideration of the centrality and meaning of early affirmations of the resurrection of the body.

EARLY ESCHATOLOGICAL SPECULATIONS

Proclamations from ancient Christian Eucharistic liturgies—like "Christ Has Died, Christ Is Risen, Christ Will Come Again!"—make clear the centrality of resurrection to Christianity. It was expressed in all three of the ecumenical or universal creeds.[1] It would not be an exaggeration to say this was *the* central, nonnegotiable belief of Christianity.[2] Furthermore, many Christians view God's raising of Jesus as not only a sign of His personal vindication but an event of ontic import that ushered into existence the new creation. While obviously not yet fully realized, the hope for its full cosmic realization when Christ comes again became integral to belief in Jesus's resurrection. Early on the "good news" included the claim that all those united to Christ would likewise enjoy this new life through bodily resurrection. Many trusted in the promise of and longed for the time when Jesus Christ "will change this lowly body to be like his glorious body" (Philippians 3:21).

It must be noted that some who called themselves Christian did not affirm the bodily nature of the general resurrection. In this era what we now label Docetism was a very influential heresy. Adherents believed that Jesus Christ was not really human, that He only appeared to be of flesh and blood. His embodiment was an illusion. If this was your starting point, then, of course, Christ's was no bodily resurrection. Without its Christological foundation, belief in the bodily nature of the general resurrection did not make sense either. Risen life, as they imagined it, was much less continuous with life as we know it now. They believed many physical aspects of our lives would be "spiritualized," if not transcended altogether. There might not even be recognizable gender differences.[3]

In contrast, others argued vehemently against such conclusions.[4] But what exactly did these early Christians mean when they affirmed their belief in "the resurrection of the body"?[5] At the level of specifics, there was little unanimity among them. Caroline Bynum argues their hoped-for transfiguration was usually imagined to come at the hands of a Master Potter or Builder, who would reassemble the person in all essential respects, albeit in more glorious fashion. Many believed all important identity markers would be preserved in the "reassembled" life to come, and among the saints, enhanced.

For example, consider Athenagoras. He wrote the earliest surviving treatise specifically focused *On the Resurrection of the Dead* (175–180 CE). After refuting commonly held objections to the doctrine of a general bodily resurrection, he argued for both its possibility and its probability. Similarly, in a tract

Against the Heresies (175–185 CE), Irenaeus of Lyons argued that those who did not affirm the salvation of the whole person, including the flesh (*universam reprobant resurrectionem*), were in effect despising the handiwork of the Creator and denying the bodily resurrection of Jesus Christ. He contended the souls of disciples who died awaited the resurrection of the flesh just as Christ had.[6]

This concept of a general bodily resurrection was a matter of keen debate at the end of second century, not only between Christians and their detractors but among the faithful as well. So it is not surprising that Tertullian of Carthage (160–220/5 CE) wrote *On the Resurrection of the Dead*.[7] This is the first Christian speculation of significant length about risen life. Tertullian could not accept the decay of the corpses of the early martyrs as a just end to their witness.[8] Since in every case death was ultimately "violent" and putrid decomposition inevitably followed every death, any claim to a genuine victory over death required victory over such physical dissolution. Everything intrinsic to a person's identity had to be raised up, and much of human particularity was located in the body.

Tertullian insisted Jesus was fully incarnate, and his resurrection was likewise fully corporeal. An analogous form of risen life in Christ is, Tertullian argued, the ultimate destination for all the faithful departed. It would be unjust of God not to raise up our bodies along with our souls: "Both therefore will be glorified together, even as they have suffered together."[9] For Tertullian, it was only the sinful work, not the substance, of the flesh, that would be excluded from the life of the world to come.[10] However wounded or defective our bodies may be before or after death, in the new creation they will be perfect and enjoy perpetual bodily integrity according to Tertullian.[11]

While interpreting the exchange between Jesus and the Sadducees, Tertullian explained that in the life to come people will be equal (but not identical) to the angels, because they will not die. Since there is no death in heaven, there will be no need for procreation. Hence, in risen life people will not marry.[12] Tertullian was aware that many who ridiculed the notion of bodily resurrection often jumped from the evident reproductive "uselessness" of risen sexual organs to the "uselessness" of the body per se in risen life. He refuted such reasoning. Like teeth, bowels, and limbs, apparently "useless" sexual parts, and so on, "although liberated from their offices, they will be yet preserved for judgment, 'that every one may receive the things done in his body.'"[13]

Tertullian went on to note: "If, indeed, it has existence, it will be quite possible for it also not to be useless; *it may possibly have something to do*; for in the presence of God there will be no idleness."[14] Consider his speculations about teeth. They will be liberated from the "lower" duties they had in this life, like chewing for relief from hunger. And yet, teeth might well serve a purpose with respect to praise and worship in the life of the world to come, or even serve a purely aesthetic purpose.[15] Though Tertullian did not specify what other purposes genitals might serve, it would certainly cohere with his line of thought to speculate that secondary sexual characteristics and sexual organs could serve analogous aesthetic purposes in the hereafter and thereby glorify God. However, whatever their new purpose, it did not include the enjoyment of sexual desire and delights. Tertullian held suspect all visceral, but especially sexual, desires. He concluded only virgins, those who practice celibacy, and those who are involuntarily sterile or without libido could serve as a present sign of our life to come.[16] "See here [in virgins and celibates] *faint outlines of our future strength*!"[17]

ESCHATOLOGICAL SPECULATIONS IN LATER ANTIQUITY

Various forms of dualism emerged in the world's religions in part to resolve the difficult questions posed by the ambiguity of the body discussed in chapter 1. Dualistic systems usually divide all of reality into two, antithetical forces. One dimension is spiritual; it is frequently associated with goodness, light, and our intellect. It is often also associated with what is masculine and with (at least the best of) human culture. The other dimension is material; it is frequently associated with evil, darkness, and our emotions. It is often also associated with what is feminine and with (often the worst of) nature. In many dualistic conceptions of reality, the ultimate goal is to escape from this material world into a purely spiritual one.

As Christianity emerged from Palestine and spread into the ancient Mediterranean world, those called upon to articulate its central tenets naturally depended on the Greek language and Hellenistic concepts to communicate their faith. Many evangelists found some forms of dualistic thinking to be especially helpful in their battle against purely materialistic views of the cosmos that denied the reality of a human soul or divine spirit. Always inevitable, the risks associated with inculturation were perhaps greatest in these early centuries, since what would become associated with orthodoxy and orthopraxis was still largely under construction. The adaptation of Christianity to Neo-Platonism and Gnosticism certainly proved to be a two-edged sword. Within their frameworks, salvation was often (mis)translated as deliverance from the body in its ambiguity. Redemption became largely otherworldly in orientation and often purely spiritual in the end.

Grace Jantzen argued that ever since Plato represented *eros* as born of need, it has been virtually taken for granted in the West that bodily desires, especially *eros*, are suspect.[18] The antipathy in the West toward sexual desire is firmly rooted in Plato's philosophy.[19] Six hundred years later key elements of it found a persuasive advocate in Plotinus (204/5–270 CE). In his Neo-Platonism the first step in the human journey back to God was to withdraw from things material and to be purified of everything sensual.

The body, along with the rest of the material creation, was associated almost exclusively with sin by Neo-Platonic and Gnostic Christians alike. When Christianity encountered Gnosticism, the two worldviews melded together into a blend that proved attractive to many in antiquity. Gnostic Christians saw people as "sparks" of spirit trapped in material bodies, from which salvation promised release. An uncritical accommodation to these dualistic ways of thought led some Christian thinkers in later antiquity to identify the human person with a disembodied spirit or immortal soul. Far from recognizing them as double-edged swords in reference, if not antithetical, to the faith, both Gnosticism and Neo-Platonism were considered compatible and enlightened allies in the task of spreading the Christian faith by some.

Joanne E. McWilliam Dewart argues that early on Clement of Alexandria (150–d. before 215 CE) "taught that sexual differentiation will disappear: men [*andrasin*] and women [*gynazen*] will be 'human' [*anthropos*], but the question whether this will be change in the body, or a change in attitude, arises when we read that the state will be a result of liberation 'from the desire which separates them here.'"[20] However, since his detailed treatise on resurrection is lost, it is only possible, and far from the certainty Segal suggests, that Clement might have concluded that in risen life, humans would not in any sense be sexual creatures.[21] Nevertheless most scholars agree that for Clement, the body and its visceral affections were sharply distinguished from what could be(come) part of the "Life of the Spirit."[22]

Clement also commended ascetic practices (such as fasting and celibacy), arguing that they would free humans from enslavement to viscerally based passions.[23] He recommended that the Christian "train himself [*sic*] for impassibility" and "put off the passions."[24] But Clement was careful to avoid too ascetic a tone. He viewed as mistaken arguments for continence based on ingratitude or hatred for what he recognized God created good.[25] In a more carefully nuanced text "On Marriage," Clement notes in his interpretation of Luke 20:35 that Jesus was not disparaging of marriage but simply refuting the expectation "that in the resurrection there will be carnal desire."[26] (This suggests, of course, that while some in his intended audience may have held marriage in disdain, others might have believed there would be sexual desire in heaven!) Clement contends *both* marriage and celibacy offer, albeit in different ways, "forms of service to the Lord."[27] He held a single monogamous marriage in high (though not ideal) esteem. Far from being "of the devil," marriage and the sexual activity therein were created by God, "even the seed of the sanctified is holy."[28] Citing its apostolic precedent in Peter and Philip, the latter having also given his daughters in marriage, Clement decries as heretical those who scorn marriage.[29]

Many theologians believe Origen (185–253/254 CE) thought the risen body would be "spiritual" in ways that were, as Brian E. Daley puts it, "dangerously close to the Platonist hope for an immortality of the soul, or to a Gnostic devaluation of the material cosmos."[30] Most scholars today do not think Origen denied the bodily resurrection, but it is difficult to say with much confidence what precisely Origen thought because his treatise on resurrection is lost. We do know however that he thought relatively stable identity markers like one's sex/gender and memories of significant relationships would not be preserved in risen life. Unlike most of his peers, Origen imagined that the body would undergo unending positive developments in risen life. Such fluidity would express perfectly the essence (*eidos*) of the person.[31] We also know Origen associated erotic love with both God and risen life. His positive understanding of *eros* had its roots not in any Platonic notion of lack but in God's extravagant "outreach." Theologian Bernard McGinn argues that Origen thought the most appropriate way to speak of God was as Passionate Love.[32] Interestingly, this leads McGinn to conclude that if God is best thought of as Passionate Love, "then the [perfect] ordering of *eros* does not *necessarily* entail the exclusion of sexual activity."[33]

Gregory of Nyssa (335–d. after 394 CE) believed that the body would reassemble on the day of resurrection.[34] According to Orthodox theologian Verna Harrison, it would undergo a metamorphosis, so as to facilitate a harmonious reunion with its now deiform soul.[35] Of course, only those aspects of the body Gregory associated with our likeness to God will be so transfigured. As he saw it, originally people were created sexless,[36] that is, "in the image of God," in whom there is no male and female.[37] Sexual differentiation was a lower part of our corporeal nature, added to our rational nature, as Virginia Burrus interprets his thinking, "as an advance compromise with the need of a fallen humanity to reproduce itself in the face of mortality."[38] Gregory suggested that sexual desire and reproduction were dimensions of the "garments of skin" (Genesis 3:21) that God mercifully provided Adam and Eve for the sake of survival after their expulsion from the Garden. As Gregory imagined it, there was no marriage in Paradise. He associated gender, reproduction, the process of aging (old age as well as childhood), the need for nutrition and to eliminate waste, lustful passions, disordered aggressions, and, of course, mortality itself with the sinful material world of decay.[39] It is interesting to note that Gregory believed some visceral passions would be transformed, rather than transcended. For example, in the world to come, while misplaced rage would be left behind, the capacity for anger would be transformed so as always to be righteous. Though reproductive energies would be reoriented so as to give spiritual "birth to various forms of goodness,"[40] sexual desire itself would not be transformed.

According to Elizabeth A. Clark, in his early writings Jerome (342/340–420 CE) declared there would be neither sexual intercourse nor sexual differentiation (gender) in risen life. But in his later writings, he partially reversed this view, noting that people might have their sexual organs, but they would feel no desire and would not use them.[41] Virginity was the gold standard for Jerome, but celibacy was also superior to marriage.[42] All sexual activity resulted from "the Fall." (According to Jerome, the "fruitfulness" commended in Genesis 1 is an exhortation to increase in virtue.) In sum, Christians schooled in Alexandria did affirm the general resurrection, but their hope excluded visceral emotions (except perhaps for righteous anger), especially sexual desire, delight, and activity. This was modeled on their beliefs about the Risen Christ, whose humanity—even if anatomically correct—knew nothing of sexual desire, since an experience of sexual desire uncontaminated by sin was apparently unimaginable.

While it is hard to overestimate the devastating effects on Christian anthropology of these dualistic influences coming from the Hellenistic world, it is equally important to remember that during its early formative years, other voices in the church recognized the body as constitutive of human personhood. Many from the church at Antioch had more positive views of the body and the material world and emphasized the full humanity of Christ.[43] John Chrysostom (349–407 CE) emphasized that in Christ the Word became fully human. He emphasized the physicality of the risen body, both Christ's and those anticipated in the general resurrection. He pointed to the example of the Risen Christ when refuting those who had denied that our earthly bodies would in some significant sense be the very same physical body raised into new life: "For wherefore shows He the very prints of the nails? Was it not to prove that it is that same body which was crucified, and the same again that rose from the dead?"[44]

Chrysostom preached that the body and all its parts, even our genitals, were God's precious handiwork. A sermon on Paul—this one on a portion of the First Letter to the Corinthians—is worth quoting in this regard.

> For nothing in us is dishonorable, seeing it is God's work. . . . But woe to the dissolute who bring reproach on the handiworks of God. For as many are wont to curse wine on account of the drunken, and womankind on account of the unchaste; so also they account these members base because of those who use them not as they ought. But improperly. For the sin is not allotted to the thing as a portion of its nature, but the transgression is produced by the will of him that ventures on it.[45]

For Chrysostom, it was lust, not the body or its genitals, that the faithful should reject. Still he could imagine, as Clark notes, only a genderless vision of risen life in Christ.[46]

As is the case with many who were judged unorthodox, none of Jovinian's (d.405 CE) writings have survived. What we know of his thinking comes from those interlocutors who sometimes chose to quote him at length. This means we know at best some of his conclusions but next to nothing of the theological reasoning he used to defend them. We know he opposed the idealization of the monastic life associated with Alexandria. He contended that the thankful enjoyment of food was equal in value to ascetic fasting. He argued that virginity, celibacy, and marriage were equal in value. We know that Jovinian's perspective on these matters enjoyed considerable popularity. Many left what they had originally thought to be a morally superior path—the celibate way of life—as a result of his teachings. Likewise, many married Christians abandoned the habit of practicing continence for long periods of time.

Given his teaching, it would have been just a small step to conclude further that not only sexual differentiation but sexual desire and delight might all be sanctified in the life to come. But Jovinian certainly did not take that step, at least not in writing, since such a conclusion would surely have been quoted at length among the ideas for which he was condemned. We know he adamantly opposed anti-body, dualistic worldviews, along with the elitism and ascetic extremes they fostered among the faithful,[47] though he himself remained celibate, noting that this way of life was his particular calling from God.[48]

In summary, there was no single view of sexuality in the early stages of Christianity. Speculations about the eschatological prospects for gender varied considerably. Of particular importance in these vigorous debates were axioms about whether sexuality was part of the Creator's original blessing, or an exemplar of original sin. For sexual desire to be part of what the faithful experience as healed and transformed in the communion of saints, it must be part of what characterizes the Risen Christ. What could the heavenly purpose of sexual attraction and delight be? Trapped in Platonic assumptions about desire, most in this era could not imagine. Jantzen concluded that only when the dominate paradigm for passionate desire shifts—from having its origin in need to having its origins in the extravagant overflow of abundance of the Creator's passion for beauty and goodness—can erotic desire be properly (re)conceptualized as made in the *imago Dei*. Once it can be so (re)imagined, transfigured expressions of it (including sexual desire) can be seen to glorify God.

Also worth noting is the fact that those visions that emphasized the continuity into the future of present-day sexual identity markers (like one's gender, marital status, and so on) tended to preserve the patriarchal structures surrounding them on earth. These models often treated bodily resurrection as the (re)assemblage, albeit in an enhanced fashion, of the original according to Bynum. In contrast, speculations about risen life that emphasized discontinuity with present-day identities sometimes gave rise to quite different approaches to these realities on earth. Bynum suggests these models treated the risen body as more fluid, less fixed. Fluidity for these thinkers was not conflated with disintegration. As convictions about all these matters fluctuated, so did teachings about sex in heaven.

AUGUSTINE OF HIPPO

For better or worse, the debate about these matters was largely settled by Augustine of Hippo (354–430 CE), whose perspective on the questions has proved definitive for much of Christian history in the West. This section is devoted to a critical analysis of the development of his thought, the influence of which is without parallel. From his time forward, churches in the West have confessed belief in the bodily nature of the general resurrection (though for some in our modern and postmodern eras "body" has become so "spiritualized" as to be nearly without significance).[49]

Augustine insisted that the expectation of the bodily resurrection of the dead was "the special belief of Christians."[50] Like Paul before him, he rooted this general expectation in his belief that Jesus Christ was raised bodily from the dead. Since conversion was a matter of the whole person, resurrection had to encompass the whole person in some sense: intellect, emotions and body. Only in this way could persons in their wholeness be raised from the dead.

Since his vision of risen life grows increasingly embodied as his theology matures, I will trace Augustine's thought chronologically. I will attend to Augustine's evolving convictions, particularly about sexuality, in "Paradise" (that is, as he imagined life before "the Fall"), on earth (that is, after "the Fall" or on earth as we know it), and in the risen life to come, when the new creation inaugurated in Christ is completed. I will demonstrate that while Augustine did not envision sex in heaven, nevertheless, the trajectory of his eschatological imagination could (and indeed should) have headed in that direction.

Augustine gave a speech, *Of Faith and the [Apostles'] Creed* (393 CE), before a general assembly of the North African

Church at the Council of Hippo Regius. He declared of the risen body that "it will no more be flesh and blood, but only body."[51] At this early point in his theological journey, Augustine's focus was almost exclusively on the transformation that takes place in risen life, not on any of its continuities with embodiment as known here and now on earth. Some thirty years later he felt obliged to correct the misimpressions to which this emphasis might have given birth. (See the comments on his *Retractions* discussed later.)

Most of the *Confessions* (397–398 CE) is devoted to the autobiographical account of Augustine's struggles with his passions, particularly his tumultuous journey from what appears to be sexual addiction to continence. When he wrote this text, he was deeply suspicious of the body and the material world, as well as alert to the dangers of conflating all our experiences of earthly pleasure with heavenly delight. In addition to sharing the commonplace view that desires had a tendency toward excess and so needed to be governed, Augustine sometimes veered toward calling not just for their proper ordering but for their extermination.

Consider Augustine's description in his *Confessions* of his conversion in 386 CE.[52] It entailed a turning away from bodily passions and a turning toward God.[53] In book 3 Augustine is quite candid about the polluting passions of his student days in Carthage, a city he describes as a "caldron of unholy loves seething and bubbling around me," wherein he succumbed frequently to the "slime of lust."[54] It is precisely his struggles with these "old mistresses"[55] of his "wretched youth" that dominate this later account of his conversion.[56]

When Augustine wrote *On the Good of Marriage* (401 CE) a polemic regarding the superiority of the virginal over married life was troubling the church.[57] This cult of virginity, though not itself new, had been given a powerful new rationale by one of its proponents, Carterius, who cited the perpetual virginity of Mary as proof of the superiority of the virginal life. While the virginity of Mary at the time of the conception of Jesus enjoyed considerable acceptance in early Christian traditions and has some biblical basis in Matthew (and possibly Luke), Mary's virginity *in partu* and *postpartum* has comparatively little biblical support and it had received little popular attention in the West until the early third century. When around 385 CE Ambrose, the bishop of Milan, began to emphasize the superiority of virgins over married persons in several important sermons, many of his listeners began to conclude that they had to repudiate sexual relations (with their spouses) if they wished to be baptized. Indeed, Peter Brown suggests this may have been the teaching that Verecundus, Augustine's friend and the owner of the country house made famous in his *Confessions*, found "impossible."[58]

It was in this context that the monk Jovinian, whose thought was briefly sketched earlier in this chapter, began around 393 CE to argue that Mary was model of both virginal and marital virtues and that virginity and marriage were equal paths of holiness for disciples. The notion that Jesus was not born normally—the notion of virginity *in partu*—struck Jovinian as a denial of the full humanity of Jesus and smacked of Manicheism. In response to such reasoning, Jerome, also introduced earlier, wrote his infamous (even then) argument for the superiority of virginity. Jerome's *Against Jovinian* was so severe an indictment against marriage, sexuality, and women, that it was widely condemned, even by those who shared Jerome's basic conclusions. It evoked so much outrage and confusion that Augustine wanted to make it clear that belief in the superiority of celibacy did not hinge on the denigration of marriage. Compared to Jerome, Augustine was certainly a moderate and this is reflected in his text *On the Good of Marriage*.

For our purposes, two features of Augustine's argument in this work are especially noteworthy. Though he names this as a possibility, Augustine does not yet affirm that Adam and Eve could have engaged in sexual and reproductive activity as a sign of their mortality in Paradise. Second, while Augustine argued that marriage served three goods—procreation, fidelity, and the bond of "natural companionship between the sexes"[59]—sexuality served only the first of these goods.[60] Augustine did not see sexual activity as love making; for him it did not have what some today call a unitive potential or function.

Sometime before 410 CE, by which time he had drafted book 9 of *The Literal Meaning of Genesis* (which was completed in 415 CE), Augustine had decided that God would have wanted Adam and Eve to enjoy additional companions in Paradise. Thus, he concluded that sexual reproduction must have been part of God's original design.[61] Of course, this did not mean that God intended humans to experience "animal desire" (*bestialem motum*), "the same drive by which there is in animals a desire to copulate and thus provide for offspring to take the place of those that die."[62] But he does not yet say much about what human sexual activity might have been like apart from it.

After sin entered the world at best married couples could witness only to God's willingness to forgive sexual pleasures that were unintended and despised, or to God's willingness to forgive intended pleasures, if they served as a remedy for (even greater) sin. Through their fidelity to one another, spouses could bear a pale witness to God's own fidelity, but spouses who were sexually active were not (in respect to their conjugal relations at least) able to experience "already" or thereby embody sacramentally the resurrected order. At this point in Augustine's theological journey, earthly sensuality could be forgiven but not raised up.

In book 3 of *On Christian Doctrine* (397–426 CE), a text written the same year as the *Confessions*, Augustine distinguished love (*caritas*) from lust (*cupiditas*).[63] And it goes without saying that for Augustine heaven was a place of love, not lust. In heaven everyone truly loved and enjoyed God, as well as others and themselves in proper subordination to God, the Center of all that is good. For Augustine the problem was not the loving desire to enjoy family or friends "in the Lord," but rather the lustful passion to do so in ways that were disconnected from the love of God. To love fully in Christ—as will be the case in the new creation—meant for Augustine that the exclusivity and jealousy associated with special spousal ties and particular friendships would dissolve. Everyone will be "special" and "family" in the Kin-dom; there are no strangers, aliens, or closed hearts in Christ.

For Augustine, the practice on earth of such an inclusive love required asceticism. Virgins and celibates alone were able to bear witness to the radically universal, inclusive character of love. When there is no longing (except for and as centered in God), there is no possessiveness or passionate jealousy for others. While Augustine maintained that people would rise as male and female, as he imagined it, there would be no sexual passion in heaven, just as he speculated there had been none in the Garden of Eden. There would be no mandate there to procreate, even "purely," as he judged the heavenly chorus to be full enough![64]

In his sermon "On the Resurrection of the Dead" (sermon 362 written in 411 CE), Augustine preached that temporal goods will have no place in heaven. Like the Risen Lord, we will have the power to feast, but we will not do so in heaven because there will be no need. There will be no eating or drinking in heaven because there will be no hunger and thirst. The blessed dead will not toil or even do corporeal works of mercy, because there will be no need for such. They will not sleep because there will be no lack of rest. Those who rise with changed heavenly bodies will not marry in order to have children because there will be no need to increase the heavenly choir. Heavenly life will be a life of peaceful, perpetual Sabbath praise and worship.[65]

Take special note here of Augustine's tendency to read the sensuous desires behind all these activities—of work, for example—as stemming only from want or need. He is not able to imagine them springing from a constructive, pleasurable outpouring of creativity. Convictions about whether such an overflowing, extravagant energy springs from the life abundant centered in God will prove to be key to our inquiry about whether there might well be sex in heaven.

In the *City of God* (413–427 CE) Augustine pauses to reflect several times about risen life. He is quite clear about his belief in a bodily general resurrection. Augustine argues here that Christians seek release from the "corruptible body," not from the holy "tabernacle" that is the body per se.[66] In resurrected life, the body would become "spiritual" only in the sense that there would be perfect cooperation between the purified will and body. Augustine stated this perhaps most succinctly in the handbook he wrote slightly earlier (sometime after 420 CE) known as *The Enchiridion (on Faith, Hope, and Love)*. Resurrected bodies will be "spiritual" in the sense that they would be morally incorruptible and physically immortal.[67]

For Augustine the risen body would not only be better than our earthly bodies at their best, but it would be better than Adam and Eve's bodies were in Paradise before sin.[68] Augustine speculated in the *City of God* that we would rise with the body we had (or would have had) at our physical prime. Whether we died as infants or in old age, it seemed obvious to him that our risen bodies would have all the vigor and vitality associated with people at the prime of life. Augustine thought this to be around thirty years old (the approximate age of the Risen Christ!), and he associated the risen body with all the beauty one associates with the flower of youth.[69]

From this life of perpetual, beatific union with God in communion with all the angels, no saint would be left behind. Augustine argued even if one's earthly body had been "ground to powder by some severe accident, or by the ruthlessness of enemies, and though it has been so diligently scattered to the winds, or into the water, that there is no trace of it left, yet it shall not be beyond the omnipotence of the Creator—no, not a hair of its head shall perish."[70] Note how much more communal at this stage his speculations are about how the saints will enjoy perpetual Sabbath and delight in God. Perhaps "God will be so known by us, and shall be so much before us, that we shall see Him by the spirit in ourselves, in one another, in Himself, in the new heavens and the new earth, in every created thing which shall then exist; and also by the body we shall see Him in everybody which the keen vision of the eye of the spiritual body shall reach."[71]

In his vision of resurrected life there will be perfect proportion among all the body's parts when they are glorified. Indeed, risen bodies will be beautiful in all respects, neither fat nor thin, without defect, blemish, or scar, with one exception.[72]

> But if it will be seemly in that new kingdom [for martyrs] to have some marks of these wounds still visible in that immortal flesh, the places where they have been

> wounded or mutilated shall retain the scars without any of the members being lost. While, therefore, it is quite true that no blemishes which the body has sustained shall appear in the resurrection, yet we are not to reckon or name these marks of virtue blemishes.[73]

It seems that for Augustine we will in several senses be personally recognizable in the life of the world to come. The continuity of our individual identity demands the persistence of sexual differences (that is, gender) in the life to come, even though procreation will no longer be necessary for the perpetuation of the species.

By this stage in his thinking, Augustine imagined that in Paradise Adam and Eve could have engaged in coitus, if there had been enough time before "the Fall." Note however that Augustine held (quite specifically) that the male erection and ejaculation necessary for such activity would not have been triggered by Adam's lust at seeing Eve (naked) or smelling her, and so on. Their desire would not have been expressed as a spontaneous response but would rather have been expressed as an act of the will, a simple matter not unlike the routine experience of lifting an arm or a leg.[74] Erection, lubrication, and ejaculation would not have been dependent upon passion, which was by definition for Augustine always unruly, always "irrational." Ejaculation would have been experienced perhaps like a sneeze.

In their essay on "The Gender of Grace: Impotence, Servitude, and Manliness in the Fifth-Century West," Kate Cooper and Conrad Leyser rightly argue that in his thinking Augustine understood sexual passion to be problematic in daily life as we know it, not only because of its tendency toward excess but also because of it could not always be predictably mobilized. It both intrudes and cools off at unwelcome times.[75] But in the Paradise Augustine imagines, sexual desire would never have been experienced as an unwelcome intruder or frustratingly unresponsive. Prior to sin, there would have been no rift between the will and sexual desire. The body and its emotions were not understood by Augustine to have been the cause of sin, though they certainly became a paradigmatic site of sin's subsequent expression. Cooper and Leyser clearly establish that

Augustine affirmed human embodiment as part of the Creator's original intention and blessing in Paradise.

In his essay "Feeling Right: Augustine on the Passions and Sexual Desire," John C. Cavadini notes that for Augustine sin found expression in the disintegration of the emotions from the will.[76] Thus after "the Fall" humans experience only what Augustine labeled passionate sexual impulses. There is no capacity for well-integrated, thus potentially loving, sexual desires. Desire and lust are conflated for Augustine. Cavadini helpfully highlights the precision with which Augustine distinguished postlapsarian passion, which he found always to be lustful from sexual desire that could have been good or bad before sin. As a result of "the Fall," however, human reproduction became concupiscent and bestial, subject to the involuntary vicissitudes and irrationalities of passion. Erections could no longer be ordered up or down at will. The "uncontrollability" of sexual passion was a basis of shame for Augustine. This reached its peak at orgasm, according to Augustine, when all reason and voluntary control was suspended.[77] If Cavadini's argument about the precision of Augustine's terminology is correct, then Augustine had a notion at least of the possibility of innocent sexual desire in Paradise at this stage. Sin alone generated the "disconnect" between sexual desire and the will. Sin alone introduced lust into the reproductive process and made sexual desire and lust indistinguishable.

For Augustine there will be both men and women in the life of the world to come.[78] Both sexes will be restored, but in contrast to life on earth as we know it, as Augustine imagined it in heaven, there is no shame in nakedness. Childbearing would no longer be needed, so there would be no good purpose served by sexual activity. Thus, there would be no sexual activity. And yet, clearly in Augustine's thinking, the fundamental purposes of sexuality can change. Originally, sexual differentiation was procreative in design, but in the life to come procreation would no longer be necessary. Therefore, as Augustine saw it, sexuality would undergo an adaptation in risen life.

> For my part, they seem to be wiser who make no doubt that both sexes shall rise. For there shall be no lust, which is now the cause of confusion. For before they

> sinned, the man and the woman were naked, and were not ashamed. From those bodies, then, vice shall be withdrawn, while nature shall be preserved. And the sex of woman is not a vice, but nature. It shall then indeed be superior to carnal intercourse and child-bearing; nevertheless the female members shall remain adapted not to the old uses, but to a new beauty, which, so far from provoking lust, now extinct, shall excite praise to the wisdom and clemency of God, who both made what was not and delivered from corruption what He made.[79]

Sexual beauty will serve a new purpose: to excite praise of God!

While Augustine had no doubt that blessedness would include bodily perfection and joyful activity, the center of life in the world to come would be the loving, endless seeing of God, in the company of the saints and angels.[80] Of this Augustine famously declared: "There [in heaven] we shall rest and see, we shall see and love, we shall love and praise."[81] And yet unlike many of his predecessors and peers, and in contrast to some of his earlier speculations, in this text Augustine imagines that in heaven the blessed will eat. The saints would do so, of course, not out of need or want, but only when they choose to enjoy the power of doing so.

> The bodies of the righteous, then, such as they shall be in the resurrection, shall need neither any fruit to preserve them from dying of disease or the wasting decay of old age, nor any other physical nourishment to allay the cravings of hunger or of thirst; for they shall be invested with so sure and every way inviolable an immortality, they shall not eat save when they choose, nor be under the necessity of eating, while they enjoy the power of doing so. For so also was it with the angels who presented themselves to the eye and touch of men, not because they could do not otherwise, but because they were able and desirous to suit themselves to men by a kind of manhood ministry.[82]

This development in his thought will prove to be of great interest when we consider what else Augustine might have imagined regarding heaven.

In the *Retractions* (426–427 CE) he developed while rereading his life's scholarly works, Augustine—by then in his early seventies—felt obliged to underscore his belief in the bodily nature of risen life and correct the language he employed in *Of Faith and the Creed*.

> But if anyone takes these declarations in a sense leading him to suppose that the earthly body, such as we now have it, is changed in the resurrection into a celestial body, in any such wise as that neither these members nor the substance of the flesh will subsist any more, undoubtedly he must be set right, by being put in mind of the body of the Lord, who subsequently to His resurrection appeared in the same members, as One who was not only to be seen with the eyes, but also handled with the hands; and made His possession of the flesh likewise surer by the discourse which He spoke, saying, "Handle me, and see; for a spirit has not flesh and bones, as you see me have."[83]

Augustine pulled no punches when criticizing the "spiritualizing" tendencies of his own early eschatology.

Brown argues that in a "later" piece of correspondence known as Epistle 6 (421 CE), a more mature Augustine conceded in a letter to Atticus, bishop of Constantinople (present-day Istanbul), that it might be possible to distinguish sexual desire—that is, a lawful concupiscence expressed in the urge to marry—from carnal lust.[84]

> Therefore this [lawful] concupiscence of the flesh, if it existed in paradise so that by means of it children were begotten to fulfill the blessing of marriage by the multiplication of human beings, was not the same kind of carnal concupiscence we experience now, when its movements covet indifferently what is licit and illicit. . . . But if [lawful] concupiscence had existed in paradise, it would have had to be of a different type, in which the flesh would never have lusted against the spirit, but not go beyond the inclination of the will in a

> wonderful harmony; . . . But since this is definitely not the way concupiscence is now, and it is necessary for chastity to overcome its adversary, let them admit that it has been corrupted by the sin, so that by its movements, they who previously were naked and unashamed are now put to shame.[85]

The direct admission here of the possibility of the existence of such a lawful experience of sexual desire in Paradise—as distinguished from what Augustine identified as the carnal experience of concupiscence known all too well on earth after "the Fall"—confirms what Cavadini suggests found subtler expression in Augustine's terminology.

According to Elizabeth Clark, Julian of Eclanum was one of Augustine's final theological opponents and the scope of their disagreement was extensive. Augustine found Julian's teachings to be problematic for several reasons, but it is his ideas about sexuality that are of primary interest to us. In his *Answer to Julian* (430 CE) Augustine indicates that Julian viewed sexual desire as "part of created human nature and, when expressed in a lawful marriage, should be seen as good."[86] Noting that sleep overcomes us, Julian argued that Augustine's inclination to stigmatize whatever is involuntary was mistaken. Julian labeled such reasoning "Manichean" in his letter "To Florus," which was drafted around 423–426 CE.

In an unfinished rebuttal to this charge, Augustine explicitly affirmed that Jesus had male sexual organs, a capacity to father children, and that the nature of his celibacy was voluntary. He was neither asexual nor impotent. But in the portrait Augustine draws of him, though Jesus is not without the capacity for sexual desire, since such a potency is perfectly aligned with his will, and his will is to be celibate, Jesus did not experience sexual passion or desire. "The faith of the Christian is not embarrassed to say that Christ has sexual organs," replies Augustine, "but you [Julian] ought to have trembled in fear to have said that Christ's sexual organs were at times aroused by sexual desire, even against his will . . . and to have said that that part of his holy body became erect for some forbidden uses against his holy choice."[87] For Augustine Jesus Christ is a man complete (and potent) in all his parts, but his sexual desire is a potency held perfectly in check by his will to be celibate. Whether in fact Julian painted such an all-too-human portrait of Jesus, in which the slide from finitude into temptation into sin proved inexorable, is not the point here. That Augustine found it impossible to imagine Jesus having an innocent experience of desire (for example, an erection) because it was His will to be celibate is what proved critical.

COULDA? WOULDA? SHOULDA?

Could have Augustine concluded that there is some transfigured experience of sex in the new creation? Perhaps. Given the changes noted earlier in the trajectory of his mature thought, it is somewhat plausible to think he could have done so. Why? At least three reasons come to mind. First, as documented by Clark, Augustine like many of his contemporaries imaged the Risen Christ metaphorically as a "celibate Bridegroom" wedded to his faithful virginal brides in the life to come. But these brides included not only the church as a communal whole but also individuals who it was imagined would enjoy this intimate, ecstatic, and blissful coupling. And in contrast to the elitism that frequently accompanied ascetic Christianity, for Augustine these "brides of Christ" included not just (literally) virgins but the faithfully married, widows, males as well as females, the sinful, and soiled alike.[88]

Second, while it is true that Augustine's mode of thought was primarily dialectical, constructive theologian John Thiel has pointed out that the young Augustine in *On Free Choice of the Will* evidenced a capacity to think in less oppositional terms. Instead of pitting the desire for lesser created goods over against desire for God, in this early work Augustine decried only desire's prioritizing of such created goods over God. As Thiel puts it, in another possible universe, Augustine need not have treated sexual desire and desire for God as "disjunctive alternatives."[89]

Third, Augustine had already noted that the beautiful secondary sexual characteristics associated with gender would in heaven evoke praise for God. As Augustine's thought matured, he moved from thinking of the body as a source of our alienation and of visceral desires for various created goods as in a zero-sum competition with our desire for God. He came to more fully affirm persons, body and soul. He eventually conceded that in heaven the blessed will feast (eat and drink), but, of course, like the angels only when they choose to enjoy its delights, never out of any experience of hunger or thirst, nor out of any other want or need.

Hypothetically, once Augustine could imagine Adam and Eve enjoying an innocent experience of sexual desire and delight in Paradise and Jesus of Nazareth incarnating at least the potential for that same experience, then it would be more possible to imagine sexual desire and delight being glorified, not just forgiven. It would be more possible for Augustine to imagine the Risen Christ as embodying the fullness of his sexuality, as did the Italian Renaissance sculptor Michelangelo.[90] Sexual desire could have been imagined as serving purposes distinct from those associated with any sense of a temporal need for reproduction. It certainly could be distinguished from lust. Sharing sexual delight like marriage could have been associated with friendship and love making. Like the capacity to feast in nongluttonous ways, Augustine could have imagined sexual desire as graciously enjoyed in the life to come, apart from lust and any earthly concerns about the survival of the species, the empire, property transfer within the clan, or a certain kind of personal "immortality" linked to being remembered by heirs. There are some grounds for entertaining hypothetically the notion that Augustine could have concluded there will be sex in heaven, of course, in some transformed sense.

Would have Augustine reached this conclusion? Probably not. Why? Too much interfered with his being able to imagine the sanctification of sexual desire. Let me suggest four reasons why this would have proved so unlikely a speculative trajectory for Augustine. First, sexual passion is an aspect of human experience to which Augustine was both addicted (as evidenced in the *Confessions*) and which horrified him. Sexual lust waxes, wanes, and wanders. Even the most faithful of its objects will someday die. If Bynum is correct in her interpretation,

Augustine sees such involuntary fluidity—along with its other expressions in aging, death, and decay—as precisely that which most threatens human identity.[91] Consequently, as Augustine envisions risen life, God will freeze all that fluctuates.

Second, Augustine seemed to think about the desires for food and sex differently. Eventually, Augustine was able to imagine a simultaneously sensuous and holy feast in the hereafter for several reasons. He had long imagined the visceral delights of eating and drinking to have been innocent in Paradise. As he imagined them angels evidently could so feast, and the New Testament witness made it pretty clear that Jesus enjoyed eating with friends both before and after His resurrection.

In contrast, for the vast majority of his life, Augustine had no analogous conception of the created goodness of sexual desire. He was never able to incorporate a notion of innocent sexual desire and delight into the conception of risen embodiment he came to affirm. Morally good sex acts for him were always genitally organized so that they could intentionally serve reproductive purposes. Period. This is true even though Augustine seemed to have recognized that childbearing could have had something to do with the grace of companionship before "the Fall" and not just be good because of the threat of death. Theoretically, at least, the affirmation of the goodness of building community in the Garden of Eden, not in response to the threats and needs posed by death but out of creative, loving joy, could have translated into affirming the possibility of both love making and even baby making in the company of heaven, but it did not. And, of course, it was not until very late in his life that Augustine conceded that if such reproductive activity had occurred in Paradise before "the Fall," that it could have been accompanied by innocent experiences of sexual desire and delight.

Third, it may be that his personal experience of sexuality made it hard for him to imagine sex in heaven. Though aware of the wildly inclusive nature of God's passionate pursuit of intimate covenant with all of humankind, Augustine's experience of sexual passion may have conflicted with what he knew of God's steadfast way of loving. From what we can tell,

Augustine appears to have had only a very limited experience of what a just, faithful, loving, and hospitable sexual partnership might be like. Such qualities certainly could not have been said to have characterized his parents' relationship. Given his father's adultery and abuse of his mother, his parents' sexual relationship could have hardly seemed a source of grace to him. His adolescent sexual experiences were (to use one of his own words) "slimy."

In his first long-term sexual relationship, Augustine and his concubine of fifteen years had a son whom Augustine named Adeodatus, which means "Given by God." This seemed to be a meaningful partnership at least on some levels. While they were together, Augustine appears to have been faithful to her. Though he would eventually describe his sexual passions (presumably most of which were for her) as powerful distractions from God in his spiritual journey, Augustine never blamed her. However, given his own and his mother Monica's aspirations that he rise in social status, this unnamed woman was judged unsuitable for marriage and sent away. A marriage was arranged for Augustine with a young heiress from a more suitable family. While he waited for this girl to come of age, Augustine took a second, "interim," mistress (to whom he also appears to have been faithful until his conversion). Even so, none of these relationships—except perhaps that with the mother of his son—seemed to have provided him with a glimpse of the graces that can accompany shared sexual desire and delight.

This brings us to the fourth and probably most important reason why Augustine *would not have* envisioned a place for a transfigured sexual desire and delight in heaven (though theoretically he *could have* moved in this direction at the end of his life). Augustine felt he had to make a choice between "lust" (with which he conflated all experiences of sexual desire) and the love of God. Truly loving God meant renouncing all other desires because he believed that they always distract us from God. According to Augustine, continence alone could be fully expressive of the love of God. This ontology had roots in his theology. Augustine did not see the Triune God's expressing a genuine involvement with and concern about the world. God was Beyond. Despite his experience of the warmth of God's love, in the last analysis Augustine could not imagine that God was delighted by and desirous of anyone or anything finite.

Should have Augustine speculated that there will be sex in heaven? My answer not surprisingly is a resounding yes! While none of us will miss the lust that we know firsthand plagues us here and now, many people of faith—unlike Augustine—have experienced some moments of sexual desire and delight as full of grace. Many of us have tasted and glimpsed in the beauty that sexual attraction and joy uncover the face of God. Indeed, in a very important and original essay, historical theologian Margaret R. Miles notes that an account of human fulfillment that omits the perfection and fulfillment of sexual desire strikes many Christians today as a simply inadequate account of that for which we groan.[92]

Thankfully, as is so often the case in Christian community, what one is unable to do, another takes up. Melodies that cannot be sung by one member are carried by brothers and sisters in other parts of the choir. What Augustine perhaps could and should have constructively imagined about life in the world to come, now falls to us. We honor him and all the faithful before us when we take up the challenge of reimagining life abundant in the new creation.

The Christian eschatological composition is unfinished (and will always be so) until the End Time. Happily, the Spirit remains at work among the people of God across the ages, so to the task of reimagining sex in heaven, let us now turn with confidence. As a theologian of the church I can only dare to articulate and share my speculations about the eschatological destiny of sexuality because I trust that my brothers and sisters in the faith will test, correct, and otherwise amend the following reflections.

CHAPTER 5

Reimagining Sex in Heaven

As was made evident in the preceding chapter, relatively few theological voices across the ages associated sexuality with what is being sanctified and incorporated into resurrected life. By and large the earliest Christian traditions had little, if any, room for sex in their speculations about heaven. Sketching a vision to the contrary will take both imaginative boldness and a willingness to refute the best objections to such an account.

It must be noted from the start that such an alternative view of the new creation is no more a product of theological imagination than the now "standard" speculations to the contrary. Neither vision of our transfiguration can be objectively verified. So, how might one make a case for sex in heaven? In order to establish the probability that there is a transformed experience of sexual desire and delight in our life with Christ, the theological foundations for such a claim must be articulated. "Proof" in this kind of argument might well involve several steps. First, such a thesis must be established as intelligible. Second, its broad coherence with reasonable interpretations of the Christian biblical witness and with tenets central to the Christian faith must be verified. Together, such "compatibility" tests render the notion of sex in heaven as plausible. Then, the theological difficulties associated with nonsexual (if not nongendered) conceptions of risen life need to be uncovered. In other words, some of the problems with the now standard view need to be identified. These three steps were in many respects the overarching goals of the earlier chapters of this book.

"Proof" however also requires constructive theology, not just critical analysis. A new theology of sexual desire—one in which desire is not simply conflated with lust—must be delineated. The primary purpose of this chapter is to delineate the theological foundations for and the elements key to this alternative eschatology of sexuality.

Before turning to this more positive task, however, it is necessary to explain in some detail how it is that such "suspicion" of the standard way of thinking can express the faithful appreciation of our tradition. For some, bringing a critical eye to tradition is in itself problematic. From its inception, the church has encouraged believers to "stand firm and hold fast" to its traditions so that their faith would not be shaken.[1] For this reason any argument (including this one) that calls for a break with what has generally been taught by the church through the ages bears the burden of proof.

Yet, even those who view tradition conservatively recognize that what is wisdom for one generation of Christians may well be foolishness to another, not only because our circumstances dramatically differ, but also because the Spirit may be graciously leading the people of God out of comparatively immature conceptions and into deeper understandings of God's Good News. The scriptures themselves are clear about the need for people of faith to test every idea, particularly ways of thinking that deny the full and complete incarnation of God in Jesus Christ (see, for example, 1 John 4:1–3). Authentic faithfulness to our Christian heritage requires that we evaluate what we have received and contribute, when called to do so, to its ongoing development. For these reasons, every faithful review of speculations about risen life will rest not only on a hermeneutic of appreciation but on a hermeneutic of suspicion as well.

The turn to and retrieval of traditional church teachings is thus inevitably evaluative. A recent Vatican document noted that a faithful person might experience a particular church teaching as out of sync with his or her understanding of Christian faith (as off-key, to expand upon the musical analogy used by Rome in the following).

> The *sensus fidei fidelis* also enables individual believers to perceive any disharmony, incoherence, or contradiction between a teaching or practice and the authentic Christian faith by which they live. They react as a music lover does to false notes in the performance of a piece of music. In such cases, believers interiorly resist the teachings or practices concerned and do not accept them or participate in them.[2]

It is understood by Catholic Christians that they have a right to give voice to their concerns *sotto voce*, that is, privately to their priests and bishops, or through a scholarly publication or forum, but not via popular news venues. This right to give quiet voice to any difficulties that they have surrounding their reception of a teaching proposed as belonging to the faith is also a solemn responsibility. Why? Because, the ongoing guidance of the Holy Spirit into the mysteries of our faith has been promised to the church as a whole, not just to its official teachers.

But, as that same Vatican document pointed out, a teaching's lack of reception may stem from two quite distinct sources. Its poor reception among the faithful could indicate a serious weakness in or a lack of faith among Christians "caused by an insufficiently critical embrace of contemporary culture. But in some cases it may indicate that certain decisions have been taken by those in authority without due consideration of the experience and the *sensus fidei* [sense of the faith] of the faithful, or without sufficient consultation of the faithful by the magisterium."[3] When such doubts about a teaching occur, the Vatican suggests not only that "the faithful must reflect on the teaching that has been given, making every effort to understand and accept it," but also that teachers of the church must "consider whether it needs clarification or reformulation in order to communicate more effectively the essential message."[4]

Like any other faithful theologian, I have not come to my review of the Christian heritage about sex in heaven without assumptions that inevitably influence my reception of the standard view and that determine what I choose to highlight and weave into my constructive contributions to its development. Obviously, judgments about what is part of the "living Tradition," as Roman Catholics would put the matter, rest on the mutual interplay of several criteria for Christians that go well beyond a teaching's general intelligibility and elegance. An idea's comprehensiveness of and coherence with all Christian sources of wisdom is often a decisive criterion. These generally include the Bible, tradition (very broadly understood to include doctrines, creeds, theological distinctions and arguments, church teachings, liturgies and hymns, as well as practices like the corporal works of mercy and expressions of piety, among others), and life-giving accounts of experiences of the Spirit among God's people, along with conclusions established by reason itself.

The very structure of this book displays some of what most Christians take to be axiomatic in this regard. To be part of the church's "living Tradition," speculations about whether there might be sex in heaven should cohere with cogent interpretations of the relevant biblical texts (as discussed in chapters 2 and 3). Similarly, eschatological speculations about sex in heaven should cohere with at least some closely related traditional theological perspectives on resurrection life (as discussed in chapters 1 and 4, as well as later in this chapter).[5] These imaginative conclusions should enjoy compatibility with contemporary understandings of sexual desire as informed by the sciences and the experience of the faithful (as will be discussed by chapters 6 and 7). Genuine elements of "the living Tradition" should prove generative as well. They should help answer questions (such as those identified in the introduction) or solve problems (such as those to be discussed in chapter 8).

The Good News suggests to me there might be sex in heaven. I think commonplace speculations to the contrary rest on inadequate accounts of the way God has designed humans for communion in and through the body, in all its parts. So it is for deeply theological reasons that I believe the denial of a transformed experience of sexual desire and delight in the life to come is inconsistent with the heart of the Christian gospel. And yet I would note simultaneously that even though I think this issue to be important (after all I have devoted years to writing this book!), I do not believe such speculations are themselves at the core of the deposit of faith. Hence, this is precisely the sort of issue about which there might be considerable disagreement among persons of deep faith, which nevertheless does not disturb our unity on other matters.

So, it is with both boldness and humility that I claim the denial of sexuality's full eschatological future rests on an inadequate theological anthropology and that this conclusion should be reformed. In order to remain consistent with Christ's invitation to abundant life together, our speculations about risen life should include transfigured experiences of sexual desire and delight. In order for this eschatological vision to make sense, a new theology of desire requires articulation.

This reconstructed anthropology begins with theology, that is, with the rehearsal of God's own erotic longing for communion with humankind, indeed all of creation. For it is only in light of God's yearning that creation itself can be recognized as made precisely for such communion. Then glimpses of how sexual desire has been reenvisioned as holy by theologians, Christian poets, and mystics are briefly reviewed. This is followed by an exploration of the connection between this understanding of God and our sexual desire as well as the communal nature of our eschatological vision of our life together in Christ. It is precisely our wholehearted love of God, neighbor, and self that invites us to enlist, evaluate, and reeducate our sexual desires. The chapter concludes with a consideration of more specific eschatological speculations about the possibility of gender becoming more fluid and about steadfast sexual relationships becoming more inclusive.

AN EMERGING THEOLOGY OF DESIRE

Let me "lay my cards on the table." I take it to be axiomatic that God truly desires to be and takes delight in communion with us and all that is and that the love of God is at the heart of the life of the world to come. There is perhaps no better contemporary account of this experience of the gospel's invitation to such godliness than that provided by moral theologian Edward Collins Vacek, S.J., in his masterful book, *Love Human and Divine: The Heart of Christian Ethics*.[6] As Vacek interprets it, one melody in the Christian tradition defines the gospel primarily as God's gift of mercy to sinners, in response to which those who are saved strive to live in grateful obedience to a merciful God. This theme, he suggests, has deep roots in the synoptic gospels and Pauline literature. While not denying the importance of this emphasis on mercy and justification, in his work Vacek emphasizes the Johannine literature that testifies to a second melody found in the Good News: God's invitation into love of God, love of one another, and love of self, indeed into love for all that is. It is this emphasis on love and sanctification that grounds the theological anthropology articulated here.

Among the ideas foundational to the claim that there might well be sex in heaven are certain ways of conceiving of the Triune nature of God and the extravagantly abundant character of the love that pours out from this Triune God as creation. At the heart of the Good News is the revelation in Christ that God is love: "Whoever does not love does not know God, because God is love"(1 John 4:8). In this vision of God, we glimpse something of the nature of Divine Love. Tradition teaches that the Passion of God—among the Persons of the Trinity: Father, Son, and Spirit—is perichoretic, that is, it is so reciprocal and responsive, so lavish and generous, that it spills out as the munificent gift of creation. All that is springs as creative, plentiful overflow from God's joyous love. The medieval theologian John Duns Scotus suggested that God so delights in the world that God would have become human—become Incarnate—even if we had not sinned. In Christ we see that our exuberant Lover wants to be close to creation. Similarly, scripture reveals that our ebullient God has what constructive theologian Susan A. Ross aptly labeled "extravagant affections" for all that is.[7] God is an eager Lover: desirous of an intimate communion with all that is.

In their fine book *Holy Eros: Recovering the Passion of God*, James D. Whitehead and Evelyn Eaton Whitehead interpret the biblical portrayal of God's love as simply prodigal: "In story after story the Hebrew Scriptures record a God who is profoundly engaged with humanity—moved by our suffering, dismayed by our folly, angered by our injustices, zealous for our well-being, and always, persistently, moving toward us in love."[8] Jesus's incarnation, public ministry, and suffering unto death reveal even more the reckless, passionate nature of God's pursuit of relationship with us: "For God so loved the world that he gave his only Son, so that everyone who believes in him might not perish but might have eternal life" (John 3:16). Indeed, John's account of Jesus's prayer in this regard clarifies beyond a doubt the thoroughly communal vision of God's desire.

> "I pray not only for them, but also for those who will believe in me through their word, so that they may all be one, as you, Father, are in me and I in you, that they also may be in us, that the world may believe that you sent me. And I have given them the glory you gave me, so that they may be one, as we are one, I in them and you in me, that they may be brought to perfection as one, that the world may know that you sent me, and that you loved them even as you loved me." (John 17:20–23)

God desires to covenant with and befriend humankind, indeed all of creation.

Obviously, God's desire does not stem from any sort of lack, need, or emptiness on God's part. On the contrary, God's creative and redemptive love for all that is floods out from a Triune fountain that cannot be depleted. God wants to include us—indeed all that is—into this Triune life. Some Christians hesitate to hear such descriptions, but the scriptures are filled with images of God pursuing—nearly stalking—us with precisely this fervor. To accept ourselves as so beloved by God is to accept God's invitation into an intimate, vital covenant. To love God this way is to enter into and participate in the Divine Life, and to take on God's own affections and so to participate in a delightful web of tender relationships with all that is. God's

Way of life is a great, inclusive, and Holy Communion in which all is mutually enhanced and beloved.

This ancient image of our Lover God is expressed not only in Paul's language of Christ as Bridegroom but also in the writings of Dionysius the Areopagite, who long ago identified Eros as one of the Names of God Himself.[9] There is growing endorsement of this theological image for God. In her essay "Beguiled by Beauty: The Reformation of Desire for Faith and Theology," Wendy Farley describes God's "outrageous" desire for us as a kind of "prevenient grace that constitutes our creation and calls us to redemption."[10] Similarly, David Jensen in his book *God, Desire, and a Theology of Human Sexuality* describes the Bible at heart as a witness to what he calls "the long arc" of God's desire for communion with us.[11]

MADE FOR LOVE: HUMAN DESIRE CREATED AND STIRRED

God's longing for communion is such that we are created with a capacity (now damaged by sin) for reciprocal love. God first implanted in humankind, and now continues to stir up in us, a desire to know and connect with God and with all that is good and beautiful. God's love kindles in us an energy for the delights for which we have been created. For these reasons Vacek argues that the call to love God, self, and neighbor expressed in the Great Commandment is not only a moral obligation and impossible duty but also a gracious invitation into a divine/cosmic communion that we yearn to join.

In his essay "Desire: Gift and Giving," Jan-Olav Henriksen draws our attention to the way the experience of God's desire for us stirs in us a corresponding desire for God and others. He argues that this firing of our desire for God, for communion, and for all "the goodness, beauty and justice of which God is the source" is precisely what God's love awakens in us.[12] God not only desires us but animates in us a restless desire to join God in communion with all that is. One way we experience God's Presence among us, the Whiteheads argue, is as a Holy Eros, an erotic grace-filled energy, moving us to reach out and touch one another and our earth in life-giving ways. God-with-us is what inspires us to be with—to get close to—each other.

Though hinted at occasionally by Augustine in his *Confessions*, this conception of desire differs dramatically from the conception of *eros* as conflated with lust operative in much of the Christian tradition.[13] And yet, there is considerable biblical support for reenvisioning desire as holy in this fashion. Citing narratives as disparate as Genesis and Revelation, Jensen contends this desire is expressed in God's creation of people made for loving relationships with each other and God. It is expressed in the redemption of *eros* and our recreation in a renewed, glorious heaven and earth where such desires flourish.[14]

An understanding of desire as holy, Jensen contends, is confirmed as well in the great mystical strains in the church's theological traditions. Mystics teach us much of importance about desire, he argues, particularly that our desires for one another are grounded in God's desire for us. Like God's, when intensified, our desire for the beloved overflows and gives "birth to a wider world of love."[15] While erotic desire is stilled (if not altogether "left behind") in many accounts of risen life, this may not be so inside the mainstream of the Christian mystical tradition.

Consider for example the mystical visions of Mechthild of Magdeburg, a thirteenth-century Beguine.[16] Mechthild's account of her experiences of God in *The Flowing Light of the Godhead* affirms the body and sexuality as primary venues in and through which people can encounter God. Instead of our sensuality with its yearnings and desires being interpreted as spiritual distractions, they are in her interpretation hungers that orient us toward God. Instead of retarding our progress, they are seen as drawing us toward God, toward all that is good and beautiful. In light of her mystical experiences, Mechthild reimagined desire.

Sooner or later our bodies return to dust. But Christians do not believe death is our eternal destiny; our energy for and sensuous delight in the Holy Communion for which we have been made does not end in death. Consider Jesus's encounter with the Samaritan woman.

> Jesus answered and said to her, "Everyone who drinks this [ordinary well] water will be thirsty again; but whoever drinks the water I shall give will never thirst; the water I shall give will become in him a spring of water welling up to eternal life." The woman said to him, "Sir, give me this water, so that I may not be thirsty or have to keep coming here to draw water." (John 4:14–15; interpolation mine)

Desires conceived of as "wants" springing from need or lack will certainly be banished completely by "the living Water" that is the Presence of God we will know in full in risen life. In this sense it is true that there will be no thirst, hunger, or the ache of loneliness in the life to come. Such needs will be left behind. In risen life God's Presence is a beautiful "spring of water gushing up to eternal life" to which we are eagerly and continuously drawn. Mechthild understood our longing for God to be rooted in the body. Thus, for her the promise and hope of resurrection is the good news that this thirst for communion will not die but will instead eternally fuel our communion.

Think again about desire. When desire is fulfilled, it does not die. Delight further enflames the desire that invigorates it.[17] We sometimes get glimpses of this pattern; have you ever been drawn toward someone and find that attraction growing even stronger the closer you get? Attraction to what is beautiful—in a person, in nature, in art—often grows as we come to "know" them better. This can be true of sexual desire. This is part of the sweetness of erotic stimulation. It serves as a vital, self-renewing force, as part of the *jouissance* of life.[18]

Though not part of either systematic or mystical theological traditions, consider as well the vision of risen life created by the fourteenth-century Italian poet Dante in his masterpiece the *Divine Comedy*. From him we come to understand that those Dante the pilgrim encounters in his travels are mere shadows of their real whole (risen) selves. We learn that we long for the resurrection of the body not to still our heart's desires but to enflame them. In his vision of *Paradiso* Dante encounters King Solomon, who explains that we long for the resurrection—not only of our body but of the bodies of our friends, family, and lovers, indeed of all creation—so that we may all delight in God and all that is together eternally. Our hope is that passion will be quickened, rather than quelled, in risen life, so that we may love ever more generously and personally. There will be nothing greedy, controlling, or jealous about the relationships energized by the transformed desires we will experience in glory. They simply grow ever more tender, radiant, fruitful, and appreciative.

To love God erotically is to love as God loves, insofar as is possible, with God's all-embracing grace. It is to love—in principle (if not in fact)—all that is, everyone and everything. It is to love ourselves and others in the same passionate way God loves us and others. Vacek is clear: we don't first love God and then our neighbor as ourselves. Rather, loving our neighbor as ourselves is part of how we wholeheartedly love God.[19] Though tensions among these loves may abound existentially, ultimately—that is, in the fullness of life in Christ—there will be no conflict between loving God wholeheartedly and loving ourselves, others, and all that is. Our rapturous love of God overflows with God's own love into the latter. God invites us to join and draw others into the Divine Dance where love for God pours out into love for all that is.

People can respond to God's invitation to participate in this great communion through three distinct but interrelated ways of loving according to Vacek. They are: love for the sake of the beloved (*agape*), love for one's own sake (*eros*), and love of the sake of the relationship (*philia*). Each can embody love of God and our participation in the life of God. In his schema for the Christian way of life, each way of loving corrects an expression of sin in our lives. *Philia* corrects personal tendencies toward aloneness. *Agape* corrects erotic tendencies toward selfishness and *philia*'s tendencies toward exclusive special relationships. *Eros* corrects agapeistic tendencies toward self-abnegation. Each way of loving bears an important witness to the nature of authentic intercommunion.

Agape is a spontaneously selfless, extravagantly generous passion, directed toward God and neighbor, friend and enemy alike. It is self-giving, and when necessary, even self-sacrificial. It is marked by steadfastness and focuses especially on those most in need. *Philia* aims to foster intimate, mutual relationships in a communion of saintly solidarity with and in God.

> I no longer call you slaves, because a slave does not know what his master is doing. I have called you friends, because I have told you everything I have heard from my Father. It was not you who chose me, but I who chose you and appointed you to go and bear fruit that will remain, so that whatever you ask the Father in my name he may give you. This I command you: love one another. (John 15:15–17)

While deeply personal, love of God cannot be private or solitary. The feast into which we have been invited demands the presence of friends and lovers, indeed, all that is.

Eros—of particular concern to this argument—genuinely values and passionately seeks the good and beauty of the beloved (whether God or neighbor) but loves for the sake and delight of the lover. As Vacek sees it, it is sinful not to enter into this dimension of the way God loves us. We have a special responsibility for our own welfare, which includes enjoying ourselves. This is why pleasure can be not only of premoral value but can be under certain conditions a moral good (even a duty). The pursuit of pleasure is never an indifferent thing. Vacek refers his readers to scriptures such as "I recognized that there is nothing better than to rejoice and to do well during life. Moreover, that all can eat and drink and enjoy the good of all their toil—this is a gift of God" (Ecclesiastes 3:12–13), as well as to the explicitly erotic and sexual pleasures celebrated in the Song of Songs. He notes, of course, that this is not the same thing as living solely for pleasure, as clearly condemned elsewhere in the scriptures.[20] In addition to warning people of the dangers of the many disordered expressions of *eros*, however, Vacek rightly contends the church should also proclaim that there are not enough properly ordered forms of *eros* in our lives. Erotic desires need to be cultivated!

Similarly, in *Befriending Our Desires*, Philip Sheldrake suggests that while our attractions need to be tested, they need also to be befriended, not ignored or bypassed.[21] God creates and stirs in us erotic—including but not reduced to sexual—desires for communion with God, others, and the world. To be faithful to such a Passionate God requires that we enlist and educate so that we might quite literally properly incarnate such passions in our own life, here and now. A call to nurture and cultivation of sexual desire follows from this understanding of God's mission. Let us turn to the task of defining and locating the place of sexual desire in this theological framework.

Within Christianity today there is, notes Roland A. Delattre, no consensus about the proper moral and spiritual connotations for sexual (and other erotic) desires.[22] On the one hand, even though desire is always relational—always tying its subject to the good to which it is drawn—we have all seen how much can go wrong in human sexual connections. For this reason, much of the Christian tradition treats desire per se as a grave threat to human well-being. Desires that seem "good" to us may in fact not be good for us, others, our relationships, and/or the community as a whole. We sometimes experience sexual desires as inclining us to treat people as possessions or merely as gratifying objects. Some experiences of sexual desire are inordinate, that is, prove to be all consuming or addictive. Discipline, if not detachment altogether, is called for in such circumstances. Obviously, the pejorative denotations of terms like "lust" and "concupiscence" are not without warrant.

On the other hand, as we just saw within Vacek's account of love, *eros*—including its expression in explicitly sexual desire—can draw us as God's children together into a communion in which we recognize ourselves and each other as beloved. This is a glimpse of the life of the world to come for which we not only groan but for which we are made and even now—by God's grace—occasionally enjoy. It is a life "already but not yet." Because we enjoy what is good for us and others, we are drawn by desire toward the good. Without such attraction and enjoyment, our ongoing capacity to recognize and delight in the good might well wither. In Plato's *Symposium*, Socrates suggests how it is that *eros* is so energizing. We are drawn to what is beautiful and good, and our delight evokes or gives birth to a beauty and vitality within us. From this perspective sexual desire stems not from an inner emptiness or lack but rather from nascent attractions that mobilize us for relationship. As such, human desire is made in the image of our Creator's own passionate desire for and pleasure in covenanting with all of creation.

Henriksen suggests three points about sexual desire that are worth underscoring in our evaluation of it. First sexual desire often "opens" both its subject and object to considerable risk. Second, sexual desire grows even as it is fulfilled. Third, delight accompanies both desire's fulfillment and the process of desiring itself. Let us consider each of these important claims in more detail.

It is actually misleading to see desire as always a grasping for or coveting relationship. (I would humbly suggest that Augustine, and Kant after him, were both wrong about this.) Desire does not always "close in" on a vulnerable "object" that it seeks only to "use." On the contrary, among persons, desire often seeks the recognition of the other. People want to be wanted, that is, desired by the other. We want to become the object of our beloved's desire. This leaves the desiring subject "open" to rejection, abuse, abandonment, and so on.[23] What this means is that sexual desire renders us vulnerable to the response of others. Whether this relationship brings us joy is at least partially in the hands of the beloved, in whom the lover has put trust. So to some extent relationships fueled by sexual desire create mutual vulnerability.

Second, desire for what is good (or at least what we perceive to be good) is in a certain sense happily insatiable. Henriksen notes that we "are 'pushed back' toward it [the object of our desire] repeatedly."[24] Pondering first biologically based desires but then others as well, Henriksen comments that the absence of a "final" gratification for desire makes it possible for us to continue to relate to and enjoy the goodness and beauty of the world ever more fully. Sebastian Moore in his groundbreaking text *Jesus the Liberator of Desire* also took note of this dimension of desire. When it is fulfilled, desire does not disappear. On the contrary, desire increases precisely as it is satisfied. It intensifies because we "can always become more trustful, more connected, which means more desirous."[25] Henriksen concurs: "To enjoy my desire and the other's desire for me is to exist in a trusting relationship in which I can grow."[26] Henriksen notes from the perspective of natural theology, humans have been designed by the Creator to enjoy life continuously. Our capacity for delight and relationship is designed to be ever expandable and intensifying. Finally, Henriksen notes that delight is experienced not only when desire is fulfilled but also (and this is the important point for our purposes here) enjoyment accompanies the longing itself. Desiring—the process itself—is pleasurable. There can be a "sweetness" (as well as an ache) to longing.

SPECULATIONS ABOUT SEXUAL DESIRE AND DELIGHT IN HEAVEN

There is no question that sexual desire does not now often live up to its potential for holiness. We have all experienced sexual desires twisted into desires to consume, grasp, possess, take, control, use, and violate others as mere objects. But one need not conclude from those experiences that sexual desire per se can only be forgiven. One need not conclude that sexual desire cannot be sanctified or that we best quiet it, if it will not pass away.

Might there be sex heaven? As you must certainly have guessed by now, the answer to that question depends significantly upon how you define its terms. (1) What do you think heaven is? What are God's ultimate intentions for human beings? Indeed, for all of creation? And (2), what do you think sex is all about?[27] I have answered the first question this way: the destiny that God desires for us is to enjoy together in mutual delight a Holy Communion with all that is to the glory of God. As Vacek clarifies, we cannot be ourselves apart from passionate love for self, each other, and God, because we have been made for such a loving interrelationship. The great love commandment calls us to become no more or less than who we have been created to be.

Might sexual desire and delight play a part in this? Many in the early church taught that a person's whole self—body and soul—would be transformed and sanctified in risen life. However, some aspects of life as we know it—like distress, disease, and death—will simply be "left behind." In this volume we have been wrestling with the question of whether sexual desire and delight are being sanctified, or are they—like disease and death—realities from which we will be healed?

I contend that sexual desire might well have a place in the life to come, and not just the flaccid version of it first imagined by Augustine and then later by C. S. Lewis. According to Lewis, gender—and what I would call a flaccid experience of sexual desire—will be retained in heaven. Of this he wrote:

> In denying the sexual life in heaven. . . . it is not of course necessary to suppose that the distinction of sexes will disappear. What is no longer needed for biological purposes may be expected to survive for splendor. Sexuality is the instrument both of virginity and conjugal virtue; neither men nor women will be asked to throw away weapons they have used victoriously. It is the beaten and the fugitives who throw away their swords. The conquerors sheathe theirs and retain them. "Transsexual" would be a better word than "sexless" for the heavenly life.[28]

This made sense to Lewis because the beauty and goodness—the desirability—of all created objects of erotic desire in his vision are overwhelmed by God's great splendor. Like lovers in the throes of sexual rapture, he argued, in heaven we will not be distracted, not even by the finest pieces of chocolate. But to my mind his analogy is precisely the problem: the dance into which we have been called by God is not a *pas de deux*! Love for self and others does not distract from love for and devotion to God, but the communion with God and the saints that is our destiny springs from God's own inclusive, all-encompassing passion for the universe. Though deeply personal, we are not invited into an individual or private encounter with God![29] As Dorothy Day famously noted, "We cannot go to heaven alone."[30]

The question of whether there might well be sexual desire and delight in heaven also depends upon whether one thinks sexual activity can be love making. Though taken for granted at least rhetorically in our culture, such a holy purpose was not traditionally associated with sexual activity. While marriage has long been identified as a potential school of friendship and love, traditionally the sexual activity therein was not thought to play a role in this edification. It was permitted only by virtue of its procreative purpose and/or its proleptic service to spouse(s) who might otherwise engage in illicit sexual activities of even greater evil.

A tremendous change in Christian teaching on this matter has occurred in recent centuries. In Roman Catholic circles these developments began in the nineteenth century.[31] It is reflected now in all those official Roman Catholic documents that recognize the love-making potential of expressions of sexual desire and delight that are truly humanizing. Consider this remarkable passage from the Second Vatican Council:

> The actions within marriage by which the couple are united intimately and chastely are noble and worthy ones. Expressed in a manner which is truly human, these actions promote that mutual self-giving by which spouses enrich each other with a joyful and a ready will. Sealed by mutual faithfulness and hallowed above all by Christ's sacrament, this love remains steadfastly true in body and in mind, in bright days or dark.[32]

For much of Christian history theologians failed to see that sexual activity could be love making. But once this potential is recognized, the notion of sex in heaven becomes more plausible. This expansion in our understanding of God's design for sexual desire is truly revolutionary. It opens the door to the notion that sexual desire has an eschatological capacity and to a variety of theological speculations in that regard.

God is about the business of perfecting all that is, including persons and the sexual desires that spring from us. Risen life—much like the "one flesh" experience that is part of good sexual activity—will be a boundary-blurring experience. As I imagine risen life, though still identifiable and distinct, embodied persons will be ever more open and available to one another. There will be a mutually porous quality to relationships, wherein we are each both permeable and penetrating. Let us consider the implications of such speculations for the ways we might imagine gender, celibacy, and marriage.

I have written extensively on the question of gender in heaven elsewhere and so what follows is a brief summary of my conclusions in regard to that issue.[33] Miroslav Volf has developed a typology of theological opinion in this regard. According to him, most theologians take as axiomatic a binary account of gender. On the basis of this premise, they reach one of three conclusions. (1) Gender in heaven will be erased. We will be neutered, "neither one nor the other." (2) Gender will in heaven be abolished through an androgynous synthesis. People will be "both the one and the other." Or (3) gender in heaven will be affirmed as complementary (enabling a mutual indwelling), so that we can be "not-without-the other."[34] He opts for this third conclusion.

Rather than accept as axiomatic a gender binary, I propose instead that we (re)interpret scripture in light of what we *now* know about the polymorphic range of sexual and gender differences among persons.[35] Neither intersex nor transgender would be presumed to be embodied expressions of sin; neither would they be left behind, untransformed by grace. Such a rereading of Galatians 3:28—"There is neither Jew nor Gentile, there is no longer slave or free, there is no longer male and female; for all of you are one in Christ Jesus"—might well support an alternative view of gender in glory. In glory we might well become people desirous of and drawn into fully complementary relationships in Christ in the holy and holistic sense delineated at length by Todd A. Salzman and Michael G. Lawler in their brilliant book *The Sexual Person: Toward a Renewed Catholic Anthropology*.[36] Though they do not make this particular suggestion, perhaps in the life to come we will be transformed into people of fluid, ever-shifting, *apposite* (as in appropriate, rather than opposite) genders.

Self-giving, mutual indwelling, and complementarity need not be structured along a polar axis. Interdependence and communion do not hinge on a binary structural design. In ways analogous to the distinctions among the Persons of the Trinity, whatever gender, sexual, or other differences among human persons that continue in heaven will not impact the equality, mutuality, and reciprocity of the erotic love expressed within the communion of saints. All manner of such sexual differences—intersex, male, and female—may become more fluid, or they may remain fairly stable. They may well be matters of comparative indifference to the life of faith in Christ. Certainly they will no longer be sources of alienation and discrimination. What is retained about gender differences must surely be only what enables communion; what is "left behind" will be whatever obstructs it.

Celibacy—at least one element of this lifestyle—has long been understood to have an eschatological future. Traditionally, it was the absence of sexual (genital) activity for the sake of God's Kin-dom that was imagined to have this heavenly future. This was so largely because it was assumed the fires of sexual desire would be quenched. Detailed speculations about the heavenly future of celibacy are perhaps best left to those among the faithful who have lived out this sexual vocation and tasted of the ways their experience of sexual desire has been sanctified therein. But I would humbly suggest that celibacy's extraordinary witness to the open, all-inclusive nature of God's love might well be included and further sanctified in the new creation.

Whatever will characterize the Kin-dom of God to come, it is not likely to be structured by social forms of marriage and family "that would develop predictably from this world."[37] We do not have to select which of the many sexual vocations that have developed across cultures and history will be raised up; none of them as is will be. Indeed, so transformed will our new heaven and earth be, there are not likely to be easily recognizable institutions therein, neither monastic nor marital.

And yet, can we not say more about the heavenly future of the sexual partnerships made "in the Lord" on earth? Some spouses discern their relationship to be sacramental. Some (Orthodox) Christians believe such marriages to be indissoluble, even by death. Are there elements within these relationships that are holy that will endure in some graciously transfigured form? What might we say about marriages that have at least at times been sanctifying bridges to God for spouses and others alike? Such couplings will, of course, be transformed, but that does not mean necessarily that the depth and intensity of love that has proven sanctifying within them could have no glorious future. Surely the steadfast, enduring character of the loving bond that shelters the gift of mutual vulnerability shared by some spouses might well be strengthened beyond imagination in eternal life.

We cannot truly be ourselves in this holy, boundary-blurring communion apart from our bodies. Part of what it means to claim as Christians that we are now being and will be bodily transfigured is to say we are being healed and will enjoy life abundant in full in the new creation. This means our experience of erotic desires—which might well include but not be exhausted by sexual desires—are and might well be even more transformed by God's grace. God desires that we be increasingly inclined toward intimacy and drawn into one another's arms in ways that are genuinely humanizing.

I have no doubt that commitments to sexual exclusivity, and to some degree emotional primacy, are what enable lovers to pay sufficient attention to each other so that their steadfast partnerships may deepen and their love grow. Indeed, I have argued in detail elsewhere that monogamy is requisite to the practice of fidelity within our present earthly limitations.[38] But I am less certain that sexual exclusivity will abide in our heavenly future. Certainly, the possessive, jealous, and controlling aspects of some marriages that close them to the practice of hospitality and to friendship with others will pass away. But will the practice of sexual exclusivity so evidently necessary here and now be altogether left behind in the new creation?

The depth and intensity of the steadfast intimacy sometimes enjoyed in marriage on earth might well be more broadly enjoyed in heaven. There might well be among the saints some kind of holy polyamory imitative God's own radically inclusive, yet absolutely steadfast and fully attentive, way of loving. It is unfair to dismiss all arguments for polyamory here and now as thinly disguised endorsements of promiscuity, incest, pedophilia, and so forth. The practice of polyamory could be marked by a commitment to steadfastness and by much of what characterizes just love. Certainly exclusivity per se does not image God's passion.

Nevertheless, I still have reservations about moving too far down this line of speculation. Upon closer analysis of its varying forms on earth, polyamory seems troubled by kyriarchy, as is the case of polyandry and polygyny. Even in the case of omnigamy there is a tendency for one pair bond to take precedence over others in a person's life, so that one partner is considered primary and the others find their more tertiary places on a sliding scale.[39] Surely those lovers afforded such "second-class," "third-class," and so forth, status do not find it humanizing. It is difficult to see how such lower class relationships could bear witness to the Christian hope for life abundant.

Inevitably, anything particular and concrete about the fullness of resurrected life that we imagine from our vantage point here and now is bound to be distorted, at least in the sense that both our experience and talk of *eschata* grow out of the present, still-broken moment. The actual contours of resurrected life are in this important sense truly and necessarily unimaginable. As the scriptures testify, it remains a mystery! And yet, we should not lose heart and abandon this speculative venture, for the Kin-dom of God is also truly already at hand. However partial and tentative, however mistaken, our speculations about sex in heaven may be, imagine and speculate we must. John E. Thiel is correct in noting that it is lingering Kantianism, rather than humility, that keeps us from fantasizing about the life to come.[40] We are called to bear witness here and now through our lives to this new life revealed to be already at hand. To do that, we must sketch, however tentatively, some vision of that destiny! Whether you agree with the particulars and cautions previously detailed, my goal has been to spark your imagination in this regard. My aim has been to convince you that we may taste and glimpse now, through God's grace, in some of our experiences of sexual desire and delight, what we will enjoy in full in the life of the world to come.

Whether all this means people will engage in coitus, fellatio, cunnilingus, genital rubbing, or the like, I care not to speculate. Whether men will ejaculate and women ovulate, again I care not to speculate. Like questions about digestion and excretion in regard to feasting in heaven, these queries miss the point. Mine is a claim about God's sanctification of and the potential tender sweetness of our sexual fires. What precise shape sexual desire will take and how we will come to such delights might well prove quite surprising, as is often the case even now.

PART 2

Sex on Earth

CHAPTER 6

Transforming Sex on Earth

Up to this point, most of this book has focused on unpacking the various components requisite for a serious theological conversation about sex in heaven. Clearly, bodily resurrection must be established as axiomatic. Scriptural and traditional arguments against sex in heaven must be, if not refuted, at least shown not to cohere well with other equally plausible interpretations and theological convictions. An alternative theology of sexual desire and constructive account of sex in heaven must be sketched. We turn now to the task of tracing the implications of these speculations for sex on earth. There are three chapters in this second part of the book. This chapter delineates why and how the reformation of our sexual desires (and not only their repression) is part of Christian discipleship. God's invitation to transform our wounded experiences of sexual desire, along with our capacity to do so, are explored. Most of this chapter is devoted to explicating how, and in what sense, the transformation of sexual desire on earth is even possible. In this sense this chapter addresses anthropological issues that precede most normative arguments in sexual ethics.[1]

FACING THE WHOLE TRUTH ABOUT SEX

I noted in the introduction to this volume that Christians understand they are called to embody on earth the love of God. To do this, we know our experience of sexual desire must be transformed. Why? Anyone who is truthful with themselves knows at least some of their sexual desires are morally problematic. In addition to being wet, wild, and wonderful, we know our passions are cunning and powerfully deceptive. Sometimes they wound us as well as others. We know our sexual attractions sometimes waver and wander; we know that our desires wax, and even if we are under twenty, we know they can sometimes wane. We know some of our sexual desires to be weird, worrisome, wanton, even wicked. In sum, we know our sexual selves to be profoundly ambiguous. It is not surprising that the Bible sends mixed messages about sexual desire. In the next chapter we will review briefly some of the sex-positive messages in the Bible. Here we shall consider some of the places where the morally problematic nature of sexual desire is highlighted in the scriptures.

In the story of "the Fall" found in Genesis 3:6–16, we are reminded that our sexuality was damaged by sin. In this account of the origin of evil, Adam and Eve find themselves suddenly ashamed to be naked. They are portrayed as not being vulnerable in their nakedness until after they have sinned. The roots of sexual relationships marked by objectification, domination, and submission are traced in this narrative back to sin, not to the Creator's original design for creation.

Testimonies about the depth of our sexual misbehaviors and the scope of their consequences are found throughout the scriptures. Warnings about prostitution and adultery abound. The capacity of sexual attractions to seduce the unwitting, naïve man and reduce him "to a meal ticket" are frankly discussed in Proverbs 6:23–26. The scriptures are replete with tales of other kinds of sexual relationships twisted by the abuse of power. Kings and judges are shown to be subject to "fatal attractions."[2] The passions of both men and women are revealed to be ensnared by and ensnaring of others.

As Deanna A. Thompson so aptly described life as we know it: "the present is not nor will it ever be a paradise."[3] Our hopes about sex in heaven grow out of this lament. Paul gives voice to what we all know to be true. Sometimes we fail to do the right thing: "For I know that good does not dwell in me, that is, in my flesh. The willing is ready at hand, but doing the good is not" (Romans 7:18). We know in our hearts that the wound that is sin runs even deeper. Sometimes we don't even want to do what is right and good. Sometimes we find ourselves groaning—with all of creation and the Holy Spirit—for the transformation of our desires themselves. We find ourselves, as Paul put it, eagerly awaiting the redemption of our bodies (Romans 8:22–23).

Nevertheless, it would be a mistake simply to conflate, as both Augustine and later Immanuel Kant are infamous for doing, all sexual desire with lust. Like many falsehoods, we recognize that there is a half-truth in Kant's claim: "Sexual love makes of the loved person an object of appetite; as soon as the other person is possessed and the appetite sated, they are thrown away 'as one throws away a lemon that is sucked dry.'"[4] Objectification and domination (especially in the forms of rape and commodification) can come to characterize a person's or even a culture's scripts for sexual desire.

There is some truth in this description of sexual desire but it is not the whole truth. Though some sexual encounters might be accurately described this way, this is not what is confirmed by all of scripture (as shall be evident in the chapter that follows) or by some of the gracious aspects of the experience of sexuality pointed to throughout this volume. Persons who call only for the repression and curtailment of sexual desire, since its obliteration strikes them as impossible, rest their arguments on such half-truths about sexuality. The whole truth about sexual desire leaves us with much more complex moral questions, both personal and social.

THE CALL TO REFORM SOME EXPERIENCES OF SEXUAL DESIRE

Obviously, there are good reasons to transform some of our experiences of sexual desire. That transformation may entail the "chastisement" of some sexual desires, as well as the nurture of others. As Jo Ind notes in her interesting book *Memories of Bliss: God, Sex, and Us*, we are all wounded and in need of healing in regard to our sexuality.[5] One very important and basic personal moral question in this regard is whether we should attempt to change what turns us on.

Clearly, some of us are more burdened in this arena of our lives than others. For example, some of us have been gravely wounded sexually by childhood experiences of incest, sexual abuse, and rape. Some of us are sexual addicts. Some of us get turned on by children (pedophilia), adolescents (ephedophilia), corpses (necrophilia), inflicting pain (sadism), and/or suffering pain (masochist). Some of us regularly find ourselves powerfully attracted to persons other than our spouse (adulterous desires). Others have experiences of sexual desire that—though not aptly described as gravely wounded—are nevertheless frustrating and less than ideal. Some of us have sexual desires incompatible with our spouse's. Everyone's experience of sexual desire waxes and wanes. One person's rhythm may not necessarily be in sync with the passions of their sexual partner. Others of us have fetishes that may trouble or disturb our sexual partner.

Nearly all of us (in the West at least) have grown up in cultures that have eroticized scripts involving dominance and submission, if not outright violence. (For ample evidence of this in the United States, it is only necessary to pick up any so-called "beach" novel at a local grocery store or turn on MTV.) Indeed, this is "the story" about sexuality told by most of the pornography consumed, whether soft or hard core. So, many of us might well pray for personal sexual healing, as well as seek medical and psychological treatment for certain kinds of sexual problems.

The social moral questions that arise in reference to sexual desire are analogous. What kinds of sexual relationships should we criminalize? What kinds of sexual scripts should we legally prohibit, regulate, and/or encourage through public policies governing the distribution of benefits (medical, inheritance, and so on) and burdens (like taxes and debts). What sexual roles and lifestyles should be blessed in Christian communities? What kinds of experiences of sexual desire should we culturally foster and/or sanctify with church teachings? What are the stories about sexuality we want told and what kind of world will they foster?

If a particular kind of sexual desire has mistakenly been judged immoral (as I have argued elsewhere is the case regarding same-sex desire), we need to recognize that changing cultural beliefs that support and reinforce this error will be very slow, and perhaps involve many generations. Martha Nussbaum suggests that the best analogy here is with racist fears. While ostensibly "reasonable," these emotions are supported by racist ideologies, stereotypes, and myths. We have a personal and communal obligation to work toward transforming such prejudicial responses to ethnic diversity, but it may take a long time to dislodge the subtle myths and systematic practices underwriting them just below the surface.

Similar (but more openly controversial) arguments have been mounted regarding homophobia and male chauvinism, and the heterosexist and patriarchal ideologies that inform them. In this volume, I am addressing erotophobia, particularly in regard to sexual desire. I have explored Christian eschatological convictions about the resurrection of the body and concluded that sexual desire and delight might well remain part of our transformed destiny in the life of the world to come in fullness. In this vision of glory sexuality serves the holy, intimate, and joyful communion for which we have been made. Far from being the spiritual distraction one might well be rid of, in the light of this vision some experiences of sexual desire should be welcomed joyously as they shed light on the pied beauty of all who glorify God.

But key questions remain. What are the criteria for making judgments about particular experiences of sexual desire? Consider again same-sex desire. Some mistakenly argue that people will be healed of homosexual desires in heaven. I am suggesting instead that same-sex attraction may be welcomed by all as an enlivening grace that empowers and expands the human capacity for intimacy and joy. Like all our speculations about our eschatological future, our answers to these and similar questions have implications for our life together now on earth. Christians claim God's promises to be both "already but not yet" fulfilled, which means that this transformation by the grace of God of our sexual desire and delight is a reality we may have already tasted or glimpsed. It is both a gift and a task that faithful disciples are presently called to embody.

THE CAPACITY TO REFORM SEXUAL DESIRE

For many people today the very idea of being able to educate—to reform however slightly—their experience of sexual desire does not make sense. After all, sexual desire—what "turns me on," if anything—seems to be quite spontaneous and involuntary. In what remains of this chapter I will explore the human capacity to shape and transform sexual desire. This section begins with an expansion of the definitions of sexual desire detailed in the introduction, with an eye toward questions about the very possibility of reeducating sexual desire. I will attend to some of the most important biological foundations of sexual desire, as well as to factors that shape its social and biographical construction. The voluntary dimensions of emotions in general, and of sexual affections in particular, are analyzed here as well. The Christian call to transform sexual desire is discussed in terms of the very limited, yet real, malleability of our sexual feelings here and now on earth.

All of us have a restless attraction toward what is beautiful to which we awaken and through which we connect with the world. I have argued, as has Diarmuid O'Murchu, that because *eros* or erotic love is a divine propensity, we need to recognize that our "capacity for desire is from God."[6] It is not just a human inclination. Furthermore, sexual desire is a subset of this erotic attraction to what is good and beautiful. It is a subset of this inclination toward connection and companionship. Sexual arousal can reveal the goodness of sensuous, genital touch and it can connect us to the one with whom we are so in touch.

When we think about sexual morality, everything from individual sexual acts (like coitus or fellatio), to various habits (like "hooking up," dating, or viewing internet porn) to various sexual lifestyles (like singleness, marriage, and vowed celibacy), requires attention. Yet the assessment of each of these practices is rooted in an overarching evaluation of sexual desire per se, which often receives little explicit review. And so, it is to this task of examining and evaluating sexual desire per se that we turn in this chapter.

If there is sex in heaven, then our experience of sexual desire (like everything else about that glorious existence) will glorify God and contribute to the flourishing of all that is. With God's grace in the new creation our erotic desires will dispose us toward one another in ways that fully image and bear incarnate witness to God's own Passionate Presence. In light of this heavenly vision, Christians are called here and now on earth to transform our sexual desires so that we likewise give glory to God and contribute to human flourishing.

Whether we are single, dating, married, or vowed celibates; gay, straight, or bisexual; young, old, or middle aged; and/or male, female, intersex, or transgender, we are called by God to (re)form our sexual desires. Learning to live this way invites us to pay more, not less, attention to the roles of sexual desire and pleasure in all our relationships (whether we act on those desires or not). When well formed, what one feels intuitively when we are sexually impassioned is the goodness and beauty of shared pleasure and mutual delight. But before we can attend to its moral (re)formation, sexual desire needs to be more thoroughly described and the question of whether it even can be reeducated addressed.

From the point of view of the species as a whole, the desire to engage in coitus (that is, male-female vaginal intercourse) is biologically linked to reproduction. The exact nature of that link is a matter of considerable controversy. Clearly, human reproduction is sexual, but it is equally clear that unlike many other mammals most of human sexuality is not reproductive in orientation. Indeed, near constant sexual activity throughout the reproductive cycle distinguishes humans from most other primates. Nonreproductive sex is in this sense what is "natural" to humans (along with dolphins and bonobos and a few other mammals). Although the tie between one form of heterosexual activity (coitus) and reproduction has been significantly reduced in the twentieth century with the development of increasingly effective forms of contraception, the reality is that coital activity involving a premenopausal woman often results in conception.[7]

From the point of view of physical anthropology, it is clear that human reproduction is for the most part sexual and that both reproduction and social bonding fostered through sexual contact contribute to the survival of the species.[8] Logically, of course, this does not establish that all normatively human sexual activity ought to be reproductive, whether in fact, in intention, or even only in potential. One cannot jump from these biological facts to the conclusion that sexual desire ought always to serve this purpose (or be open to that possibility intentionally or otherwise in each and every sexual act, as presently taught by the Roman Catholic Church).

From a biological perspective, the nature of the connection between reproductive and sexual activities among human beings is actually far more complex. For example, those who are exclusively homosexual have virtually no desire to engage in coitus and thus may have no experience of a connection between their sexual desire and reproduction. Likewise, some heterosexual persons—for example, postmenopausal women, many of whom remain sexually active for decades—do not connect their experience of sexual desire with reproduction. Sexuality's precise connection to reproduction appears to be quite variable. But for the moment, it is sufficient to acknowledge that there can be a link between sexuality and reproduction.

There are several additional ways in which the human experience of sexual desire is physiologically grounded and delimited. For example, particular biological stages like puberty mark an intensification of the human experience of sexual desire.[9] There are neurological parameters to the experience of sexual desire. In addition to one's general health and level of energy/fatigue, and so on, there are particular vascular factors that "push" or "fire" desire. The engorgement with blood of erogenous zones usually both signals and heightens arousal. Our genitals—the vulva, clitoris, penis, scrotum, testicles, and perineum—all these structures have nerve endings and vascular structures far beyond what is requisite for reproduction. Indeed, from a physiological perspective, the clitoris appears to have no purpose other than its service in the production of exquisite pleasure.

Physical touch is crucial for our well-being. Though not documented scientifically until the twentieth century, many cultures recognized that infants need loving touch and that intimate attachment (though not necessarily with their birth mother) is necessary for healthy human development. Most people continue to need touch in order to flourish.[10] The pleasurable release of oxytocin—the so-called "cuddle" chemical associated with parental attachment and companionate forms of love—has been documented in association with the birthing process, lactation, and loving touch of many kinds. This accounts in part for significant ways we may bond through sexual touch.

The need for loving touch is not something we outgrow as we age. Most evolutionary biologists report that like other species, the giving and receiving of sexual pleasure among humans clearly serves broadly social as well as reproductive functions. It can strengthen relationships.[11] Sexuality appears to be biologically aligned not only with reproduction but also with social bonding processes. In his essay on "The Desiring Brain," practical theologian David A. Hogue concludes that desiring is a profoundly embodied experience and the central reward circuit in the brain is active in virtually all forms of human desiring.[12] Hogue reviews the work of Helen E. Fisher, who has been mapping the anatomical and neurochemical signatures of various dimensions of love since 1998. In summary Hogue concludes, "Clearly identifiable systems in the human brain underlie our sexual interest, romantic attractions to others, and our ability to form long-lasting, even life-long bonds with others."[13] Estrogen and androgens fuel our sex drive; increases in dopamine and norepinephrine (along with decreases in serotonin) account for the addiction-like qualities of passionate (romantic) love; and the release of oxytocin and vasopressin enable attachments and more companionate forms of love. Biologically, these can operate independently of each other or work together.

While other biological factors like age and general health can be influential, there are clearly chemical components to the experience of the absence, loss, or chronically deficient experience of sexual desire. Neuroscientists have mapped their resultant pathways in the subcortical, so-called "primitive" brain. The structures and neurochemical networks of the brain's central "reward circuit" illumine those embodied processes that are part of all human desiring.

Hypoactive sexual desire disorder (known clinically as HSDD) may result from the release of too few chemical stimulants from the brain's dopamine system (like oxytocin, norepinephrine, and melanocortins) or from the release of too many chemical inhibitors from the brain's opioid, endocannabinoid, and serotonin systems, or from a combination of both.[14] Molecular biologist John J. Medina summarizes what we know at this point about the physiology of sexual desire this way: "The feelings of sexual desire are best understood as an emergent property of at least four interlocking physiological systems, at least eleven different regions of the brain, more than thirty distinct biochemical mechanisms, and literally hundreds of specific genes supporting these various processes."[15] Pleasure is a constituent quality of and can sometimes trigger certain emotions like happiness (and pride, and so on). Of course, my point in rehearsing all this here is to naturalize our experience of sexual desire, not reduce us to what is only chemical or biological.

Our experience of sexual desire is also and simultaneously psychologically, socially, and culturally constructed.[16] Individual childhood experiences and memories, as well as social, ethnic, and religious scripts and practices, are "written onto our flesh." These personal, social, and cultural factors do not just contribute to our understanding of sexual desire; they impact our very experience of it. Whatever its origins, our libido is shaped by our autobiographical and cultural histories, as well as by the contemporary context in which we find ourselves.[17] We often think of this or that desire as "natural" or "unnatural," but to a large extent, what seems natural to us is as much a product of what we are drawn toward by social conditioning as it is by virtue of biological factors.

Jo Ind offers a fascinating comparative set of snippets about what different cultures recognize as sexually attractive. In Africa and the Caribbean, large "women with protruding bums" are considered especially attractive. While the "Twiggy" look no longer dominates Euro–North American fantasies, neither do most people in these cultures find full-figured women—think Mae West and Sophia Loren—especially desirous anymore. Similarly, while people in the United States currently find plump, full lips attractive, few would describe as "hot" the lower lips extended for cosmetic purposes by wooden plates by the Surma women of southwest Ethiopia.

What is considered "sexy" varies in different eras within the same culture as well. Consider skin color among Caucasians. Porcelain white skin was considered "hot" among middle- and upper-class Victorians of the nineteenth-century Industrial Revolution in the United States. "Tans" were linked to manual, outdoor labor, and the lower classes. Consider the connotations of the label "red neck." Just one hundred years later, by 1975, "tans" (especially in the Northern states) had become associated with wealth, power, and freedom from economic constraint that enabled some to vacation in the sun; tans suddenly became "sexy"! (Only recently have concerns related to skin cancer and premature aging begun to diminish this trend.)

Even body parts are experienced differently, depending on the culture and the context. In northern Namibia, women of the Himba tribe do not ordinarily cover their breasts (except perhaps with a string or two of beads.) There, women's breasts are not considered especially "sexy." Alternatively, in the United States today the bare, jiggling cleavage exposed in a slinky cocktail dress is frequently considered "sexy." And yet those same breasts, when partially exposed while suckling an infant in public, are seen by some as abhorrent.

In her brilliant essay "Constructing Love, Desire, and Care," philosopher Martha C. Nussbaum explains how even the way sexual feelings are labeled or classified has varied across both cultures and time. The concepts we use to think about human sexuality are socially constructed. They have—as Michel Foucault put it—a "genealogy" or history. In her essay Nussbaum compares two different, conceptual taxonomies for sexual desire.[18] Today we tend to divide sexual desires into heterosexual, homosexual, and bisexual preferences. But the ancient Greeks did not think this way about sexual desire.[19] They simply distinguished between active and passive partners and the sexual roles proper to them. Within the ancient framework it was considered "natural" for men to be the active sexual partners with passive recipients, and so raping a male slave or a defeated enemy soldier, like penetrating a woman, simply expressed a "real" man's proper dominance. In contrast, a desire to be penetrated—to be the passive sexual partner—on the part of a man was considered "unnaturally" feminine and thus immoral.[20]

A useful digression taken by Nussbaum is worth rehearsing here. She considered other feelings like fear, grief, and anger, before turning her attention to the consideration of sexual feelings, about which we may be less comfortable thinking. All emotions are passions in the older sense that they happen to us; they impress us. We undergo our feelings.[21] Nevertheless, Nussbaum notes, all our feelings are tied to particular interpretations of the world. They have a cognitive foundation as well. Emotions, then, are at least in part learned; this is what it means to say they are socially constructed. Therefore, emotions—including those associated with sexual feelings—can be unlearned, redirected, and otherwise transformed.

Consider grief. Our grief over the death of a loved one strikes us as "natural," and this emotional experience is virtually ubiquitous. This is so, Nussbaum argues, largely because almost all humans believe death is a bad thing, and were this construing belief to change, however, so might the emotion that accompanies death.[22] The point is: changing an emotion hinges in part on changing the interpretation of the experience to which that feeling responds. Because of their relationship to what we think, emotions can be properly situated—at least partially—in the moral domain of life.

People make judgments about emotions in general and particular expressions of them. Consider anger. Judgments about anger vary. Nussbaum reports that among the Utku, an Eskimo tribe, any expression of anger by an adult, regardless of the circumstances, is considered shameful. In contrast, genuinely "manly" men, in the ancient Roman Empire, were expected to rage against even the smallest of "slights" to their honor. Variation in cognitive beliefs about what constitutes adulthood and masculinity (among other factors) account for differences in the ways anger (as an entire type of emotion) is judged. In our culture today, anger is considered for the most part to be a "negative" emotion. Nevertheless, in exceptional circumstances it is judged appropriate. In fact, "righteous," prophetic anger in response to injustice is even judged "good" anger.[23] So, we might say in summary that in our culture we regularly make judgments about whether a particular expression of anger is a "reasonable" response to a given provocation.

What do the philosophical reflections of Nussbaum and the cross-cultural perspectives of Ind on emotions have to do with sexual desire? Let me make two connections explicit. First, every sexual ethic presumes a judgment about sexual desire in general, and not simply particular experiences and expressions of sexual desire. Some judge *all* feelings of sexual desire as shameful and repulsive. As noted in chapter 4, one of the most influential Christian examples of this conflation of lust with desire was Augustine of Hippo. In overreaction to such views, many contemporary North Americans have what Nussbaum aptly describes as a naïve, "rosy picture" of all sexual desires and pleasures.[24] It is important to assess the theological adequacy of both these axioms. Sexual desire and pleasure are neither always morally good nor always morally bad. Much depends upon the kind of sexual encounter in which one delights.

Second, because emotions in general, and sexual desire in particular, are socially constructed, they can, to some degree, be altered.[25] Thus, moral questions regarding human sexuality are not only deeply personal but social and cultural as well. For example, to disconnect shame from the feeling of sexual desire would require in part altering the cognitive beliefs (some of which are eschatological!) upon which that link was built and rests. However, because we usually leave puberty with our sexual feelings and worldviews fairly well established, the extent to which they can be changed individually may not be great.[26]

In summary, this feeling called sexual desire has physiological and anthropological foundations. It is socially constructed and biographically shaped. We have some, but only a limited, ability to shape our sexual desires. To be human is to experience the voluntary as inscribed in the involuntary; to be human is to be limited. Nevertheless, to the degree our sexual desires are "voluntary," both as individuals and communities we have corresponding moral obligations to form them virtuously. This is why our desires can be moral or immoral, and why we can make such judgments about them.

Let me make another caveat about sexual choice clear. How we react to our sexual feelings is completely—100 percent—volitional! We do not have to act on every, or even any, sexual attraction we have. Despite cultural, seemingly romantic lies to the contrary, no one is swept off his or her feet by sexual desire. Physical attraction and even the experience of "falling in love" do not justify irresponsible affairs. We can always keep our pants on, no matter how powerful the passion. And we can always stop what we are doing, even when our pants are off! Admittedly, our passion can acquire a momentum of its own that makes resistance to its intense expressions a matter of great difficulty and distress. Indeed, it may be difficult to impossible to make such feelings simply disappear. And yet, though it is often no small feat to do so, people can and do suddenly stop their sexual activity, as is evidenced when a child, mother, or priest walks unexpectedly into the room!

We may sometimes feel like we are impelled to act on our desires, but in fact we do not have to act on them. Humans are aware of their inclinations and make judgments about the attractions that fuel them. The point here is simply to underscore the fact that we have deliberate control over our sexual activities, practices, and lifestyles. But this ability to refrain from acting on a sexual desire is not what I want to make my focus. It is a very important topic, but here I want to draw our attention to something else.

We have some capacity to nurture and shape, and consequently some moral responsibility for, not only our sexual activities and practices but our sexual feelings as well. To be blunt, I am saying we have some influence over "what turns us on" (and off). While also powerfully involuntary, our sexual desires are to some limited extent malleable, capable of being nurtured as well as repressed, and disposed toward this or that, good or bad end. We can grow in our understanding of what attracts us and become somewhat (again in a limited sense) responsible for those attractions. To some extent, we can shape our sexual tastes, and this is one very important reason why the promiscuity associated with the "hook up" culture and the eroticization of violence associated with pornography are so morally problematic. The evidence that their habitual engagement hardens our hearts to intimacy with real-life partners and reorders our affections is convincing. (We shall turn to that conversation toward the end of this book.)

The fact that we have some limited ability to (re)form our sexual attractions is important to grasp, because both scripture and tradition suggest that God calls us to transform not only our sexual activities but also our sexual desires. God calls us to sexual virtue in both of these senses. God wants us not just to restrain but to retrain our emotions, so that even our sexual desires are fitting. In the gospel of Matthew, Jesus is reported to have taught: "You have heard that it was said, 'Do not commit adultery.' But I tell you that anyone who looks at a woman lustfully has already committed adultery with her in his heart" (Matthew 5:27–28). Many North American Christians tend to dismiss this command about lust as a human impossibility. And, of course, apart from grace, it would be impossible. But like all such directives, this is not simply a moral task. It is a gracious word about the depth to which divine grace can penetrate our lives and decisions.

We have learned that sexual feelings of arousal can be affected by the experiences, activities, memories, and practices that become "written on our flesh." Nevertheless, people frequently deny this. As Diana Fritz Cates notes in her masterful book *Aquinas on the Emotions: A Religious Ethical Inquiry*, they say something like: "emotions are not good or bad; they just *are*."[27] There is a certain real, but only partial, sense in which this is true. Emotions provide us with information, and we must choose how to respond to that information. But this purely passive way of approaching our emotions, Cates rightly argues, is morally dangerous. We need a different grammar for emotions in general, and I would add, for sexual feelings and desires in particular. Sexual desire has limited but real malleability.

Paul himself noted in his letter to the Christians at Rome that this isn't an easy task. Recognizing a desire as inordinate is difficult. There he writes: "What shall we say, then? Is the law sin? Certainly not! Indeed I would not have known what sin was except through the law. For I would not have known what coveting really was if the law had not said, 'You shall not covet'" (Romans 7:7). The law, of course, to which Paul refers is the tenth commandment: "You shall not covet your neighbor's house. You shall not covet your neighbor's wife, or his manservant or maidservant, his ox or donkey, or anything that belongs to your neighbor" (Exodus 20:17). While we need to develop a contemporary grammar that illumines the moral dimensions of our feelings, it is important for Christians to recognize that this enterprise has an ancient foundation in Mosaic Law.

Consider anger again. Like all emotions, it can be morally good or morally bad; it is rarely morally neutral. Road rage is morally problematic, but so is the absence of anger in the face of injustice. From a Christian perspective, virtue doesn't aim to make us unemotional; it aims to cultivate affections consistent with morally good lives. To feel nothing and thus to just stand or walk by a classmate who is screaming for help while she is being gang raped outside a school dance is clearly wrong.[28] Emotions like anger and compassion are precisely what incline and move us toward action—for good and ill—when we confront such situations.

It is sexual desire that inclines us toward and moves us into sexual relationships. These feelings are never morally neutral. Consider a situation where an adult feels desire for a newly pubescent person. If my experience of this desire lasts for more than a few seconds, then it is important for me to recognize that I have consented to it. I have very little, perhaps no, voluntary control over or moral culpability for whether this attraction pops into my head. Like other emotions, sexual desires are spontaneous. However, it is important to recognize that I have the power not to welcome it. We can choose to deconstruct or distract and otherwise distance ourselves from sexual desires we judge to be morally problematic. For such we are morally responsible.

One way we can shape our experience of sexual desire is by pondering it. Nearly all human beings for that matter have the ability to step back from and reflect on our sexual affections and thus make judgments about their appropriateness. We can then withdraw our consent from an emotion and refuse to let it occupy our attention if we judge it immoral. This is the work of deconstruction. As Cates makes clear, we do this all the time with a variety of feelings. For example, I can deliberately distract myself from feeling the blues by listening to upbeat music. I am inclined to play music that helps me weep when the time is ripe to do so. This sort of self-awareness can be empowering, enable us to have some hold over our feelings, which in a sense often grasp hold of us. They may not go away, but their rule over us may be lessened, even if not broken.

You and I can do similar things with our sexual feelings. We can deliberately distract ourselves from them by considering the object of our desire from a new and different perspective. This human capacity was brilliantly portrayed in the award-winning 1999 movie *American Beauty*, when Lester Burnham (played by Kevin Spacey), the depressed, middle-aged protagonist, suddenly "sees" how very young and innocent the object of his desire truly is.

Reason's ability to reinterpret the object of desire can do more than distract us. It can render the object of our desire less attractive or, at least, make this attraction more troubling. This is probably why those who are trying to sell fast food resisted having calorie counts printed on menus. And more significantly, this is why mind-numbing forms of alcohol and drug abuse often precede irresponsible sexual activities. Opting to distract and distance ourselves from an immoral sexual desire by reinterpreting it is quite different from merely attempting to ignore or suppress it. While repression might work in the short run, buried attractions are notorious for their capacity to resurface and catch us unaware, especially when our guard against them is down.

Generally speaking, I would argue that our culture grossly underestimates the capacity of people to educate sexual affections (as well as other desires, like our desires to eat or shop).[29] There are, of course, notable exceptions.[30] But the malleability of desire should not be overestimated either. Like all emotions, sexual feelings can surface without warning and shut down just as spontaneously. We cannot just "order up" penile erections or vaginal lubrication. We can make decisions about how we will respond to our attractions, but our ability to schedule the appearance, or order the disappearance, of desire is on average notoriously absent.[31]

Our ability to shape our sexual feelings is limited. Do you find broad shoulders exciting? Long legs thrilling? Black "undies" or a "big booty" a turn-on? If so, are these turn-ons something you specifically chose? Probably not. The same is true for experiences of sexual desires that worry us morally. Can we stop an adulterous fancy from popping unbidden into our heads? No. Can we order up desire for a spouse when it just isn't there? Not always. Can we change what we find arousing? Probably not, or at least we can do so only slightly here on earth.

And yet, we know that we can choose to linger over fantasies that nurture incestuous, adulterous, pedophilic, sadistic, or other immoral desires. The voluntary is inscribed in the involuntary. Given the fact that the prospects for the significant change of deeply seated sexual feelings even with the assistance of psychotherapy prior to resurrected life may be profoundly limited, most of us have to accept (even if we may not celebrate) many of our experiences of sexual desire. Ignoring or simply trying to repress our sexual desires may actually enable them to catch us off guard. This is just one reason why the brilliant work of Cristina L. H. Traina on erotic attunement is so important.[32] Of course, this does not mean we act on any or all of our desires. Even within the most rigid of sexual scripts into which we may be hardwired by the mix of organic and social factors that largely determine the parameters of our experience of sexual desire, people have some room, as Nussbaum puts it, to improvise.[33]

Christian sexual ethics has many tasks. We must identify those norms that might best enable us to avoid harming one another, as Marie Fortune has done so well.[34] We must identify those norms that enable our encounters to be expressions of just love, as Margaret Farley has taught us. I am suggesting here that we must also explore how, if at all, our capacity to be aroused and to arouse others ought to be transformed, so as to embody sex on earth as it is in heaven. There are many important additional questions with which Christian sexual ethics ought to wrestle. I would include among them: How should we interpret the waning or absence of sexual desire? Is no or low sexual desire always adaptive? Might the decline of desire sometimes be morally problematic? Should people try to cultivate sexual desire? If so, how? What might be the role, if any, of pornography in the nurture of sexual desire? I see a focus on questions like these as a complement to the justice approaches of Fortune, Farley, and others. These are questions that have received comparatively little explicit attention both in the tradition and among contemporary moralists. I will focus on them in the final two chapters of this book.

CHAPTER 7

Cultivating Sexual Desire

As noted earlier in this volume, for much of its history Christianity (mistakenly) viewed celibacy as the sexual ideal for all humanity, not just for those with a special calling to it. Consequently, routine sexual abstinence and celibacy was encouraged even in marriage, when its mutually agreed upon practice didn't lead to masturbation or infidelity.[1] Martin Luther rejected such commendations because he viewed them as unrealistic and, hence, unwise counsel, but he did not reject celibacy as the moral ideal. Over the centuries Protestant and Catholic theologians concluded that because there would be no sex in heaven, if and when desire wanes, as long as its "loss" was mutual and not a problem for one's spouse, it might well be ignored or even considered a blessing. This inattention to the loss of desire was reinforced by the stigma associated with it. It was often considered so emasculating that its admission by men was rare.

However, if as I have argued sexual desire and delight should be envisioned as sanctified in the life to come, then any decline in the experience of desire should be considered *prima facie* problematic, even among those who are called to renounce its genital enjoyment here and now. Properly formed sexual desire ought to be nurtured and celebrated, not only because its reciprocal enjoyment may serve marriage but as a holy sign of the life to come. The development of ways—disciplines, in the technical sense—to foster virtuous experiences of sexual desire becomes an important Christian moral task. (I argue from this perspective in the final chapter that the use of pornography should be seen as problematic not because it stimulates desire but more precisely because the erotic desires it enlivens are malformed.)

In this chapter I explain why the nurture of sexual desire is an important moral task for those who experience no or low sexual desire. Initially, I review why teachers of the church have hesitated to discuss the cultivation of sexual desire. Then I highlight often ignored insights about the cultivation of desire from several sources of moral wisdom such as the Bible, tradition, and the experience of faithful Christians as well as scientific studies. I conclude that we need to expand our very conception of sexual virtue. Chastity should connote practices that strengthen and intensify, that nurture and humanize expressions of sexual desire, as well as disciplines that curtail its lustful expression.

CALLED TO CULTIVATE NOT ONLY CURTAIL SEXUAL DESIRE

A significant number of individuals and couples experience the decline and/or absence of such feelings as not only a sensual and interpersonal loss but also as a spiritual loss. While Christianity has had much to say about the wild and wicked ways of sexual desire, theologians have had relatively little to say about the waning or absence of sexual desire. In fact, the silence on this point continues to be deafening in some denominations. Though they do not consciously conflate sexual desire with lust as was typical of their predecessors, most contemporary theologians still do not address seriously the questions of whether and/or how sexual desire should be cultivated. Why is Christianity relatively silent about the absence of sexual desire? Why do we overlook the need to cultivate, but not to curtail, sexual desire?

There are many interrelated reasons for this. Ultimately, the waning of sexual desire is ignored by theologians of the church, perhaps even met with a pastoral "sigh of relief," because its absence per se is often not viewed as a spiritual or moral problem, certainly not in the long term. Why? First, like other passions, sexual desire has a tendency to flame out of control, so its cultivation is considered too risky by some. Second, like other passions, sexual desire is often presumed to have no eschatological future. Let us examine critically each of these traditional reasons for neglecting to cultivate sexual desire.

First, as noted earlier in this volume, sexual desire was often simply conflated with lust. Hence, its remission—for whatever reason—was generally welcomed. Indeed, one might well translate the silence about the absence of desire as a quiet celebration. From this traditional perspective, it goes without saying that all efforts to cultivate sexual desire were seen as morally too risky, if not evil per se.

Few theologians consciously hold this viewpoint today, but remnants of this perspective still survive and shape what are considered ethical priorities. The cultivation of sexual desire is seen by many pastors as so fraught with moral danger that it is foolhardy to try and talk seriously about the need to foster it. Like anger, sexual desire has a worrisome tendency—once fired up—to flame out of control. As discussed in the previous chapter, many expressions of sexual desire can be wounding. This makes commending the cultivation of sexual desire very tricky business. Some may welcome the waning of desire simply because of the relief it brings from the very real struggle we all have with its potential for vicious expression.

But to neglect cultivating sexual desire for this reason is an overreaction to the moral dangers posed by lust. It is the ethical equivalent of "throwing the baby out with the bath water." It fails to recognize the multiple ways virtuous expressions of sexual desire—the many ways "that loving feeling," as the Righteous Brothers crooned—can be good. It fails to reckon with the ways the loss of "that loving feeling" can be problematic.

I would argue instead, as did Catholic moral theologian Christine E. Gudorf, that generally speaking, it is bad for spouses to lose sexual interest in each other. Of course, there are important qualifications to make about such a claim and notable exceptions. But mutually pleasurable sexual activity can create and multiply love and bonding. It can school us in love. According to Gudorf, "As we learn that giving ourselves fully in sex is rewarding, we feel encouraged to give ourselves fully to the spouse in other non-genital ways as well because we trust that these other gifts—of time, effort, confidences—will also be returned multiplied."[2] Sexual activity can be love making. In such grace-filled relationships partners are rewarded with both pleasure and intimacy. This joy spills out from the couple onto others. It enables couples to reach out in love and trust to friends, children, neighbors, and their wider community. When so formed, sexual desire is a tremendous source of overflowing, loving energy. It is for this reason, Gudorf notes, that grace-conveying, sexual activity is the sacramental symbol of marriage for Roman Catholics.

Given such convictions about the important role sexual desire plays here on earth, Christians must begin to have serious conversations about faithful ways to cultivate virtuous expressions of sexual desire, even if such cultivation is risky. Obviously, this moves the focus of Christian sexual ethics into a relatively new, if not for some disturbing, direction. Undoubtedly there are many expressions of sexual desire that need curtailment and many experiences of desire that might well be idolatrous. Our moral task as Christians is to cultivate in ourselves and others expressions of sexual desire and delight on earth that bear witness to experiences of the transfigured sexual desire that we glimpse here and now and will enjoy fully in the life to come. Despite the real limitations on the human capacity to do so, Christians are called with God's grace to transform our experiences of sexual desire in light of its eschatological destiny. As the analysis of internet pornography that concludes this book will make clear, Christians must try to identify various virtuous ways of nurturing sexual desire. Otherwise, without such much-needed guidance, people will turn to alternatives like pornography to stimulate desire.

The questions of whether and how to cultivate sexual desire are often ignored by teachers of the church for a second reason.

As the first four chapters of this volume detail, sexual desire was presumed (mistakenly, I have argued) throughout much of Christian history to have been left out of the new heaven and earth. Though Christian ethicists conceded the proper formation of sexual desire to be of real temporal concern, they did not see any longer term spiritual or moral value in "growing" sexual desire. Without much careful consideration, many theologians still presume that everyone's eschatological future will be asexual.

One reason why many contemporary theologians hesitate to argue seriously for the cultivation of sexual desire stems from their mistaken conviction that sexual desire—like anger—is only of interim value. While sexual desire may serve procreative purposes (at least for some heterosexual couples prior to menopause) and foster intimacy here and now, some Christians believe there will be no need for sexual desire to fuel either human capacity in the life of the world to come. From such a purely asexual eschatological perspective, concern about the cultivation of sexual desire probably seems prurient. Let me unpack this argument in more detail and explain why it is mistaken.

In the preceding chapter I argued that despite what we may have heard to the contrary, our feelings—including our sexual desires—can be good or bad, morally appropriate or not, in specific situations. We can even make some ethical generalizations about our emotions. I suggested, for example, that while rage needs to be curtailed for obvious reasons, a strong case can be made that generally speaking, it is good to be angered by injustice and that it is morally problematic to be unmoved by evil. Given the tendency of some people to be "bystanders" when faced with evil, I suggested that there may well be a moral obligation for people to cultivate their capacity to respond to evil with prophetic or righteous anger.

And yet, I would add now that our sense of the goodness of anger should remain qualified. Here and now on earth as we know it, righteous anger can be truly good. Without it we can become complicit (albeit by omission) with evil as it unfolds. As noted previously, anger does have a real place in the work of love now.[3] But anger has no eschatological future. As Christians envision the life to come, there will be no injustice and hence no need for righteous anger.

The author of Revelation gives voice to the Christian vision of the peace and justice that will be the new heaven and earth:

> I heard a loud voice from the throne saying, "Behold, God's dwelling is with the human race. He will dwell with them and they will be his people and God himself will always be with them [as their God]. He will wipe every tear from their eyes, and there shall be no more death or mourning, wailing or pain, [for] the old order has passed away." (Revelation 21:3–4)

The old order, marred as it is by injustice, will no longer exist. There will be no need for righteous anger in our coming life together. There will be no need to confront injustice prophetically.

Our eschatological vision qualifies our sense of the goodness of anger and rightly so. Anger has a rightful place in this world but not the next. Anger is of only interim value. Pleasure and delight, not wrath, mark the world to come. For this reason, moral efforts to cultivate anger are dampened not only by its worrisome tendency—once unleased—to explode into rage but also by its purely temporal value.[4]

Unlike anger, however, I have argued that we will continue to feel a transfigured, fully holy form of sexual desire in the life to come. While several contemporary texts in Christian ethics critique the conflation of all sexual desire with lust, this book moves beyond that worthy agenda and offers a sustained and critical deconstruction of the assumption that there will be no sexual desire or delight in the new creation. I hope I have established at least as plausible an alternative, imaginative reconstruction of Christian speculations about sexuality in risen life. Though certainly we will not feel the ache of loneliness that stems from unmet emotional needs or the need for sexual relief from physical tensions, nevertheless glorious expressions of the affective warmth, energy, and *joie de vivre* that are embodied in sexual attraction and expression may well be part of our experience of the communion that is our holy destiny in Christ.

Let me expand on this last point. Consider how we might feast together in the life to come. We will eat in the new creation not out of a need for nutrients in order to survive, but because the sensuous process of sharing food together is delightful and richly embodies our communion with one another. How, or even whether, we will digest food and/or eliminate its waste products are questions that are irrelevant to belief in the resurrection of the body and its feasts to come. In like manner in the new heaven and earth, we will not hunger for human touch. But just as we will feast together and enjoy sharing food, we will be drawn by one another's beauty into each other's arms in the life to come. Not all of these sensuous expressions of erotic touch will be sexual (genital), but some might well be. Again what these sexual activities might be, I have no clue. There will be no individual isolation or interpersonal alienation in the new heaven and earth for sexual desire to bridge, as it does here and now. Only depth and intensity will characterize our joyful connections in glory. But unlike anger, I think we might best imagine that erotic (including but by no means exclusively sexual) desires will continue to fuel the pleasurable expression and intensification of loving intimacy in the life of the world to come.

WARRANTS FOR THE CULTIVATION OF SEXUAL DESIRE

I have shown the premises that support the contemporary silence about the need to cultivate sexual desire to be false. It may well be mistaken to presume that sexual desire is of only temporal value. Likewise, it may be wrong to conclude that its cultivation is morally too dangerous to undertake. Let us turn to various sources of moral wisdom and explore whether there might be positive warrants for cultivating sexual desire to be found in the scriptures, in tradition, and in the experience of the faithful.

The scriptures are far from silent about the import of nurturing sexual desire. In the Bible the sexual drive for pleasure and intimate companionship is repeatedly portrayed as good.

We know from the second creation account found in Genesis 2:18–25 that we are designed to be totally at ease in our own skin and blissfully unashamed of our nakedness before God and one another. The Bible suggests that it is precisely sexual desire that fuels our inclination to move into each other's arms and lives. Sexual desire enables some partnerships to become extraordinarily intimate, "one flesh" unions.[5]

It is of such a union that the woman sings in the Song of Songs: "I belong to my lover, his yearning is for me. Come, my lover! Let us go out to the fields, let us pass the night among the henna. Let us go early to the vineyards, and see if the vines are in bloom. If the buds have opened, if the pomegranates have blossomed; there will I give you my love" (Song of Songs 7:11–13). The biblical witness to the import of sexual desire continues. Among marital responsibilities, mutual sexual endearment was so important that the book of Deuteronomy recommends that newly married husbands be excused from military service and other public duties, so they could stay home and fulfill the Lord's command to make their wives happy.[6] Within Judaism the so-called laws of *onah* were technically directed toward men and required the husband to give his wife pleasure during their sexual activities, rather than think just of himself. But this emphasis in the scriptures on sharing sexual pleasure was routinely understood to be mutually obligatory.

Paul implies this in his first letter to the Christians at Corinth when he writes: "The husband should fulfill his marital duty to his wife, and likewise the wife to her husband" (1 Corinthians 7:3). This talk of "marital duty" here may well have been meant to address precisely the issue of the decline or absence of sexual desire in one or both spouses. Though such talk might well prove counterproductive vis-à-vis the cultivation of desire, notions of duty and law underscore the recognition of its importance. In that same letter Paul noted as well that the practice of sexual abstinence within marriage—even just for a brief period of prayer—required mutual consent (1 Corinthians 7:3–5).[7] Again, this underlines the importance of sexual activity. Far from forbidding people to marry, the author of 1 Timothy reminds us: "For everything created by God is good, and nothing is to be rejected when received with thanksgiving" (1 Timothy 4:4).

Additionally, across the ages some more pastoral theologians recognized that among spouses a decline in desire (at least if unilateral) spelled trouble. These practical theologians continued to speak—if only briefly—of conjugal "duties." We cannot be certain, but Augustine may have thought that male impotence, as well as unwelcome penile erections, were both expressions of the "unruly" nature of sexual desire he found so disturbing.

Thomas Aquinas's approach to this issue is worth noting. In his discussion of lust in the *Summa Theologica* Aquinas wrestled with the question of whether the excessive desire for venereal pleasure (commonly known as lust) had—like other such vices—an analogously sinful opposite. His answer was a quiet "yes." Aquinas labeled this excessive aversion to venereal pleasure "insensibility." Though Aquinas mentions this sexual vice, he clearly did not think such "insensibility" to be of much moral concern. He presumed it was "not found in many, since men [*sic*] are more inclined to pleasure." It "occurs in one who has such a dislike for sexual intercourse as not to pay the marriage debt."[8] Because of his (inaccurate) presumption that it was extremely rare, Aquinas paid the vice of "insensibility" little notice thereafter. It must be conceded that, overall, the direct mention of no or low libido in itself was infrequent. Nevertheless, its recognition as a moral problem implies that its cultivation might well be good.

Aside from a few references like those previously noted, there is little direct theological comment about the absence of sexual desire. Even less is said about the moral significance of nurturing or cultivating sexual desire. And yet, today a significant number of faithful individuals and couples experience the decline and/or absence of such feelings as not only a sensual and interpersonal loss but also a spiritual loss. In another wonderful essay Gudorf summarizes well the experience of sexual desire as a real grace: "For many persons in our society, sexual intimacy is their primary experience of inclusive love, of openness to another, of being accepted and enhanced, and of being empowered by love to reach out in love to others."[9] The lack of sexual desire is experienced as a spiritual loss because the sweetness of desire and its energy—the *joie de vivre* that accompanies its delight—are recognized by many as great gifts from God.

In light of this fairly common experience among the Christian faithful of shared sexual pleasure as a gracious gift, the diminishment of desire should be understood to leave life impoverished, even when it is judged adaptive and understandable in particular circumstances. Similarly, speculative accounts of our life to come strike many as impoverished when they fail to envision a place for sexual desire. While many people of faith might be grateful for the "passing away" of particular, morally problematic sexual desires, the prospect of a risen life altogether without sexual desire strikes many as lifeless. An asexual vision of glory seems at best to be an incomplete expression of the promise of bodily transfiguration.

Theologians need to pay careful attention to such affective experiences among the faithful. They may signal the need to revise our eschatology. I use the word "may" because every feeling we have should not be presumed trustworthy. But such feelings should not be presumed untrustworthy either. Rather than automatically dismissing such disappointment as a product of ignorance or the undue influence of a secular, hypersexualized culture, why not test such a feeling? Upon reflection, I found such feelings of dismay to uncover insights that occasioned needed developments in my imaginative conceptualization of life in glory.

Though I do not think he had this particular issue in mind, Edward C. Vacek in his essay on why "Orthodoxy Requires Orthopathy: Emotions in Theology" stated the matter succinctly: "Put simply, change in doctrine happens when a standard belief no longer coheres with the evaluations given in affective experience."[10] To those for whom sexual intimacy and joy have been gracious blessings here and now—truly experiences of transfiguration—it doesn't make sense to imagine the life to come as altogether devoid of them. Surely, the fullness of the new creation to come will be characterized by even more blissful, loving, fruitful experiences of sexual desire. Likewise, if this joy is "already" to some degree present, it makes little sense to ignore or neglect the decline or absence of sexual desire here and now on earth.

SCIENTIFIC INSIGHTS INTO NO/LOW SEXUAL DESIRE

When we take seriously the scriptural affirmation of sexual desire and delight, and the experience of dismay over the waning of sexual desire expressed by many of the faithful, then it becomes clear that the brief remarks about "insensibility" and "marital duties" to be found in the margins and footnotes of Christian tradition warrant development. But the fact is that many of us know (or admit to know) very little about the waning of sexual desire. Indeed, this is so much the case that we do not "see" any need for its cultivation. My aim in this section is to summarize some of what we can learn from various scientific disciplines about the loss of sexual desire, some of the practices associated with faking desire, and both the extent and the correlates of no or low sexual desire. This will necessitate that we consider, even if only briefly, the contemporary debate among sexologists about whether asexuality (itself a contested label) is a disorder or variation.

Human sexual dysfunction takes many distinct forms, from vaginal dryness to anorgasmia to erectile dysfunction (popularly called ED), to name just a few.[11] Here we are interested in the experience of no or low sexual desire, which can affect both men and women. Despite cultural narratives to the contrary, many people know their sexual desire to fluctuate. Often, the waning of sexual desire can be accounted for in one of two ways. Sometimes, a drop in desire is due to a specific issue like physical or emotional exhaustion, to health problem(s), and/or to the side effects of medications used to treat those problems. The loss of sexual desire is a well-known side effect of a common class of antidepressants (specifically, selective serotonin reuptake inhibitors, hereafter SSRIs). Studies indicate the lack of libido correlates, not surprisingly, with depression itself. It is also frequently associated with diabetes, ED, thyroid disorders, and medications for high blood pressure, as well as low levels of testosterone. It is also the case that low or no libido has been clinically shown to stand alone, apart from these and other conditions.

Happily, in some instances, the waning of desire is comparatively short term and relatively easy to address. There are other times, however, when people experience a precipitous and extended loss of sexual desire. Interest in sexual activity sometimes does more than just wander off, or go "underground" for some "R and R." Indeed, sometimes it disappears altogether. In such instances, the plummeting of desire can leave people suddenly asexual and trying to cope with this dramatic change.

While this chapter focuses mainly on the experience of women in this regard, ethicist Howard L. Harrod, a beloved mentor and friend of mine, gave poignant and brutally honest voice to the impact of the loss of sexual desire on men in "An Essay on Desire." Following surgical and hormonal treatments for an aggressive form of prostate cancer, Harrod wrote, "the sudden loss of libido produced forms of suffering I had not anticipated." He described himself as "tormented by memories of desire," even though through the experience he eventually learned that the socialization process that shaped his experience of sexuality had been "excessively genital" in focus and "goatishly" (his word) reduced his experience of sexual pleasure to orgasm.[12]

In our culture it is at least embarrassing, if not humiliating, to be without sexual desire. To lack this sign of vitality over a long period of time is almost unmentionable. The steady decline or long-term absence of sexual desire is often "closeted" both by individuals and couples. Many find speaking about this "secret" very difficult, even with their sexual partners, close friends, pastors, and/or physicians. To reduce the threat of isolation and stigma, many couples—and men and women individually—try to "pass" as consistently and highly libidinous.

Since neither genuine desire nor pleasure is requisite for their sexual activity, women especially can and do fake both.[13] The capacity of women to fake orgasm was made famously "public" when Meg Ryan (who played Sally) faked an orgasm during a lunch scene at a New York City delicatessen in the 1989 movie *When Harry Met Sally*. In that same film, the fact that not all women are routinely orgasmic was humorously underscored by another woman at the deli who said to her waiter: "I'll have what she's having!" While humor sometimes helps us face difficult issues, the whole truth about "passing" as passionate is not so funny.

In her book *Performing Sex: The Making and Unmaking of Women's Erotic Lives*, Breanne Fahs documents in concrete detail the stories of ordinary women who routinely fake both sexual pleasure and interest.[14] The studies she examined and the interviews she conducted suggest that young heterosexual women not only fake orgasm but also pass themselves off as bisexual—that is, as interested in other women sexually—and engage in "bisexual" threesomes in order to please their male partners. Similarly, heterosexual women of all ages pretend to favor penile-vaginal intercourse, even though it does not consistently lead to orgasm for most women. Why would heterosexual women do this? All these behaviors facilitate and prioritize men's pleasure over women's. Fahs concludes that women do these things because that priority is central to the cultural narrative about sexuality in the United States.

The social pressure on women to be steadily libidinous, if not "wanton," is currently so high that women with low or no sexual desire often seek "off-label" prescriptions for testosterone or "share" their male partner's prescription. Fahs reports: "In 2006 alone, doctors wrote over a million prescriptions for off-label testosterone."[15] Obviously, women who use testosterone in this way hope that it might increase their sexual desire, but there is no clinical evidence it will do so. There is, however, clear evidence that such use of testosterone by women will significantly increase their risk of breast cancer. Women feel pressure to "perform" sexual desire this way both in order to please their partner and/or to avoid facing the personal identity issues posed by the absence or loss of sexual desire.[16]

Because of this capacity (especially among women) and pressure to "fake" not only orgasm but also pleasure and desire, it has been easy for theologians to ignore the question of whether sexual desire needs cultivation. To complicate matters, like many other topics in the relatively new field of sexology, even the "experts" do not yet know very much about low or no libido. Let me rehearse briefly some of what scientists are saying.

The absence of desire is more a mental, than a physical, issue. More precisely, it is not a physical issue typically located below the neck. Almost all women with no libido respond to sexual stimuli with increased vaginal blood flow. It seems that it is the mind (not the genitals) that is the control center for sexual desire. The key driver (neurotransmitter) for sexual desire appears to be dopamine. It radiates out from two centers in the brain. Sex hormones (both testosterone and estrogen) fuel the production and release of this erotic impulse, while serotonin is thought to organize and calm (inhibit) it. The neural networks for this process are only vaguely understood, though the neuroplasticity of the brain explains how it is that the social construction of sexuality might result in this being a condition that affects mostly females.[17]

Early studies done in North Atlantic countries made the disruptions in people's experiences of sexual desire, arousal, or orgasm seem like a problem unique to developed Western countries, but a more recent global study showed that it is of concern worldwide.[18] Still the estimates of the number of people who experience no or low libido vary tremendously. We know it affects both men and women, though overall it is more prevalent among women. One early study suggested 39 percent of women in the United States experienced diminished desire.[19] But in her book, Fahs reports that in a cross-cultural study only 10 percent of British women reported low sex drive.[20]

A 2004 study suggests about 40 to 50 percent of adult women and 20 to 30 percent of adult men have at least one form of sexual dysfunction. For men, the most common problems are early ejaculation (14 percent) and erectile difficulties (10 percent), while for women the most common are lack of sexual interest (21 percent), inability to reach orgasm (16 percent), and lubrication difficulties (16 percent).[21] A more recent study of women between the ages of twenty to sixty suggests that "only" 10 to 15 percent of them are indifferent to (or repelled by) sexual activity, but Daniel Bergner suggests that rate rises to 30 percent "when you count the women who don't quite meet the elaborate clinical threshold."[22]

The absence of libido has been "associated" with aging, sexual exclusivity, and egalitarianism. While it is associated with the aging process, some young women and men suffer from no or low sexual desire as well. But a lack of sexual desire is certainly more common among the elderly, both male and female. A recent study found that sexual desire generally decreased by late menopause. However, in addition to age many other factors have been associated with desire's decline in women: race/ethnicity, marital status, change in relationship, and vaginal dryness.[23]

Though this might well prove to be a consequence of other illnesses or of the aging process itself, a testosterone deficiency (popularly labeled "Low T") has been associated with the depression of sexual desire and fewer spontaneous erections in men. At least this is the claim of the pharmaceutical companies marketing "off-label" testosterone replacement therapies for men. In some cases, however, hormone replacement itself may actually have no significant impact on a person's libido. One small, but random and double-blind, study has raised serious questions about the efficacy of testosterone therapy. Both the men who received "T" replacement therapy and those who received a placebo experienced an improvement in sexual function and mood, but no differences between the two groups were distinguishable. No significant statistical difference was found between depressed older men who were given testosterone and those who were given a placebo.[24]

Furthermore, while there have been small studies of the risks accompanying testosterone therapy, the results of these studies have proven indecisive. Though the stakes are high for the men who are taking the drug—testosterone therapy might well significantly increase the risk of sleep apnea, pulmonary embolism, heart attacks, and stroke, among others—we have no data yet from a large-scale, clinical trial to settle the current disagreement about these risks among medical researchers. In sum, we have little sound clinical evidence about either the benefits or risks of testosterone replacement therapy.

Some studies suggest a flagging sex drive among married couples is the result of monogamy itself. This line of thinking is reinforced by studies that suggest a lack of libido frequently accompanies any long-term practice of fidelity. Other studies report that when couples adopted egalitarian approaches to housework and child-raising activities, even though they reported feeling closer and happier overall, their sexual activity declined. According to this study a reduction in gender differentiation correlates with a reduction in desire.[25] Pepper Schwartz, infamous for describing "lesbian bed death," suggests that sexual partners who become committed best friends experience less frisson or excitement/thrill in sex. Contrasting conclusions have been reached by others. Marie M. Fortune argues that neither commitment nor friendship need reduce desire.[26]

And, of course, even if expressions of power and control are currently eroticized in many countries that border the North Atlantic, such a trade-off between justice and eroticism is not written in stone. Expressions of mutual respect and shared pleasure could be woven into what is culturally identified as "hot" in our sexual socialization. If the script for what is sexy were to be rewritten, then egalitarian friendships could well correlate with sexual heat. Such a reimagination of what would count as good sex is precisely what Marvin M. Ellison called for in his fine book *Erotic Justice*.[27]

It is also important to note that not all people—especially women—with no or low libido are troubled by this "disorder." One survey suggested that only about 24 percent of heterosexual women suffer from—that is, not only experience but are also distressed about—low sex drive.[28] In a later study, only about 12 percent of the women surveyed reported being subjectively distressed.[29] Currently, low sexual desire is defined by most clinicians as the consistent and enduring (for a six-month minimum) experience of no or low libido (defined as the lack or absence of sexual fantasies or desire for sexual activity). This interpretation is presently a matter of considerable controversy. The question is whether the absence of libido should be treated as a "clinical problem" or simply recognized as a sexual difference or normal variation.

This is not as easily resolved as the language in the fifth edition (2013) of the *Diagnostic and Statistical Manual of Mental Disorders* (popularly known as the DSM-5) might suggest. I would argue that while the way a subject "feels" about an experience like the loss or absence of sexual desire is certainly relevant to its normative analysis, those feelings should not be treated as self-evidently decisive. Not every feeling we have is "trustworthy." Sometimes we "internalize" unwarranted biases. Consider again the way many of us absorbed for the most part the racist, sexist, and heterosexist biases afloat in the culture in which we were raised and how that has been, and perhaps still is, reflected in what we find comfortable and what we experience as distressing. This is why there is at present a vigorous debate among sexologists about how to evaluate no/low sexual desire.

On the one hand, when it is accompanied by "marked distress and interpersonal difficulty," it is defined in the DSM-5 as a clinical problem and labeled Hypoactive Sexual Desire Disorder (hereafter HSDD). Why is this controversial? It is very difficult to determine how much of a person's "dis-ease" with their lack of sexual desire is the internalized by-product of a socially constructed narrative about what is a normal experience of desire. In North Atlantic countries the adult sexual script says that wanting to be sexually active much of the time is what is normal. Thus it is quite possible this discomfort with no/low sexual desire is a consequence of having internalized this script. It might disappear if an individual's sexual socialization recognized as normal both fluctuations in desire and variations among adults.

This question is further complicated by the way cultural messages about sexual desire inform the culture's gender ideals and standards for vitality. According to one such myth, "real men" always elicit sexual desire from their partners and "real women" are at least always sexually available and responsive, if not libidinous. And though it poses challenges for both, low libido is certainly a sexual trait far more acceptable in North American culture for women than for men.

On the other hand, some of the men and women who experience low or no sexual desire over the course of their lifetime report that they are not uncomfortable with their nonsexual orientation. It is not personally disturbing. They note that people have long recognized that changes (often, though not always, decreases) in sexual desire commonly accompany women's hormonal fluctuations around pregnancy, birth, lactation, menopause, and aging. They ask: why presume the lack of sexual desire itself to be problematic? For them, it does not trigger relationship difficulties because they are not interested in having (or apparently in maintaining) sexual relationships. They report that they otherwise enjoy many intense, even "romantic," friendships. They self-describe as content with their asexuality.

Why is this perspective controversial? Again, it is very difficult to determine how much of a person's "ease" with their lack of sexual desire is the internalized by-product of a socially constructed anti-sexual script that encourages sexual repression. Though North Atlantic cultures are in some respects hypersexualized, there remain many sex-negative forces at work in the socialization process that could result in individuals having poor body images and that could produce sexual repression. Included among these is the traditional Christian notion that sexual desire is among all that which will be "left behind" in the life to come, and so leaving it behind here and now—far from being problematic—actually embodies proleptically the future in glory.

Though I would not in principle rule out the development or use of pharmaceuticals in the treatment of the loss or absence of sexual desire, I agree with much to which "The New View Campaign" seeks to draw our attention. John Bancroft reminds us that there are situations (for example, following sexual trauma) where the absence of desire should be recognized as an understandable, even adaptive, response.[30] As Leonore Tiefer argues, a host of even more particular issues affect desire. When a partner is untrustworthy, hostile, or sexually inept, a decline in desire is an understandable consequence.[31] As Fahs summarizes the viewpoint of many feminists, "women should reimagine their interest in sex as having normal fluctuations in response to life events, biological changes and partnered relationships."[32]

And yet, even though it is not a matter of life and death, I would contend that low or no sexual desire is not a trivial, bourgeois health issue. Whether personally bothered by the problem or not, a growing mound of evidence strongly correlates healthy sexual functioning with better rates overall of health, well-being, and happiness. There is a strong correlation between staying sexually active and staying healthy, even between sexual activity and longevity.

On the one hand, my argument suggests that asexuality—like being deaf from birth—might well be a defect healed in risen life. Some for whom decline proves intractable might well find their patience taxed while awaiting the resurrection of the body, even as they are consoled by its promise. On the other hand, many who have been asexual their entire life do not report that they experience their lives as wounded or deficient simply because they have never enjoyed an intimate relationship fueled by sexual desire. I do not know how they might respond to the prospect of such a heavenly possibility, but I suspect they (like many in the deaf community) would not welcome their present life being labeled "disabled." Most human relationships are not sexual. The absence altogether of this particular thread in portions of the human tapestry both now and in the life to come might well simply be a difference, part of the dappled beauty that is our life together, rather than a defect.

Honestly, I do not think sexologists know enough about the experience of asexuality to say much more than this at this time and it is not my goal in this chapter to resolve this controversy. We need to learn a lot more about all the various factors that affect sexual desire. Still, I hesitate to recognize asexuality as simply a different (perfectly normal) "sexual" orientation because at least some people clearly experience the absence of sexual desire as problematic. Those in previously satisfying sexual relationships who experience a drop in their level of sexual desire that is not only precipitous but long term might well view this as a condition for which they eagerly seek healing. While they certainly hope and pray for its transformation in the life of the world to come, they rightly seek to cultivate the healthy and holy expression of sexual desire here and now.

REDEFINING SEXUAL VIRTUE

The need to cultivate desire results in an expansion of our notion of what constitutes sexual virtue, traditionally known as chastity. As always, though a gracious gift, the practice of sexual virtue is conceived of as a moral task, commended to all people regardless of whether they are dating, married, single, or avowed celibate. I would argue however that despite its present connotations to the contrary, sexual virtue should not be thought of as exclusively, or even primarily, about the suppression or denial of sexual energy. The work of chastity includes the nurture of sexual desire as well as its simultaneous education.[33] Chastity should denote both the "chastisement" of lustful experiences of desire and the correction of deficient experiences of desire through its cultivation. Sexual desire requires both restraint and nurture. One mistake Aquinas made in this regard was to assume that the nurture of sexual sensitivity is rarely necessary. We now know that its nurture is of moral concern to a significant number of people at least at certain times in their life.

Gudorf was among the first theologians to recognize sexual pleasure in itself as a gracious gift. She identified it as "a premoral good," by which is meant "that it is, in the normal scheme of things, good, before we morally evaluate its role in any particular situation." She argued that we all need bodily pleasures and that for some—depending upon their lifestyle and commitments—this will include sexual pleasure.[34] In an article entitled "Sex without Shame," Mennonite Keith Graber Miller details a list of sexual "do's" (instead of "don'ts"), which includes the suggestion that Christians should "talk openly and directly about sexuality in our homes and churches" and "help younger people and each other say 'yes' to some shared bodily interactions."[35] He goes on to affirm self-pleasuring for some, especially if such masturbation is not associated with lust. But that is exactly the heart of the matter, isn't it? How does one kindle the fire—stimulate erotic desire—without schooling it in ways that are lustful? The final chapter of this volume assesses the capacity of internet porn to nurture sexual desire.

CHAPTER 8

Pornography and the Education of Sexual Desire

Some readers may be wondering why a book that opened with arguments about the need to reconsider eschatological speculations about sex in heaven is closing with an analysis of the contemporary world of pornography. Admittedly, the connection between the two topics is not immediately self-evident. But think for a minute about the trajectory of this argument and consider its implications. From the very beginning I have argued that discipleship calls Christians to bear witness in their sex lives on earth to their convictions about the life to come. When we (re)envision sexual desire and delight as constitutive in some transfigured sense of our life in Christ, then the decline here and now in such sanctifying desire and its virtuous enjoyment is seen as morally and spiritually problematic. As was discussed in the previous chapter, properly formed sexual desires need to be cultivated by Christians (just as malformed desires need to be curtailed). Sexual desire can not only nurture love on earth; it can be an important holy sign of the life to come. The development of ways—disciplines, in the technical sense of that moral term—to stimulate sanctifying experiences of sexual desire and delight is an important moral task from this eschatological perspective.

The sense that it is important to keep our sexual fires burning is commonplace, and many ordinary people, including Christians, turn these days to pornography in search of sexual stimulation when their libido wanes or withers. And indeed, porn usually does prove to be stimulating. There are many problems with this turn to pornography, but the fact that it is sexually stimulating is not central to them. Indeed, I will argue here that finding alternative ways to invigorate our sexual lives is an important moral task for all the faithful. The problem with porn is not that it is arousing; the problem is that the erotic desires it arouses are malformed.

Our sexuality is constructed by many factors, including cultural narratives about sexual desire. Many stories about sexuality are being told in North America (and across the globe) through a variety of popular media including novels, films, music videos, and advertisements. In this chapter we will evaluate the messages about sexuality being sent via pornography. As Robert Jensen notes in the conclusion to his book *Getting Off: Pornography and the End of Masculinity*, "pornography is telling us stories about what it means to be a man, to be a woman, to be sexual as men and women." He reminds us of the importance of asking: "Are these the stories we want told? Is this the world we want to build?"[1]

As should be clear by now, Christianity too has a story to tell about sexuality, a narrative that might well include eschatological images of what Wendy Farley so aptly calls "beguiling beauty" and sensuous sweetness. Christians seek to embody this script here and now not only in their behaviors but in their very experience of sexual desire. The questions are: How do we school sexual desire for its "already but not yet" destiny in our life with Christ? Will the narratives sold in porn enable us to cultivate sexual desires compatible with the Christian story about sexuality?

This final chapter is divided into two parts. In the first section, Christian traditions about the formation of sexual desire are evaluated. While the relation of sex to reproduction will be reviewed, most of this discussion about the schooling of desire will focus on the potential of sexual desire to be cultivated in ways that fuel love making. Important caveats about sexual pleasure—about why it must be shared, if it is to prove to be love making, and why sexual pleasure by itself doesn't really satisfy desire—will also be laid out here. The second half of this chapter focuses on internet pornography. Given the notorious problems associated with defining it, porn is described at this juncture in some detail. While there are many compelling arguments to be made against the porn industry, this analysis focuses the effects of pornography on its consumers, particularly on their cultivation of desire.

SCHOOLING SEXUAL DESIRE

Since sexual desire and its pleasures can be good and gracious gifts from God, their nurture in ways appropriate to one's vocational commitments are rightly considered spiritual and moral disciplines. For many couples in committed relationships the formation of sexual desire is likely to include not only its discipline toward steadfastness and exclusivity but its cultivation for love making as well. The decline or absence of sexual desire may threaten sexual partnerships. When sexual desire flags or disappears altogether, many look for ways to refuel it. It is critical to remember that such nurture is never value-neutral; desire is always directed toward this or that purpose. Christians are called to stoke the fires of sexual desire on earth in ways that are compatible with how we imagine they might be in heaven.

In their anthology *Saving Desire: The Seduction of Christian Theology*, F. LeRon Shults and Jan-Olav Henriksen aim not just to rescue erotic desire (which includes but is not reduced to sexual desire) from the repressive tendencies associated with "Christian" dualism. They also want to give an account of the power of virtuous erotic desires—including virtuous sexual desires—to order our lives together positively. In her essay in their volume, Wendy Farley describes the nurture and "formation of desire as a central task of Christian life," noting that one's theology of desire provides direction for its schooling.[2] Yet another contributor to this volume, Christine Roy Yoder, argues that the possibility of directing sexual desire and modifying it if necessary is taken to be axiomatic throughout the scriptures. As she sees it, a classic example of this can be found in the opening chapters of Proverbs, where a father presumes erotic (including sexual) desires can be modified by changes in the way his son comes to think about such relationships. The father's advice aims to reshape this youth's vision of what is sexually desirable and thus to reform his sexual life.[3] Clearly, there are more or less better ways to cultivate desire. The Christian task is to kindle desire so that it can be salutary and engender human flourishing.

As Robert Jensen notes, when desire wanes many ask: "In such a situation, why not use an outside stimulus such as pornography to jump start the sexual aspect of the relationship?"[4] Certainly, the answer to that question depends upon what we think desire is ultimately for. This is *the* question in sexual ethics and the answers to it have been several. Traditionally, within Christianity, the desire for sexual pleasure was thought to serve the common good primarily by facilitating procreativity and the parental bonds that facilitate child rearing. More recently, Christians have recognized that sexual desire can be love making. Let us consider each answer.

Consider Thomas Aquinas's reply to the question: what is sex for? His argument was actually quite nuanced. Some with whom he argued taught that sexual pleasure and desire were intrinsically evil. Instead, he recognized that our capacity for sexual delight had to be good, because God created it. The key was to identify and live in accord with its God-given purpose. For Aquinas the answer seemed obvious: normatively human (naturally good) experiences of sexual desire were designed to promote the propagation and proper education of children (and therefore the survival of the species as well as the building up of the church). Sexual desires and activities were natural only when ordered in accord with these goals.

Aquinas viewed sexual pleasure as the servant of procreativity. Although Aquinas greatly valued the intimacy of marital friendship and accepted the sacramental unity of the couple as a good associated with marriage, nowhere does he commend the promotion of intimacy and love as an intention befitting sexual activity. He came close to this when he noted that sexual activity can bond parents together, but pleasure is good not in itself, nor for spousal love, but because it serves child rearing.

At the denominational level no mainstream church in the West these days teaches that procreation alone is the purpose for which sexual desire was designed. However, some still teach that this purpose must be at least symbolically embodied for a sexual relationship for it to be good. In debates about IVF, sterilization, contraception, and especially in disputes about heterosexism and homosexuality, many denominations teach more or less consistently that openness to possibility of procreation is an essential element of good sex. My own communion—the Roman Catholic Church—teaches that openness to the possibility of procreation is essential to each and every expression of good sex and that such openness is inseparably connected to its unitive, love-making function. In contrast many other Christians do not think that openness to the possibility of procreation is essential to good sex, or that it is inseparably connected to the capacity of sexual activity to be genuinely love making.[5] They recognize children as a great blessing from God and that some of the faithful are called by God to responsible parenthood. But they think sexual desire is primarily or essentially for something else.

Sexual desire opens us to love. The first awakening of (what might become) love is our spontaneous response to the beauty that has attracted us. This initial response may not be subject to choice, but as Margaret Farley points out, we can be actively receptive to sexual desire's invitation to open ourselves and pay attention to the beloved (or not).[6] Given the argument of this book—about the likely destiny of sexual desire in the life of the world to come—it should come as no surprise that I think the sexual desire has been designed by God to draw us toward each other and to build up a holy communion, to make great lovers of us all. This natural, built-in inclination to love does not conclude our inquiry; it is but the launching pad. As Farley puts it, for Christians and many others, "love is the problem in ethics, not the solution."[7]

What might it mean to say one's sexual desires should be love making? To fuel a just love, Farley notes, sexual desire must be shaped so that it will help us attend to the concrete realities of the beloved as a person. Minimally, a well-formed experience of sexual desire will be alert to and respectful of our lovers as an end in themselves. This requires that we avoid harming the beloved. A well-formed experience of desire will also respect the beloved's capacity for choice and self-determination. Such respect requires that we respect their bodily integrity and ensure the free consent of our sexual partners. To enable such genuine consent, we must be truthful and committed to honoring our promises.[8]

Farley goes on to argue that well-formed experiences of sexual desire will also be alert to and respectful of the human capacity for relationship.[9] Sexual desire can help us embody this capacity to know and be really known, to love and be loved, and so on, only if it inclines us toward certain kinds of sexual relationships.[10] Sexual desires that are love making will fuel relationships characterized by mutuality, equality, fruitfulness, and commitment. Sexual desires have the potential to incline us toward genuine love only if they do not fuel rigid, active/passive models of interaction, unequal patterns of vulnerability and dependence, and unilateral experiences of pleasure among lovers. Relationships that turn in on themselves or fail to care adequately for children conceived therein should also be avoided. Farley notes that even brief sexual encounters may open lovers to relationship, but she warns that the pursuit of sexual pleasure in such a context might well prove isolating instead.

It is important to note here that despite considerable "romantic" rhetoric to the contrary, there is actually little cultural support for the idea that sexual desire should be formed so as to fuel love making. Currently, in North America most Christian churches only give lip service to this notion. Few have taken such a claim about the love-making potential of mutually pleasurable, sexual intimacy seriously. I say this for two reasons. First, for the most part, churches still do not treat the sharing of sexual pleasure (or the failure to share it) as morally significant. Second, much of popular culture (at least in the United States) fails to recognize that the pursuit of pleasure alone will not orient us toward the genuinely intimate relationships that can satisfy our deepest desires.

Consider contemporary Christian teachings about sexuality. Most mainline denominations in the West now celebrate sexual pleasure in their official teachings and note that sharing sexual pleasure can be love making.[11] These recent developments should be applauded.[12] Yet, the discussion of pleasure therein remains superficial. The androcentric myth that coital activities are widely pleasurable for women appears to remain unchallenged by clergy of both genders. Furthermore, many denominations that explicitly teach about sexuality give little attention to the moral significance of *sharing* sexual pleasure, or even to the moral import of not causing pain during sexual activities.

The exceptions that prove the rule in this regard are the sex-affirming manuals written for conservative, evangelical Christians. They have been plentiful since Tim and Beverly LaHaye first published their blockbuster book *The Act of Marriage* in 1972. Even though this book and its many descendants emphasized the goodness of sexual pleasure (including female sexual pleasure), they are inclined generally to prioritize sexual submission (particularly ministry to a husband's sexual "needs") over the value of mutually shared pleasure.[13] Few note explicitly that if sexual activity is not mutually pleasurable, then it will not promote intimacy and it cannot be love making.

Consider as well the ongoing emphasis on openness to the possibility of procreation. Roman Catholic Church teachings continue to imply that vaginal-penile intercourse is the only form of good sex. It appears that most teachers of the church presume that most women delight in coitus, but this is simply not true. While many women enjoy coitus, research indicates that 70 percent of women do not have orgasms through coital activity alone. Studies suggest that in fact some women do not routinely enjoy coital activity at all. Many actually find it painful. In her book *Women's Bodies, Women's Wisdom*, Christiane Northrup, MD, reports that 25 percent of women say they have painful vaginal-penile intercourse virtually all the time and another third report pain a significant amount of the time.[14] For these couples, sexual intercourse that is potentially open to the possibility of procreativity is far from love making. It does not take a great deal of moral imagination to recognize that sexual activity that is not mutually pleasurable will not be bonding or prove to be love making.[15] Instead of enhancing a loving bond, such sexual activity might well prove destructive of it. Sexual activity cannot be love making apart from the sharing of mutual delight, and coitus by itself is a source of pleasure for only some women, perhaps only a relative few.

Ironically, in light of its own teachings on the importance of the unitive purpose of sexuality, the Catholic emphasis on coitus should be qualified, on the grounds that coitus alone often does not serve the unitive end of sexual activity adequately. The problem is that noncoital sexual activities in themselves are not procreative and much of what constitutes at best "foreplay" from this procreative perspective has traditionally been judged "unnatural," particularly if it should result in male ejaculation. Ongoing silence about these activities speaks volumes to couples about the comparative importance of baby making over love making, though officially neither purpose ought to have primacy over the other. Much, much more needs to be said by all denominations during sex education programs, marriage preparation, and marriage enrichment courses about the importance of sharing pleasure and about the candid sexual communication in intimate relationships requisite for such sharing.

Another problem at least in the North American sexual climate is the failure to recognize that the hedonistic pursuit of pleasure alone cannot satisfy our deepest sexual desires. It simply isn't enough. We know this to be true because deep down we don't just want sexual "release" or merely to be entertained. We want connection. We want to be wanted. We want to be the focus of another person's attention. Indeed, we want to be deeply known for who we truly are and ferociously loved in response. This is what we really want. Built into human being is this deep longing for intimate companionship. While making such a love can be terrific, the problem is that it is also terrifying.

Sexual desire incarnates our yearning for intimacy. It inclines us toward such connections. This is why people frequently experience phone sex or cybersex as so much "hotter" than solo forms of masturbation, even those involving porn. These technologies facilitate—from a distance, of course—a measure of intimacy. Sexual desire can incline us toward even more passionate attachments and can empower the maintenance of such bonds. It can draw us into one another's arms and hold us there. Sexual desire can enable people to know themselves as significant and fiercely wanted, as an occasion of joy and tender delight for another. This is why many Christians believe sexual activity can be sacramental; it is part of the body's grace, to use the apt phrase of the former Archbishop of Canterbury Rowan Williams.[16]

What does it mean to say sexual desire can be bonding? This cannot be answered exactly, because it varies with each couple. But sexual partners can become so interconnected that the other's concerns, interests, and agendas become their own. For example, I care about what happens to my husband; his business is my business. If he is treated poorly at work, it concerns me. Likewise, he cares about me. When my mother needed end-of-life care, he cared for her. A lover's concern expands to include his or her lover's concerns: his or her parents, siblings, friends, biological and stepchildren, more distant relatives, and even to the institutions with which they are associated—like the unions and public schools—that touch them.

Christians believe that this expansive relational design is built into sexual desire for deeply theological reasons. This inclusiveness of the other's concerns mirrors God's love for us. This image of God is recognized as stamped into our very experience of erotic desire. Since it is by God's design that people's boundaries blur when they so love, Christianity affirms that the many expressions of human sexuality—the attraction of desire, the heat of arousal, and the joy of genital pleasure—can be good and gracious gifts of God. The longing for connection built into our experience of sexual desire is an inherent image of God's longing to commune with humanity, indeed for all of creation.

God's love for us is unfailingly steadfast, deeply passionate and personal, yet inclusive and welcoming of all. God's incarnation in Christ—that is, God's becoming "one flesh" with all of humanity—reveals more fully still than even creation itself God's own boundary-blurring activity and the erotic destiny for which we as humans have been made. Christ's passion tells the terrific and terrifying story of the lengths to which God will go in an effort to woo us back into the great communion that is God's Dance.

Human love can be terrifying too. Our bodily availability to one another and our longing for intimate engagement leaves us at risk. We are extremely vulnerable to abandonment and humiliation, to hurt, betrayal, and rejection in sexual activity. Perhaps no one said it better than James A. Baldwin when he described what lies behind the refusal to love: "I think the inability to love is the central problem, because the inability masks a certain terror, and that terror is the terror of being touched. And, if you can't be touched, you can't be changed. And, if you can't be changed, you can't be alive."[17] Touching—especially sexual touch—is boundary-blurring behavior.

Boundary-blurring behavior nurtures intimacy. But such relationships are not just a lot of work; they are a lot of trouble. Sex is risky business. We have good reason to be afraid of getting hurt. We also have good reason to be afraid of our power to hurt others—there is something both seductive and corrupting about our power to humiliate and degrade someone who is physically and emotionally naked before us. Our touch is very powerful. So, we sometimes harden our hearts and separate our personal selves from our sexual relationships. This is why people sometimes look for relationships "without strings attached." We are afraid. This is why people "hook up" with strangers. This is why we settle for the "benefits" of sex with a casual friend. While such a friend will not take our beauty to heart, neither will he or she leave us broken hearted. Nor will we be tempted to harm him or her.

Boundary-blurring behavior can also slide easily into boundary-violating behavior. If you watched the movie *Lars and the Real Girl*, you saw the tender truth about the dangers of intimate partnerships. Lars isn't the only one afraid of really standing naked and vulnerable before another human being. We are all afraid both of being hurt and of hurting others, of being violated and of violating others. Precisely because it is so valuable and potentially harmful, sexual desire requires both discipline and nurture.

Ola Sigurdson reminds us that the process of sustaining and constructing desire takes place in communities ("cities," to use Augustine's term), that will either foster or inhibit the edification of our desires.[18] As discussed in preceding chapters, the formation of our sexual desire is social and so, of course, will be its (virtuous and/or vicious) reformation and nurture.[19] Our mothers were right! What we do regularly (our habits) and who we hang out with (our lovers and friends) really does matter! Let us consider whether pornography can help in cultivating sexual desire for love.

INTERNET PORNOGRAPHY

There are at least two ways to rekindle and stoke sexual desire. One, notes Margaret Farley, is to extend through commitment the sexual relationship sufficiently "through time to allow the incorporation of sexuality into a shared life and an enduring love."[20] To this path we will return at the close of this chapter. The other way to keep sexual desire alive is through novelty. As Farley notes, "moving from one partner to another prevents boredom, sustains sexual interest and the possibility of pleasure."[21] Novelty is what the internet offers in spades. Nothing in human history has enabled such movement from one sexual "partner" to another faster and with such ease of access and anonymity as has the World Wide Web. The stimulation associated with such novelty is why so many are increasingly inclined toward various forms of cybersex. It is undoubtedly one of the factors that explains why the consumption of virtual forms of sex has exploded.

It should be noted here—lest there be any illusions to the contrary—that the rising popularity of internet pornography is not an exclusively secular or liberal phenomenon.[22] A 2009 state-by-state study done at Harvard University reported a positive correlation between subscriptions to online porn sites and religious and political conservatism.[23] In her essay on "Pastors and Pornography" Amy Frykholm noted that well over 50 percent of the men in Promise Keepers use porn.[24] Whatever the precise numbers, porn use is growing in popularity among people who occupy both the pews and pulpits of Christian churches. While there are undoubtedly still significant gender differences both in attitudes toward and the consumption of pornography, increasingly women as well as men use porn for sexual stimulation purposes (and not only as a result of the pressure or coercion of male sexual partners).

In the United States most boys have been exposed to soft-core porn by the age of eleven and 84 percent have been exposed to hard core porn by high school.[25] Prior to the age of eighteen, 93 percent of boys and 62 percent of girls viewed online porn. Whether we like it or not, a considerable amount of sex education appears to be occurring online. According to a recent study in *CyberPsychology and Behavior*, "Boys were more likely to be exposed at an earlier age, to see more images, to see more extreme images (e.g., rape, child pornography), and to view pornography more often, while girls reported more involuntary exposure."[26]

The explosive growth in the consumption of sexually explicit materials online is widely reported in the social science literature to be linked to its affordability and to the easy, anonymous access provided by the internet.[27] In his TED Talk on "The Great Porn Experiment," Gary Wilson[28] notes that early in the twenty-first century when Simon Louis Lajeunesse began to study the impact of internet porn on college age men, Lajeunesse could not identify a control group, that is, he could not find enough college age men who were not already using sexually explicit materials on a regular basis to constitute a randomly defined control group.[29]

Given these statistics it is certainly reasonable to conclude that significant exposure to pornography is commonplace in the United States. Beyond exposure, encounters with porn appear to be part of a typical male rite of passage in North America. They are often a shared secret and their use a type of male bonding. It is important at this juncture to underline for some what others know to be obvious: most of the time porn is not just viewed or read. It is nearly always accompanied by masturbation.[30]

Should Christians view this as morally problematic? Historians of the West can trace sexually explicit materials apparently intended to spark sexual desire clear back to ancient Greece. We know from the discovery of the statues of erect penises and the images of explicit sexual activity found in many homes and public buildings entombed at Pompeii that such material was not judged obscene in the ancient Mediterranean world, at least not during the Pax Romana in Italy. Indeed, in her book *Fantasies of Femininity: Reframing the Boundaries of Sex*, Jane M. Ussher reports that sexually explicit materials were not routinely judged negatively (and hence closeted from public view) until the mid-seventeenth century. They were not repressed in private homes until the mid-nineteenth century.[31] Generally speaking, Ussher concludes, explicit representations of sexual activity were not viewed as obscene—that is, as threatening to morally corrupt viewers—until relatively recently in Western history.

The nature of sexually explicit narratives, images, statues, videos, and so on, continues to evolve, so that today in the early twenty-first century many people want to distinguish between forms of sexually explicit material that might energize desires that could prove to be just, if not love making, from those that could not. But the dividing line between the two is notoriously difficult to articulate. This is not a question just for the likes of academics, state legislatures, or Supreme Court justices either. I once received a phone call from an irate mother who had overheard her son talking with one of mine about a book—a wonderful, "coffee table" book—we brought home following the year I spent teaching in Rome. Among its pages were images reproducing many of the sensuous nude statues and gorgeous paintings so typical of the Italian Renaissance found on nearly every corner in Rome. I have no doubt that our son and his friend found these beautiful nude images to be erotically stimulating. I also have no doubt that these images were not obscene.

I see its impact on sexual desire as edifying, as drawing those who view its pages to the beauty and sensuality of the human body. But my neighbor clearly did not share that judgment.

Robert Jensen suggests we should simply agree for pragmatic purposes to label all of what is sold in sex shops and on adult sex websites as pornographic.[32] (Of course, this does not truly solve the problem; it only defers the question.) Jensen reports that in these marketplaces one can find two types of sexually explicit materials: (1) feature films that are barely organized around the thinnest of plot lines and (2) what is known as gonzo or films that simply record sexual activity, "wall to wall" so to speak. At these locations, a production is likely to be categorized as soft core (instead of hard core) if it portrays nudity and sexual petting but avoids directly showing genitals and acts of penetration. But, of course, the issue of import is not what body parts are uncovered, or what sexual activities are explicitly portrayed, but rather the script for the person or relationship that is narrated and its effects on the viewer.

What could be problematic about stimulating sexual desire through the use of such sexually explicit materials, if sexual desire is a good and gracious gift, both here and quite possibly in the life of the world to come? Might pornography have any place in the Christian schooling of sexual desire? To answer that question, we must have a clear sense of what some of the effects of using internet pornography to stimulate desire might be. We need to understand the complex relationship (1) between the consumption of porn and violent, abusive relationships, (2) between porn, sexual addiction, and the loss of desire, and (3) between porn, sexual communication, and developing skills for intimate relationship. Obviously, these three concerns are not the only important moral questions related to pornography, but their consideration will give us a better handle on porn's formative impact on sexual desire.[33]

Violence

Marvin Ellison contends that in porn frequently the source of arousal is "not merely the sexual explicitness of the images but the subjugation and humiliation" portrayed therein.[34] Pornographic books and films eroticize phallocentric, crudely (mostly hetero)sexist scripts of subordination (usually of women) and domination (usually by men) as well as violence (again usually against women and often sexual). Jane Caputi concurs and emphasizes that pornography conditions its viewers "to eroticize domination, subordination, violence, and objectification, even when, as in some contexts, a woman takes the masculine role or the man the feminine."[35] Two questions follow: (1) How much of the sexually explicit materials sold in sex shops and on the web falls into this category? (2) What are its effects?

Those who favor increased censorship of pornography believe materials that normalize, indeed make sexy, structures of domination and violence of many types are widely representative of what is available on the internet. Others however do not think such materials typify most of what is sold there. Ussher reports:

> In my own research, I found that the most common theme was of a woman on her own—no man in the scene at all—strongly reminiscent of the archetypal nude we see in "art." . . . Soft-core is certainly more ubiquitous, and if we examine the vision of "woman" in this context, it is not as easy to say that it can be explained away solely as "woman hatred." It appears to be as much about fantasies of untrammeled desire, or about warding off fear, as it is about desecration or dread.[36]

She argues that though some studies suggest the portrayal of violent, illegal activities may constitute as much as 25 percent of the porn market, other researchers have concluded "that only 3 to 4 percent of pornography is violent."[37]

In her chapter on pornography, Ussher reviews the social scientific literature generated in the 1970s and 1980s surrounding the claim that there is a straightforward cause and effect relationship between pornography and violence. She concludes that such a claim lacked sufficient support, noting that the scientific community was divided on whether there was even a positive correlation between an increase in the consumption of pornography and an increase in sexually aggressive behavior among men. And yet, in 1985 the U.S. Attorney General's Commission on Pornography concluded that there was a link between pornography and harm to women. In her summary of the research available to this commission, Edna F. Einsiedel concluded as follows.

> Sexually explicit material designed to be arousing is arousing; rapists are aroused by both forced and consenting sex depictions, but college males are only aroused by forced sex if the victim is shown to enjoy it; arousal associated with rape is positively correlated with attitudes to rape and acceptance of rape myths; both of these correlated positively with aggressive behavior toward women; and laboratory aggression toward women positively correlates with self-reported sexually aggressive behavior.[38]

The problem is, notes Ussher, that this interpretation of the evidence did not represent a scientific consensus. Other social scientists had assessed the same evidence differently and concluded "that a simple stimulus-response model of pornography and violence cannot be substantiated."[39] For this reason similar public commissions in Britain in 1979, in Canada in 1985, and in Australia in 1988 determined that there was not sufficient evidence to conclude that the consumption of pornography by "normal" (that is, not convicted sex offenders) men harms women.[40]

It continues to be difficult to assess the relationship of porn to violence because pornography itself may well simply reflect scripts even more deeply enmeshed in popular culture. Marvin Ellison makes the point this way: "the burgeoning pornography industry in the U.S. displays sexuality as a dynamic of dominance and subordination. Good sex is depicted as requiring inequalities of power and status between man and woman. In this regard pornography expresses mainstream cultural values about sex though, granted, in exaggerated display."[41] The violent (hetero)sexist scripts found in pornography are in evidence in many other genres—in art, advertising, popular music, movies, television, and so on—and porn may be far from uniquely educative in their regard.

Macrosociological studies that positively correlate increases in the consumption of porn with increases in the rate of sexually violent crime must also be carefully interpreted. Ussher cautions that other factors may be at play, given the fact that the roots of (sexual) violence are quite complex. She cites the work of Dennis Howitt, whose review of the literature on divorce highlights one such additional variable. His studies indicate that there is an even stronger positive correlation between increases in reported rape and increases in the number of divorced men in a society. He argues that when we control for this factor, no statistically significant correlation can be found between the consumption of porn and reported rape.[42] Additionally, it may well be that the consumption of porn impacts different viewers differently. For example, one study positively correlated the exposure of unhappy individuals to pornography with nearly a sevenfold increase in their having engaged in casual sex, but this same study found the use of porn had no impact on the rates of casual sex behavior among happier adults.[43]

But when Ussher examined studies that focused on the impact of pornography on women and children subject to sexual abuse, she found the evidence more compelling. For example, studies suggest that child abusers expose children to images of incest and pedophilia in an effort to "normalize" such behavior and to undermine the potential internal resistance children might have to abuse. This strategy proves effective especially among children who have considerably less capacity to interpret critically what they are exposed to, and if they do, they may simply feel shame at their own sexual response to it. (Of course, because what we see is "real" for those involved in its production, pornography that involves the abuse of children and/or adults should be illegal, regardless of its effects on viewers.) Ussher concludes: "We should be able to condemn violent pornography, child pornography and the sexual abuse of women and children without having to exert a blanket censorship over all sexually explicit material . . . "[44]

Additionally, porn often treats acts that can actually be harmful to one's partner (including substance abuse, risky sexual behaviors, and pressure, if not outright coercion) as sexy. Some studies have positively correlated risky sexual behavior with the consumption of porn.[45] But as with porn's relationship to violence, this does not establish a causal relationship. Engaging in unprotected anal intercourse (referred to in the literature as UAI) has also been found to correlate positively with age, HIV status, and substance abuse (particularly the use of inhalant nitrates). The point here is this. As has proven to be the case with sexual violence, the factors underlying dangerous sexual behaviors are multiple and their interrelationship undoubtedly complex. The consumption of sexually explicit material that eroticizes such risky behaviors alone will not account for them. What we do know is that porn use may well be one among many contributing risk factors.[46]

The Loss of Desire

The central promise of porn is that it will spark sexual desire and in the end lead to sexual pleasure. As Robert Jensen puts it, porn usually "produces sexual stimulation that can efficiently lead to orgasm."[47] This is the one well-established effect of porn. But even this claim requires some qualification. Those who develop a sex arousal addiction in response to their internet porn use—and this is a sizable minority of viewers—will eventually experience a drop in their libido, followed by erectile dysfunction in men and a numbing of desire in women.[48]

In her helpful review of the neuroscience behind desire, Joyce Ann Mercer explains why this happens. Sexually explicit images trigger the release of dopamine in the brain. The viewer learns to associate this pleasure with that external trigger. Digital technology enables viewers to see at high speed a succession of novel, sexually explicit images. One study, Mercer cites, makes it clear that any trigger that does not extinguish the release of dopamine with repeated exposure is a potentially addictive substance or process.[49] When viewing internet pornography, "dopamine rapidly and continually floods the brain," effectively rewiring its reward circuit.[50] Habituated to this flood of dopamine, porn use (this trigger) then becomes requisite for any experience of desire and its pleasures. For those who become addicted to internet porn, arousal requires an ever greater volume of, and constantly intensifying, sexually explicit imagery. No merely human sexual encounter can produce what technology has made requisite. Thus internet porn addicts frequently suffer ED and the loss of desire.

As is the case with substance addictions to drugs, food, alcohol, and the like, the addiction to internet porn, like other so-called behavioral or process addictions, is associated with multiple relationship difficulties. This should not come as a surprise since the very reward circuits of the brain likely to be changed by behavioral addictions (think here of various forms of sex addiction, including cybersex addictions to internet pornography and hot chatting) are critical to our most intimate social relationships. Labeling this the "theft of desire," practical theologian David A. Hogue concludes that sex addictions "in effect 'hijack' these circuits from their support of loving desire."[51] Admittedly, not all who consume internet porn will become addicted. Perhaps about only 8 percent of men and 3 percent of women will become addicted to porn and eventually suffer the loss of desire. But in 2015 this might well have amounted to roughly thirty million Americans. No moral assessment of the effects of consuming porn should exclude this risk, but this can only be recognized as a serious moral issue when the proper cultivation of desire is seen as constitutive of sexual virtue.

Unilateral Pleasure

While agreeing that at least some kinds of pornographic materials should be banned, many argue that other kinds of sexually explicit erotica send wonderful, positive messages about sex. After all, women are often portrayed as sexually adventurous and appreciative, voracious (indeed insatiable!) symbols of sexual desire who eagerly seek phallic penetration. But this fantasy does not square with reality. Many women are not so enthusiastic; they are certainly not always and endlessly available for and interested in sex. In contrast to what is portrayed in porn, few women walk around already aroused, nearly ecstatic at the mere prospect of penetration. Likewise, even among adolescent males, penises are not always and already rock hard.

Ussher may well be right to interpret such narratives as reflecting male fantasies about their sexual prowess and women's desires. They may well express efforts to ward off male anxieties about women's lack of sexual interest. She suggests that much of porn may aim to allay male fears about the ability to get and keep erections and to pleasure females. It is interesting to note that studies indicate that women's sexual fantasies are often similar to the scripts present in porn. And yet, research also suggests that these fantasies "rarely reflect the experiences actual women found the most pleasurable and satisfying in their partnered sexual lives."[52]

The question remains: are such fantasies helpful? Admittedly stimulating for many, do such scripts bring people to satisfying sexual partnerships in reality? Pornographic fantasies do not eroticize the good communication about sex requisite for sharing pleasure. On the contrary they teach that there is no need for sexual partners to pay close attention to whether they are sharing pleasures with each other and/or to negotiate their sexual encounters. The message they send is that there is no need to communicate, that is, to speak about one's own and to attend to one's partner's sexual preferences. In a recent article on the loss of sexual desire, a couples' expert from Boston, Terry Real, takes note of the lack of concern for the reciprocity of delight expressed in pornography.

> What will you never see in a porn video? "Honey, I don't like that, could you stop doing that, could you take a shower first?" The archetype of the porn queen is that she is a woman who derives sexual pleasure by giving the man pleasure—and here's the key—everything he does is perfect! What you don't see in porn is anything that needs to be negotiated, the woman having needs of her own or the roles being reversed.[53]

Were this "queen" to speak up, she or he would break the "magic" spell cast over the sexual activity, particularly its power dynamics. These fantasies fuse erotic stimuli with the active partner's inattention to (if not outright disregard for) the passive partner's (usually women's) pleasure, and those roles are not reciprocated.

Some users of porn might respond: Well, of course not. That's the whole point. It is a sexual fantasy! It is not meant to be a unit on the importance of good communication in a sex education course. But the fact is: like it or not, these genres are confused in our culture. Internet porn is for many people a (if not the) major source of their sex education, and tragically it communicates a lot of misinformation about what makes for mutually pleasurable sexual relationships. Likewise, porn does not eroticize safer sex practices (unless it is produced in a state that requires condoms be used) or other habits that express a sense of shared responsibility regarding the spread of STDs or family planning.

In sum, when detailing its impact, certainly the stimulation of desire can be correlated with the consumption of internet pornography. At the same time, the risk of addiction—and with it the loss of desire—should also be linked to the use of porn. The sexual fantasies envisioned in the vast majority of sexually explicit "scripts" available online do little to foster among their viewers better skills at sexual communication, sharing pleasure, or sharing responsibility for reproductive or other health concerns. And while admittedly no simple causal relationship can be established between the consumption of porn and sexual violence and abuse, some studies suggest it may be one of many contributing factors.

This is what I recommend. Because of the role they play in sustaining abusive relationships, I would argue that violent and child pornography, as well as any sexually explicit materials whose production requires the abuse of people, should be outlawed. Because of their many, likely positive correlations with unhealthy outcomes, much of the remaining sexually explicit material available for consumption on the internet should be avoided. Scripts can be harmful in multiple ways. We need to eroticize good communication and consensual sexual encounters—but not only that. As we see in narratives like that found in *Fifty Shades of Grey*, people can agree to participate eagerly in their own violation and debasement. People called to embody sex on earth as it might well be in heaven need to ask whether what they use to stimulate their sexual desire fosters both intimacy and respect for human dignity.

FROM EXCARNATION TO INCARNATION

I would also argue that we need to turn our gaze away from what is external to our sexual relationships. We need to turn away from virtual (exclusively visual and audio) realities and to "(re)materialize" sexually, as it were. We need to turn away from screens and devote more time to actually smelling, tasting, and touching our sexual partners. We need to make time in our lives for sex play. Before suggesting in a bit more detail what such a discipline might concretely entail, let me say a word about our contemporary tendency toward excarnation and why I think it is problematic.

It is critical to concede in our day and age that the contemporary social production of sexual desire is and will be primarily visual. "Without claiming that this dimension is exhaustive," writes Sigurdson, "I would suggest that it would still be a good idea to start with the so-called turn from a 'textual' to a 'visual' culture in the West, in which the written or printed word no longer has a hegemonic status when it comes to the production of meaning."[54] Indeed globally the formative power of "moving pictures" cannot be doubted.[55] There may be no more powerful medium whereby people's lifestyles are "produced" than movies. Like all narratives, movies (sexually explicit or not) provide the categories, roles, and scripts for our sexual desires.

The philosopher Richard Kearney has explored the differences between negotiating sexual relationships virtually (through sight and sound) and through touch. He traces these preferences back to an ancient debate about which way of mediating the world—visually or through touch—produces the most wisdom. Plato, whose hermeneutic was largely opto-centric, commended our visual sense because it facilitated through distance the development of theoretical understanding. In contrast, Aristotle advocated a more carnal hermeneutic, noting that proximity did not foreclose the possibility of wisdom because touch is cognitive as well as sensitive. To make a long story short, the Platonists won this argument in the West, and touch was stigmatized in the various dualisms that followed.[56]

Technology has accelerated the movement in the West toward what Kearney (presumably building upon the work of Charles Taylor in *A Secular Age*) has labeled "excarnation." Our steady divestment in matters of touch and the flesh is expressed powerfully in the phenomenal growth in the amount of time we devote to "screens" each day and in internet porn industries. We can see the impact of "excarnation" in the explosive consumption of pornography today.

It is not without painful irony that the impact of the excarnation of sex has been told so well by Spike Jonze in his movie *Her*. In this examination of the limits of virtual love, we meet Theodore, who was left deeply wounded in his real life by a divorce. He and "Samantha" (an operating system's digital persona) eventually become virtual lovers, but this does not prove satisfying. Proxies for "Samantha's" presence—even the surrogate lover Samantha sends Theodore in the flesh—cannot adequately replicate the connection established by a lover's touch. Why? Because when we touch someone, we are exposed immediately to that person, to the adventure they are, the risks their carnal presence introduces as well as its delights.

What has all this to do with the appeal of porn? Basically, as we know it pornography is a visual medium. It is voyeuristic. And in such visual relationships, power is unilateral. We have much more control over purely visual relationships than over those that are enfleshed. This is why more and more of us, especially chronic users, prefer the relative anonymity of a casual sext and to gaze at internet pornography over taking the multiple risks of trying to initiate a sexual encounter and share pleasure with a real partner. Like any "blind rut," as James Joyce so indelicately put it, porn is far less challenging than a relationship with a three-dimensional, sometimes smelly and blemished, sometimes exhausted or angry, sexual partner who can and often does both look and talk back.

Whether we watch it as a couple or as an individual, porn turns us away from knowing and being known by a real person, whose affections we can neither turn down or off when they make us uncomfortable, nor turn on with the click of a switch. No matter how eager, lovers encountered in the flesh are not always available for or even interested in sexual activity. Unlike the idealized, disembodied avatars we might encounter or become on the web—who like porn stars apparently never pick up a pound or two over the holidays, suffer menstrual cramps, and so on—sex play on earth cannot ignore the limits and messiness that accompany finitude.

Most porn is problematic, not because it is sexually explicit or stimulating, but because its narrative often (but perhaps not always) fuels a desire to take, rather than share, pleasure and because its promise of the easy release of sexual tension reinforces our fearful inclination to turn away from each other in real life. When we pay close attention to what is truly delightful, however, pornography's disorienting, if not always deadening, impact on our heart's desire for shared joy is revealed. When we habitually divorce sexual pleasure from its power to sustain and deepen intimate relationships—which is I would argue what the chronic use of porn does—we harden our hearts to the sensuous joy for which sexual desire was designed.[57]

The Christian tradition has devoted significant attention to the way sexual desire wanders off in new and different (and not coincidentally in sexually stimulating) directions. Much in traditional Christian sexual ethics speaks clearly to and negatively about such wanderings in search of novelty, to the habits of "hooking up" (fornication), to adultery, even to lust practiced "only" in one's heart (or increasingly online). The Christian literature on sexual exclusivity is extensive, but there has been comparatively little analysis of the connection between the wandering of desire and its fluctuations, between the search for novelty and the hope of reigniting that delicious fire that is desire. The church has offered little counsel as to how spouses might otherwise cultivate sexual desire, as noted earlier by Margaret Farley, through its incorporation "into a shared life and enduring love."[58]

If the sexual incarnation of love is to serve as an antidote to their heart's desire wandering off in search of novelty either online or across the street, then partners must set time aside to play sexually with each other. They must focus their time, energy, and attention on each other, so they do not lose touch with each other amid the clutter and work that accompanies building a shared life. Perhaps those among God's people who are in committed relationships ought to treat such dates as a way, along with worship, that they "keep the Lord's Day holy." Instead of "giving up sex" for Lent, perhaps "sex play" should become a Lenten discipline.[58] Since we have established that there might well be sexual desire and delight in heaven, then at least some Christian disciples are called to cultivate and enjoy such transfigured expressions of sex on earth.

Notes

INTRODUCTION

1. Nicholas Thomas (aka N. T.) Wright, *Surprised by Hope: Rethinking Heaven, the Resurrection and the Mission of the Church* (New York: HarperCollins Books, 2008), 214.
2. Unless otherwise noted, all biblical quotations will come from *The New American Bible, Revised Edition* (*NABRE*), translation approved by United States Conference of Catholic Bishops (Washington, DC: United States Conference of Catholic Bishops, 2010).
3. Many in this chorus will be cited throughout this volume. For a good introduction to this focus, see Christopher Ruddy, "In Defense of Desire: The Theology of James Alison," *Commonweal* 136/2 (January 30, 2009): 12–15.
4. David H. Jensen, *God, Desire, and a Theology of Human Sexuality* (Louisville: Westminster John Knox Press, 2013), 45. Childbearing is, of course, another obvious way this happens, though this was not noted by Jensen.
5. James Alison, "The Gay Thing: Following the Still Small Voice," in *Queer Theology: Rethinking the Western Body*, ed. Gerald Loughlin (Oxford: Blackwell, 2007), 55. This strikes some as a devilish idea. As Mark Twain wryly observed, many of those Christians concluded that "only

someone like Satan would find the loss of such joy unintelligible!" Mark Twain, *Letters from the Earth*, ed. Bernard Devoto (New York: Harper and Row, 1938), 8.

6. Arland Dean Jacobson, "Jesus against the Family: The Dissolution of Family Ties in the Gospel Tradition," in *From Quest to Q: Festschrift James M. Robinson*, ed. Jon Ma. Asgeirsson, Kristin De Troyer, and Marvin W. Meyers (Leuven: Leuven University Press, 2000), 189–218.
7. Many feminist theologians use the term Kin-dom, rather than Kingdom or even Reign of God, because it denotes the intimate interpersonal friendships that siblings ideally enjoy while connoting the nonhierarchical character of this cosmic communion (inclusive of even our Brother Sun and Sister Moon).
8. The emergence of the title for Mary of Theotokos cannot help but underscore the sanctity of motherhood through its association of pregnancy with the call of all Christ's disciples to be God-bearers, that is, to embody God in our lives.
9. In his *Nicomachean Ethics*, Aristotle first described desire as identical with the joy experienced as activity or energy (Greek *energeia*). See *Nicomachean Ethics* book 10, chapter 4, 1174a11ff.
10. According to predominant models, sexual desire is presumed to be awakened by preferred objects or stimuli. This experience can then be followed by genital arousal (vasocongestion, lubrication, and so on) excitement and orgasm. Traina suggests that this is an androcentric model, which may not even take adequate account of all men's sexual experience and certainly does not comprehend most women's sexual experience. She notes that recent research suggests that in women's experience arousal precedes sexual desire, which may or may not follow. When viewing visual stimuli, women's experience of arousal may be more flexible than men's. As Traina puts it, for women sexual desire appears to be more like a possible product of genital arousal rather than a necessary precursor of it, and physical arousal is not necessarily an indicator of psychological arousal. In this regard Traina cites the work of Meredith L. Chivers, "A Brief Review and Discussion of Sex Differences

in the Specificity of Sexual Arousal," *Sexual and Relationship Therapy* 20/4 (2005): 377–390, and Lisa Diamond, *Sexual Fluidity: Women's Love and Desire* (Cambridge: Harvard University Press, 2008). See Cristina H. L. Traina, *Erotic Attunement: Parenthood and the Ethics of Sensuality between Unequals* (Chicago: University of Chicago Press, 2011), 47–70.

11. I recognize the imperfections of this definition. Engorgement does not always signal sexual desire, and one can certainly experience erotic passion without engorgement. And yet, most of the time for most people, this signals sexual arousal. It is my hope that this working definition will prove to be both flexible and focused enough to serve this query.
12. Thomas Hobbes (1588–1678) was among the first philosophers to distinguish sexual desire from other desires, such as those for food and the like, precisely because it has this dual agenda, both to be pleased and to please.
13. Traina, *Erotic Attunement*, 7.
14. Traina contrasts her view with that of the Roman Catholic Church, which defines all desire for companionship as sexual rather than erotic. *Catechism of the Catholic* Church (New York: Doubleday, 1995), Section 2332.
15. James B. Nelson, *Body Theology* (Louisville: Westminster John Knox Press, 1992).
16. Robin Scroggs, "Paul and the Eschatological Woman," *Journal of the American Academy of Religion* 40/3 (Spring 1972): 283–303.
17. Raymond Kemp Anderson, "Corporate Selfhood and Meditatio *Vitae Futurae*: How Necessary Is Eschatology for Christian Ethics?" *Journal of the Society of Christian Ethics* 23/1 (Spring–Summer 2003): 39–40.
18. Henry H. Knight III, *Anticipating Heaven Below: Optimism of Grace from Wesley to the Pentecostals* (Eugene: Cascade Books, 2014), 11.
19. Christopher Morse, *The Difference Heaven Makes: Rehearing the Gospel as News* (New York: T&T Clark, 2010).
20. From a lecture by Nester O. Miguez entitled "Doing Theology in a Non-Revolutionary Situation," Delivered at Saint

Paul School of Theology, Kansas City, MO, February 18, 2009.

21. David Cloutier, "Composing Love Songs for the Kingdom of God? Creation and Eschatology in Catholic Sexual Ethics," *Journal of the Society of Christian Ethics* 24/2 (2004): 71–88.
22. John Paul II, *The Theology of Marriage and Celibacy* (Boston: St. Paul Editions, 1984), 18.
23. Elizabeth Stuart, "Queering Death," in *The Sexual Theologian: Essays on Sex, God and Politics*, ed. Marcella Althaus-Reid and Lisa Isherwood (London: Continuum, 2005), 58–70. In her essay Stuart is clear that risen life will be without gender and presumably sexless too, since she interprets the comment attributed to Jesus in John 20:17 as referring back to the clinging testified to in Genesis 2 and as implying that in Christ "all clinging" is to stop.
24. Andrea Bieler and Luise Schottroff, "Eschatological Imagination," *The Eucharist: Bodies, Bread and Resurrection* (Minneapolis: Fortress Press, 2007), 15–48.
25. For rich accounts of feminist concerns about traditional forms of eschatology, see Catherine Keller, "Eschatology," in *Dictionary of Feminist Theologies*, ed. Letty M. Russell and J. Shannon Clarkson (Louisville: Westminster John Knox Press, 1996), 87, and Rosemary Radford Reuther, "Eschatology and Feminism," in *Lift Every Voice: Constructive Christian Theologies from the Underside*, ed. Susan Brooks Thistlethwaite and Mary Potter Engel (San Francisco: HarperSanFrancisco, 1990), 129–142.
26. See Helen Rhee, "Wealth, Poverty and Eschatology: Pre-Constantine Christian Social Thought and the Hope for the World to Come," in *Reading Patristic Texts on Social Ethics: Issues and Challenges for Twenty-First-Century Christian Social Thought*, ed. Johan Leemans, Brian J. Matz, and Johan Verstraeten (Washington, DC: Catholic University Press of America, 2011), 64–84.
27. See Audre Lorde, "Uses of the Erotic: The Erotic as Power," *Sister Outsider: Essays and Speeches* (Freedom: Crossing Press, 1984), 53–59; Rita Nakashima Brock, *Journeys by Heart: A Christology of Erotic Power* (New York:

Crossroads, 1988); Carter Heyward, *The Erotic as Power and the Love of God* (San Francisco: HarperCollins, 1989).

28. Wendy Farley, *The Wounding and Healing of Desire: Weaving Heaven and Earth* (Louisville: Westminster John Knox Press, 2005), xvii–xix.
29. See Barbara Blodgett, *Constructing the Erotic: Sexual Ethics and Adolescent Girls* (Cleveland: Pilgrim Press, 2002), 60–83.
30. Geoffrey Rees, *The Romance of Innocent Sexuality* (Eugene: Cascade Books, 2011).
31. John Anthony McGuckin, *The Orthodox Church: An Introduction to Its History, Doctrine and Spiritual Culture* (Oxford: Wiley Blackwell, 2011), 422.
32. William Stacey Johnson, *A Time to Embrace: Same-Gender Relationships in Religion, Law and Politics* (Grand Rapids: William B. Eerdmans, 2006).
33. Margaret D. Kamitsuka, "Sex in Heaven? Eschatological Eros and the Resurrection of the Body," in *The Embrace of Eros: Bodies, Desires, and Sexuality in Christianity*, ed. Margaret D. Kamitsuka (Minneapolis: Fortress Press, 2010), 261–276.
34. Jensen, *God, Desire, and a Theology of Human Sexuality*, 68.

CHAPTER 1. GENERAL RESURRECTION OF THE BODY

1. On these points see Wright, *Surprised by Hope*, 27–30. See as well Caroline Walker Bynum, *The Resurrection of the Body in Western Christianity, 200–1336* (New York: Columbia University Press, 1995), 13, and Oscar Cullman, *Christ and Time: The Primitive Christian Conception of Time and History*, trans. F. Filson, 3rd ed. (London: SCM, 1962).
2. While defending some of his ninety-five theses in 1520, the great Reformer Martin Luther described as "monstrous" these presumptions about the immortality of the soul. He condemned them because he thought they served as anthropological foundations for the notion of purgatory and the

practice of what Luther eventually came to call "saint worship." For more details, see Martin Luther, "Assertion of All the Articles of M. Luther Condemned by the Newest Bull of Leo X," November 29, 1520, Art. 27, in the *Works of Martin Luther*, vol. 7 (Weimar: Hermann Bohlhaus Nachfolger, 1897), 131–132. See as well Paul Althaus, *The Theology of Martin Luther* (Philadelphia: Fortress Press, 1966), 414–415.

3. Bynum, *The Resurrection of the Body in Western Christianity*, 8.
4. Wright, *Surprised by Hope*, 200. As discussed in the introduction to this volume, the moral life is greatly influenced by eschatological convictions. This interpretation has been confirmed by many theologians over the centuries. For example, I am grateful to my colleague Young Ho Chun for drawing my attention both to John Wesley's sermon "Salvation Is a Present Thing" and to the work of the Dominican physician and theologian Marie-Dominique Chenu, O.P., both of whom argued that in Christ human history (our present time) is being ontologically transformed.
5. Consider texts that arguably could be interpreted to mean that believers no longer truly die (John 5:24, 8:51, 11:25–26), that the dead are with God (Mark 5:39; 1 Corinthians 15:20; 2 Corinthians 5:8; Philippians 1:23; 1 Thessalonians 4:14; Hebrews 4:9; Acts 7:59; 1 Peter 4:19), or that appear to testify directly about this "intermediate state" (Luke 16:19, 23:43; 1 Peter 3:19; 4:6). Nevertheless, it should be conceded there is still very little detail in the Bible about precisely what might happen *between* an individual's death and the coming in fullness of Christ's Reign at the end of time.
6. This notion was officially enshrined by the Fourth Lateran Council in 1215, promulgated again in the 1336 declaration by Pope Benedict XII in *Benedictus Deus*, and reiterated during the Fifth Lateran Council, when Pope Leo X in 1513 condemned those who asserted the mortality of the intelligent soul. This view was confirmed most recently by the Congregation for the Doctrine of the Faith (hereafter CDF) of the Roman Catholic Church when

it argued: "The Church understands this resurrection as referring to *the whole person*; for the elect it is nothing other than the extension to human beings of the Resurrection of Christ itself. . . . The Church affirms that a spiritual element survives and subsists after death, an element endowed with consciousness and will, so that the 'human self' subsists." See the CDF's 1979 "Letter on Certain Questions Concerning Eschatology," http://www.vatican.va/roman_curia/congregations/cfaith/documents/rc_con_cfaith_doc_19790517_escatologia_en.html.

7. The saints, canonized or not, are alive in Christ, and for Roman Catholic Christians among others this means the dead can and do pray for and with us. At its best, like the tending of ancestral graveyards, the treasuring of the relics of the saints kept alive this sense of connection between the living and the dead. But by the late Middle Ages, the veneration of relics became problematic. Superstitions about relics emerged and relics were faked, bought, sold, traded, and stolen, as if the power of prayer could be so manipulated. Protestants perhaps still worry that this focus on the saints detracts from emphasis on the saving grace of Jesus Christ.

   Still, this sense of communion is not a peculiarly Eastern Orthodox or Roman Catholic experience, as evidenced by the Protestant novelist Wendell Berry. One of his protagonists, Hannah Coulter, says when speaking of the population of her fictive hometown, Port William, "The membership includes the dead." See Wendell Berry, *Hannah Coulter* (Berkeley: Counterpoint Press, 2004), 94. In his analysis of resurrection themes in Berry's literary corpus, United Methodist theologian D. Brent Laytham notes that Berry is right to complain that Christianity is not earthy enough. Hymns like "This World Is Not My Home" deny that God has made all things well and instead call us away from this earth. See D. Brent Laytham, "'The Membership Includes the Dead': Wendell Berry's Port William Membership as *Communio Sanctorum*," in *Wendell Berry and Religion: Heaven's Earthly Life*, ed. Joel James Schuman and L. Roger Owens (Lexington: University Press of Kentucky, 2009), 173–189.

8. Perhaps the most famous Roman Catholic to hold this position is Karl Rahner, S.J. He speculated that resurrection occurs at the moment of death. For an extensive review of various Catholic views, see Bernard P. Prusak, "Bodily Resurrection in Catholic Perspectives," *Theological Studies* 61/1 (February 2000): 64–105.
9. Joseph Cardinal Ratzinger, *Eschatology: Death and Eternal Life*, 2nd ed. (Washington, DC: Catholic University of America Press, 1988), 253. This text was originally published in German in 1977.
10. Second Vatican Council, *Pastoral Constitution on the Church in the Modern World* (*Gaudium et spes*) (1965), 14, http://www.vatican.va/archive/hist_councils/ii_vatican_council/documents/vatii_cons_19651207_gaudium-et-spes_en.html.
11. These statistics come from the Pew Foundation, "U.S. Religious Landscape Survey" (2007), accessed July 7, 2012 at http://religions.pewforum.org/pdf/report-religious-landscape-study-key-findings.pdf. NB: most Christian theologians and pastors would agree that the idea that death results in personal annihilation (period) is not compatible with Christian faith.
12. Lisa Miller, *Heaven: Our Enduring Fascination with the Afterlife* (New York: Harper, 2010). Data from a 2003 Harris poll, she reports, indicated that 30 percent of the U.S. population believed in reincarnation. This is a notion traditionally associated with Hinduism, even though 21 percent of those who indicated they believed in reincarnation had self-identified as Christian.
13. The absolute ban on cremation was first lifted by the Vatican in 1963. Following funeral services, cremation was permitted for good reasons, but burial was still clearly preferred. This has been followed by increased openness to cremation, but not over internment. These changes were codified in 1983 when the Code of Canon Law was last revised. See Code of Canon Law, Canon 1176 and *Libreria Editrica Vaticana*, 1983, accessed December 2, 2015, http://www.vatican.va/archive/ENG1104/_INDEX.HTM#fonte. They were maintained in the recently revised Catholic

funeral rites. See the International Commission on English in the Liturgy, *Order of Christian Funerals* (Chicago: Liturgy Training Publications, 1989). An addition to these regulations was made by the Vatican in 1997, permitting U.S. bishops on a case-by-case basis to allow funeral Masses in the presence of cremated remains.

14. Ramsey MacMullen, *Paganism in the Roman Empire* (New Haven: Yale University Press, 1981), 56–57.
15. The careful consideration of which burial practices might best bear such witness in our world today would take us too far afield, but it is certainly an ethical question worthy of more sustained attention than it is currently receiving in most places.
16. Barbara Brown Taylor makes this point by asking this question: what else besides—that is, apart from—the body can be sanctified? She concludes that the Christian moral life must consist in "practicing incarnation" because, as the Brian Wren hymn proclaims so beautifully, "Good is the flesh that the Word has become." Barbara Brown Taylor, "Our Bodies, Our Faith," *Christian Century* 126/2 (January 27, 2009): 24–29.
17. For a recent detailed account of this, see Margaret R. Miles, *The Word Made Flesh: A History of Christian Thought* (Malden: Blackwell, 2005).
18. For a broad review of classical Western thinkers in this regard, philosophers and theologians alike, see James Alfred Martin Jr., *Beauty and Holiness: The Dialogue between Aesthetics and Religion* (Princeton: Princeton University Press, 1991). For a fine evaluation of Hans Urs von Balthasar's efforts in this regard, see Susan A. Ross, "Women, Beauty and Justice: Moving beyond von Balthasar," *Journal of the Society of Christian Ethics* 25/1 (Spring/Summer, 2005): 79–98. For a compelling account of the often overlooked but powerful role beauty plays in evoking and sustaining the work of justice, see Patrick A. McCormick, *God's Beauty: A Call to Justice* (Collegeville: Liturgical Press, 2012).
19. The nature of the sacramental character of marriage from a Protestant perspective was perhaps most famously noted by Dietrich Bonhoeffer, "A Wedding Sermon from a Prison

Cell, May, 1943," *Letters and Papers from Prison*, trans. Reginald Fuller, Frank Clark, et al. (New York: Touchstone, 1997), 41–55. For more contemporary arguments, see Timothy D. Lincoln "Sacramental Marriage: A Possibility for Protestant Theology," *ATLAS Proceedings* (1995): 205–216, and especially Elizabeth Myer Boulton and Matthew Boulton, "Sacramental Sex: Divine Love and Human Intimacy," *Christian Century* 128/6 (March 22, 2011): 28–31.

Noteworthy here too is the explicit reluctance of other Protestants to equate marital sex with sacrament. Such claims strike them as idolatrous. See Stanley J. Grenz, *Sexual Ethics: An Evangelical Perspective* (Louisville: Westminster John Knox Press, 1997), 83. To be sure, I would concur that sex per se is not salvific, but much in both scripture and tradition suggest that sexual activity can mediate the presence of God and thus be a locus wherein humans may encounter God.

20. For a sampling of texts ordinarily interpreted in support of this claim, see Matthew 25:31–46 and Acts 3:4–7, 8:4–8, and 28:3–6.
21. These are described as *prima facie*—on first appearance—duties precisely because other obligations may legitimately override their fulfillment, or because circumstances may prevent their fulfillment.
22. For more on this, see Stephanie Paulsell, *Honoring the Body: Meditations on a Christian Practice* (San Francisco: Jossey-Bass, 2002). See as well Rick Warren, Daniel Amen, and Mark Hyman, *The Daniel Plan: 40 Days to a Healthier Life* (Grand Rapids: Zondervan, 2013).
23. See the book of Ecclesiastes for biblical testimony in this regard. For a detailed description of how living with *jouissance*, honoring the body, and the love of God intersect around the delights of eating well, see L. Shannon Jung, *Sharing Food: Christian Practices for Enjoyment* (Minneapolis: Fortress Press, 2006).
24. Mary Catherine Hilkert, O.P., "Grace-Optimism," *America* 202/2 (January 18, 2010): 4.

25. Within Judaism, the *yetzer hara* or evil inclination is rooted in the misuse of what the body needs for survival.
26. Susan A. Ross, *Extravagant Affections: A Feminist Sacramental Theology* (New York: Continuum Books, 1998), 64–96. While Ross addresses this issue at many junctures throughout the text, the third chapter on "Women, the Sacraments and Ambiguity" is especially relevant. For another feminist take on these issues, see Melanie A. Mays, *A Body Knows: A Theopoetics of Death and Resurrection* (New York: Continuum, 1995).
27. Interestingly, sometimes when our possessions are defaced or our homes are invaded, we feel personally violated. But this only happens when we consider those things or that space to be in a real sense an extension of our elves. We don't feel this way about property that is not "ours" in this highly personal sense.
28. In the history of ethics it was precisely the recognition of the distinction of our persons from our bodies that enabled ethicists to distinguish surgical procedures (however invasive and risky) from violent assaults.
29. For a detailed account of the connection between embodiment and sociality, see L. Shannon Jung, "Spatiality, Relativism and Authority," *Journal of the American Academy of Religion* 50/2 (June 1982): 215–235.
30. Morse, *The Difference Heaven Makes*.
31. Genuine thanksgiving naturally produces good stewardship of and a sense of true kinship with the rest of creation. The affirmation of the dignity and worth of all persons as children of a good and gracious God, as well as of the love of God for all creation, leads Christians to care for the entire cosmic web of life in which we are embedded and by which we are sustained.
32. Miller, *Heaven*, 75. Of course, the quote originated in J. D. Salinger, *Franny and Zooey* (Boston: Little and Brown, 1966), 171.
33. This tension found voice early in church history in the differences between two schools of theological thought about the Incarnation. According to one school of thought historically

associated with Clement of Alexandria and Origen, and still presently emphasized in some Reformed theologies, it is important to keep *discreet* the two *natures* of Christ. Given the ambiguity of embodiment, it is understood to tie people to corruptibility and death. God is thought to have become human in order to help people overcome the frailties identified with material life. Union with this Incarnate God liberates us from such bodily bondage and the vanities of this world. Blurring the human and divine will denigrate the Christ's transcendent nature. One must avoid such idolatry. Thus, within an Alexandrine model of the Incarnation, only a relatively weak claim can be made about the sanctification of what is corporeal. This Christology minimizes the role the Incarnation plays in the economy of salvation. It is primarily the point of connection or mediation between a largely transcendent spiritual God and humanity/creation. Not surprisingly, within this school of thought, Christian sacraments are understood merely to sign essentially spiritual realities.

In contrast, theologians historically associated with Antioch, such as Irenaeus, gave an account of the doctrine of the Incarnation that emphasized the *interpenetration* of Christ's human and divine natures. From this perspective, Jesus Christ reveals that God pervades all of life. The earth is seen as suffused with God's immanent Presence. Within this Antiochene framework, the Infinite Triune God intends from the beginning to embrace the finite and to body forth into the material world. Human sin was not the only or even the primary reason for the Incarnation. Rather in Christ God's pervasive activity in the world is revealed. People experience the Presence of God in their midst not in spite of but rather through their sensuality. We encounter God in the body and the world. Correspondingly, within this theological school, Christian sacraments are understood to disclose God's Real Presence in our midst, here and now.

More about these two viewpoints will be discussed in chapter 4. Meanwhile, let me be clear. Though there are merits to each perspective, it is I am sure clear by now that it is within the Antiochene school of thought that I stand.

34. Gregory of Nazianzus, "Gregory of Nazianzus on Apollinarianism," in *Christian Theology Reader*, 3rd ed., ed. Alister E. McGrath (Malden: Blackwell, 2006), 229.
35. Traditionally, at least four qualities will further distinguish those raised as saints. Their glorified bodies will (1) be beyond the reach of pain and even inconvenience (that is, they will be impassible), (2) have all the energy, agility, and power they are pleased to have, (3) be luminous to different degrees (1 Corinthians 15:41–43), and (4) enjoy "subtlety," a kind of spirit-like fineness or delicacy, like that which enabled Christ to pass through doors.
36. At least *prima facie* the Islamic account of the world to come is more clearly sensual. Paradise is filled not only with cool fountains and fresh fruits, but also great sex, at least for heterosexual males. In her book on *Heaven*, Miller notes that most translations of the Holy Quran promise male residents of heaven the company of beautiful maidens (*houri*), and that later accounts of the sayings of Mohammad (*hadiths*) promise seventy to seventy-two virgins to male religious martyrs. See Miller, *Heaven*, 95–101.
37. John Paul II, "The Sacramentality of Marriage," *The Theology of the Body: Human Love in the Divine Plan* (Boston: Pauline Books, 1997), 350.
38. Grenz, *Sexual Ethics*, 26. To be fair to Grenz, he did go on to affirm that dimensions of sexuality he considers "deeper" may not be eradicated.
39. Indeed what is inconsistent in this framework is that gender so often plays a part in traditional speculations about our life to come. Feminist theologians suggest, however, that it should not be surprising that fairly rigid, binary accounts of gender are often not left out of heavenly speculations. A genderless vision of heaven might suggest the "specter" of the loss of patriarchal systems of power and authority.
40. See Ben Witherington III, *The Rest of Life: Rest, Play, Eating, Studying, Sex from a Kingdom Perspective* (Grand Rapids: William B. Eerdmans, 2012), 113–153.

41. Ibid., 127.
42. Ibid., 156.
43. Ibid., 152.
44. Ibid., 155.

CHAPTER 2. THE NEW TESTAMENT ABOUT THE GENERAL RESURRECTION OF THE BODY

1. Harry Rabinowicz, "Death," *Encyclopedia Judaica*, 2nd ed., vol. 5, ed. Fred Skolnik (New York: Thomson and Gale, 2007), 510–513.
2. Texts that are generally understood to testify to this view include Genesis 2:19, 25:8; Psalm 104:29; and Job 34:14–15.
3. I say—for the most part—because noted in the Hebrew Bible are two exceptions to the generally accepted notion that life ends with death. Enoch—a patriarch about whom little else is known except that he walked with God before "the Flood"—is not reported in the Hebrew Scriptures to have died. Instead, after a (comparatively) short life, Enoch "walked with God, and he was not; for God took him" (Genesis 5:24). Similarly, according to the Hebrew scriptures, the beloved prophet Elijah did not die but was instead taken up into heaven in rather spectacular style in a chariot of fire in a whirlwind, and so on (1 Kings 17–21 and 2 Kings 2:11).

   Generally speaking, Christians do not interpret these as resurrection stories for three reasons. First, neither Enoch nor Elijah were portrayed as having died. Second, for Christians, resurrection is not just about going away from earth to live in heaven, or even about escaping death, but rather, it is about being transfigured or transformed bodily for new life with Christ in a new heaven and new earth. Third, Christians believe that Christ's resurrection was the *first* fruits of the general resurrection of the dead.
4. BCE stands for "Before the Common Era," while CE stands for the "Common Era." They have the same value as BC (Before Christ) and AD (*Anno Domini*, Latin for the year

of the Lord), respectively. The word "common" is generally understood simply to refer to the fact that this system is based on the most frequently used—Gregorian—calendar. Though I recognize this to be a matter of controversy for some Christians (see Resolution Nine at the annual Southern Baptist Convention in 2000), I choose to employ this designation as an expression of respect for the religious liberty of all my potential readers.

5. Texts that are generally understood to testify to this vision include Psalm 6:6, Isaiah 38:18, and Numbers 16:33.
6. Ratzinger, *Eschatology*, 83.
7. While a few Christian scholars may interpret the desire to enjoy the presence of God expressed in Psalms 73:16 as an expression of hope for the vision of God after death, most scholars believe the focus of the text is on the hope for the presence of God in the here and now.
8. See Ezekiel 37, Hosea 6:2, and Isaiah 26:19.
9. Jon D. Levinson, *Resurrection and the Restoration of Israel: The Ultimate Victory of the God of Life* (New Haven: Yale University Press, 2006).
10. Early in the twentieth century many scholars believed the apocalyptic visions of these early Jewish activists of this era could be traced back to Persia. They believed that they had probably been influenced by the robust, imaginative Persian accounts of an afterlife in which the righteous were rewarded with bodily resurrection. They saw such an eschatological vision rooted in the religion of the ancient Persian Empire, known as Zoroastrianism, which was centered in modern-day Iran. It offered a powerfully influential worldview, in which the world and its creatures would eventually—on the day of Final Judgment—be purged of both evil and mortality. However, the vivid pictures of a cosmic war between the "sons of light" and the "sons of darkness" found in the Dead Sea Scrolls at Qumran laid to rest the hypothesis that largely "foreign" influences rested behind apocalyptic developments in nascent Judaism.
11. Apocalyptic revelations normally predict or presage at least in part imminent, total disaster and universal destruction. The term has Greek roots, which mean to uncover or

disclose. For more on this specific vision, see John J. Collins, *Daniel: A Commentary on the Book of Daniel* (Minneapolis: Fortress Press, 1993).

12. Neither Jews nor Protestants grant 1 and 2 Maccabees canonical status. Some Protestants include it in the Apocrypha. Roman Catholic and Orthodox Christians recognize both books as part of the Christian Bible.
13. For a detailed analysis, see Dag Ølstein Endsjø, *Greek Resurrection Beliefs and the Success of Christianity* (New York: Palgrave Macmillan, 2009).
14. Indeed the notion of an individual person gaining eternal life is an idea that dates far back into Western literature. In the "Epic of Gilgamesh" (dating from the thirteenth century BCE) Utnapishtim is granted immortality by the gods for his heroic action.
15. Dag Ølstein Endsjø, *Greek Resurrection Beliefs and the Success of Christianity* (New York: Palgrave Macmillan, 2009), 227. See notes 52, 53, 54, and 55.
16. "Dead" is plural in the original (Greek) New Testament texts relevant to this issue.
17. See note 3 in this chapter for why I have concluded that the stories about Enoch and Elijah, like the restorative healings of the dead in the Elijah-Elisha cycle, should count at most as exceptions that prove this rule.
18. In his letters, Paul himself does not speak of having a mission in Athens. It is only described as such in a later document by the author of Luke-Acts. See Acts 17:18, 31–32, 23:6.
19. See Romans 6–8 (especially Romans 8:11); 1 Corinthians 6:14, 15:12; 2 Corinthians 4:14, 5:1–10; Philippians 3:21; 1 Thessalonians 4:12–16; 2 Timothy 2:11; and Hebrews 6:2.
20. An even fuller, more complete account would also include detailed analyses of all the texts related both to the Transfiguration and the Ascension of Jesus as well as of the quite sensuous account of life to come found in Revelation.
21. See Matthew 22:29; Mark 12:18–27; Luke 14:14, 20:37; and John 5:28–29, 6:39–40, 11:25.
22. It may be best at this juncture for me to lay my theological cards on the table, even though many scholars these days

keep silent about their convictions in this regard. I believe it is wrong to conclude that the Easter events described in the Bible testify only to the arising of faith in the early church. Likewise, it is mistaken to suggest that apostolic testimonies about encounters with the Risen Christ refer only to a profound experience of the forgiveness of God. While both the gift of faith and a gracious sense of personal salvation undoubtedly accompanied encounters with the Risen Christ, spiritualizing Jesus's physical body out of the resurrection is not the *sensus literalis* of the New Testament texts—and I think this approach does grave harm to the *sensus plenior* of the witness. I interpret these texts to say that Jesus Christ rose bodily from the dead and that his resurrection is the first fruit of a general resurrection of the body to come. Given the surprising, somewhat unprecedented character of their faith claims, first-century talk of resurrection could hardly have been simply another way of saying that the soul (alone) would live on after death. The apostles would simply have said that only Jesus's spirit had ascended to heaven, not his body. Audacious as it sounds, it is unreasonable to assume that is all to which they were testifying. For a brilliant exposition of this viewpoint, see Wright's *Surprised by Hope*.

23. See Matthew 28:9; Luke 24:36–43; and John 20:27, 21:12–13.
24. See Luke 24:13–16 and John 20:19.
25. Wright is well aware that nearly from its origin this biblical portrait of a new heaven and new earth also had to compete with Plato's vision of disembodied immortal souls finding their bliss at death.
26. Alan F. Segal, *Life after Death: A History of the Afterlife in Western Religion* (New York: Doubleday, 2004), 698–699.
27. Raymond F. Collins, *First Corinthians* (Collegeville: Liturgical Press, 1999), 526.
28. Joseph A. Fitzmeyer, S.J., notes in his commentary on this text that it may record the oldest expression we have of Christian belief in the resurrection of Jesus of Nazareth. Joseph A. Fitzmeyer, S.J., *First Corinthians: A New Translation with Introduction and Commentary* (New Haven: Yale University Press, 2008).

29. One popular contemporary hypothesis is that many in the Corinthian community had begun to operate with an "*over* realized" eschatology, that is, with an eschatology that exaggerated the extent to which God's Kin-dom has "already" been realized on the one hand, and downplayed, if not ignored, on the other hand, the degree to which it is "not yet." Since most of Paul's letters tend to emphasize the continuity between our lives in Christ here on earth and in the next, it would not be unreasonable to assume Paul's preaching might have likewise underscored this continuity as well. There is some textual evidence supportive of this claim. "But each in turn: Christ, the first fruits; then, when he comes, those who belong to him" (1 Corinthians 15:23). A few Corinthians may even have believed they had already arrived at the fullness of the life of faith and completely collapsed the fullness of God's future Kin-dom into their present. While Paul preached that the resurrected life of the world to come had been inaugurated in Christ Jesus, it seems to me that a tendency toward "*over* realized" eschatology could gain this sort of traction, only if the promise of such transformation was misunderstood to be purely spiritual. I believe this was in fact the deeper misunderstanding that truly worried Paul, and so it is on that misunderstanding that I focus in this chapter.
30. Robert W. Wall, J. Paul Sampley, and N. T. Wright, *The New Interpreter's Bible: Acts–First Corinthians* (Nashville: Abingdon Press, 1994), 973–990.
31. Their questions are readily understandable. As Fitzmeyer notes, little qualifies Paul's proclamation in this passage. We might well hypothesize that Paul's preaching about Jesus's resurrection, prior to this correspondence, may have been similarly unqualified. Specifically, Fitzmeyer notes, Jesus's resurrection is not specified as bodily in nature. (The Greek term *soma* does not appear in this text. Fitzmeyer also notes that Jesus is not proclaimed to have been raised "from the dead" (Greek *ek nekron*), though that—it seems to me—is certainly implied by its literary context.) Fitzmeyer, *First Corinthians*.
32. About this Paul had no doubts. He states this claim most clearly in his letter to the Romans: "We were therefore

buried with him through baptism into death in order that, just as Christ was raised from the dead through the glory of the Father, we too may live a new life. If we have been united with him like this in his death, we will certainly also be united with him in his resurrection" (Romans 6: 4–5).

33. See 1 Corinthians 15:29. Why else, Paul asks, would those in thc latter group undergo baptisms apparently on behalf of and in the name of the dead, if those dearly departed would not—through this effort to incorporate them into Christ via a proxy—thereby be raised up? Though perhaps problematic on other fronts, this sacramental practice certainly bespeaks a lively sense among some believers in Corinth of the general resurrection.
34. In addition to his encounter on the road with the risen Lord, Paul experienced further personal disclosures by Jesus (Acts 23:11) and encounters with the Mystery of eternity after his conversion (2 Corinthians 12:1–10).
35. When Paul describes Jesus as the first fruit, his analogy may have been understood or intended to be biological as well as agricultural, in which case Jesus might have been understood as the first born of a large family in which all the brothers and sisters share in the inheritance of this new life.
36. I speak of it this way because the gospels indicate the *basileia tou theou* began prior to Jesus's resurrection. Jesus's resurrection inaugurated the final culmination of the Kin-dom of God that began in a more hidden way in his earthly life and ministry as it drew all those united with Him in faith into kinship with God, each other, and the cosmos.
37. Initially, Paul may have believed the Parousia was imminent. So, while he argued this ultimate transformation was yet to come, he probably thought the time for it was near. But Paul lived a relatively long time after his conversion. If he initially thought the Lord Jesus would return within a few years, he surely was compelled by the brute force of his pastoral longevity to adjust this view.
38. This notion finds expression in a multitude of places beyond 1 Corinthians 15 in the Pauline corpus, but Romans 8 and Philippians 3 would be good places to turn for more such testimony.
39. Segal, *Life after Death*, 429–430.

40. William Barclay, *The Letters to the Corinthians*, rev. ed. (Philadelphia: Westminster Press, 1975), 141. Other biblical theologians with roughly similar interpretations include Rudolf Bultmann and Jerome Murphy-O'Connor.
41. J. Richard Middleton, *A New Heaven and Earth: Reclaiming Biblical Eschatology* (Grand Rapids: Baker Academic, 2014).

CHAPTER 3. THE NEW TESTAMENT ABOUT SEX IN HEAVEN

1. Daniel J. Louw, "Sexual Health: Towards an Eschatological Understanding of Sexual Love and Human Embodiment," *Cura Vita: Illness and the Healing of Life* (Wellington: Lux Verbi, 2008).
2. This inordinate experience of sexual desire she distinguishes from healthy experiences of sexual desire. See Laura A. Smit, *Loves Me, Loves Me Not: The Ethics of Unrequited Love* (Grand Rapids: Baker Academic Press, 2005), 75.
3. Ibid., 70.
4. Of note is the fact that Paul offers no explanation as to why sexual activity might hinder prayer or why sexual abstinence might serve it. Some interpreters suggest that this attitude may express a residue in Paul of the purity concerns found in the Holiness Code from which Paul may not have yet been freed. Consider for example the concern expressed in Leviticus 15:18: "When a man has sexual relations with a woman and there is an emission of semen, both of them must bathe with water, and they will be unclean till evening." For more about this approach to this text, see Theodore Mackin, S.J., *The Marital Sacrament* (Mahwah: Paulist Press, 1989).
5. Like Louw, William Stacey Johnson argues that apart from sexuality, creation was not complete. The provision of gender, sexual desire, and delight enable humans to become better at giving glory to God. Sexuality has the potential to provide a foretaste of the redemptive reordering that will be the new creation. Johnson, *A Time to Embrace*.

6. See Matthew 22:1–14, 25:1–13; Luke 12:36; John 2:1–11, 3:29; and Mark 2:19.
7. Richard B. Hays, *First Corinthians* (Louisville: John Knox Press, 1997), 270.
8. There are various ancient manuscripts of this gospel. According to the New International Version (hereafter NIV), in one manuscript, more is added to verse 8 so that the gospel concludes: "Then they quickly reported all these instructions to those around Peter. After this, Jesus himself also sent out through them from east to west the sacred and imperishable proclamation of eternal salvation. Amen." This version does not include vv. 9–20. Other (even later) manuscripts of this gospel provide readers with a different, longer ending. In this later version we are told Jesus appeared to Mary Magdalene, who went and told those mourning that "he was alive and had been seen by her." But she was not believed. This is followed by the story of an appearance to two disciples walking out into the country, but their testimony was not believed either. This is followed by the story of Jesus appearing to the eleven while at table, where he chides them for not believing the earlier testimonies and commissions them to proclaim the good news. This is followed by a brief account of the Ascension. See Mark 16:9–20, NIV.
9. See Matthew 28:1–8; Luke 24: 1–9; and John 20:1–10.
10. Daniel A. Smith, *Revisiting the Empty Tomb: The Early History of Easter* (Minneapolis: Fortress Press, 2010).
11. There is some debate among biblical scholars about whether Jesus was himself a Pharisee or simply heavily influenced by this movement.
12. The name for this practice stems from *levir*, a Latin term for brother-in-law. According to the commentary on Mark in *The New Interpreter's Bible*, there is little evidence that the custom of levirate marriage was actually observed in Palestine during the first century of the Common Era. Hence, most scholars believe the case was probably purely hypothetical—"trumped up," as it were—by the Sadducees. See Leander E. Keck, *The New Interpreter's Bible: Matthew–Mark* (Nashville: Abingdon Press, 1994), 676.

Indeed, Lamar Williamson Jr. argues that the type of scoffing question put to Jesus here is known in the Jewish tradition as a "vulgarity" (in Hebrew *boruth*) because it is so contemptuous of the person addressed. However, it cannot be dismissed as an utterly ludicrous query, given the intertestamental story of Sarah who had survived seven husbands (Tobit 3:8, 6:14). See Lamar Williamson Jr., *Mark: Interpretation: A Bible Commentary for Teaching and Preaching* (Atlanta: John Knox Press, 1983), 222.

13. John R. Donahue, S.J., and Daniel J. Harrington, S.J., *The Gospel of Mark* (Collegeville: Liturgical Press, 2002), 439, 352. (This is volume 2 in the Sacra Pagina series of which Daniel Harrington, S.J., was the general editor.)
14. Joel Marcus, *Mark 8–16: A New Translation with Introduction and Commentary* (New Haven: Yale University Press, 2009). This is part of the Anchor Yale Bible series.
15. M. Eugene Boring, *Mark: A Commentary* (Louisville: Westminster John Knox Press, 2006).
16. This is certainly what is argued by N. T. Wright in *The Resurrection of the Son of God* (Minneapolis: Fortress Press, 2003), 341.
17. Colleen MacDannell and Bernhard Lang, *Heaven: A History* (New Haven: Yale University Press, 1988).
18. In the Old Testament, the "fallen" or bad angels are described as seducing women and even procreating with them. "When human beings began to grow numerous on the earth and daughters were born to them, the sons of God saw how beautiful the daughters of human beings were, and so they took for their wives whomever they pleased. Then the LORD said: My spirit shall not remain in human beings forever, because they are only flesh. Their days shall comprise one hundred and twenty years. The Nephilim appeared on earth in those days, as well as later, after the sons of God had intercourse with the daughters of human beings, who bore them sons. They were the heroes of old, the men of renown. When the LORD saw how great the wickedness of human beings was on earth, and how every desire that their heart conceived was always nothing but evil, the LORD regretted making human beings on the

earth, and his heart was grieved. So the LORD said: I will wipe out from the earth the human beings I have created, and not only the human beings, but also the animals and the crawling things and the birds of the air, for I regret that I made them. But Noah found favor with the LORD" (Genesis 6:1–8). A more elaborate version of this can be found in the book of Enoch, which is treated as canonical by Ethiopian and Eritrean Orthodox Churches, but not by Jews or believers from other Christian denominations.

19. Marcus, *Mark 8–16*, 833–834. According to Marcus, the interpretation of such sexual activity as paradigmatically impure makes sense for at least two reasons. First, like bestiality, it represents a mixing of species, which God did not intend. And second, if sexuality for humans is designed only, or at least always, for the preservation of the species, then sterile sexual liaisons could not be licit. One problem, of course, with such a presumption is that it does not address why angels would have been created with sexual desire in the first place.
20. Only here in the Lukan edition of the story is the Greek compound form—*isangeloi*—used. In both Mark and Matthew, the Greek expression *hos angeloi* is used. The former connotes only similarity and likeness, not equality as well.
21. Though others within Byzantium were more moderate, by the early Middle Ages, the best marriage within Russian orthodoxy was an unconsummated one. The "cult of virginity" was present in Western Europe as well. Historian Merry E. Wiesner-Hanks summarizes the situation there at this point as follows: "Sexual relations with one's spouse were also to be kept within strict bounds, and were prohibited when the wife was menstruating, pregnant, or nursing a child, and during certain periods in the church calendar, such as Sundays, Fridays and most major saints' days, as well as all of Lent and Advent. This left about fifty days a year when a married couple could legitimately have sexual intercourse, and even this was hemmed in by restrictions as to position (prone, man on top), time of day (night only), and proper dress (at least partially clothed). Following the rules did not free one from ritual defilement, however, for

couples were expected to wash after sex before coming to church." Merry E. Wiesner-Hanks, *Christianity and Sexuality in the Early Modern World: Regulating Desire, Reforming Practice* (New York: Routledge, 2000), 37.

22. Though there are some who question this claim, there is considerable agreement that Jesus was both single and celibate.
23. For a full presentation of this argument, see Dale C. Allison, *Jesus of Nazareth: Millenarian Prophet* (Minneapolis: Augsburg Fortress Press, 1998). NB: This is a problematic conclusion on a number of theological grounds, not the least of which is the fact, as Tom Driver pointed out decades ago, that sexuality is so pervasive a reality in the animal world that to assign it to the Fall *in toto* would eventually necessitates some form of Manicheism. Only then could a good God be absolved of its creation. Thomas Faw Driver, "Sexuality and Jesus," *Union Seminary Quarterly Review* 20/3 (March 1965): 235–246.
24. At the time of his writing this letter, Paul was evidently unmarried. (See 1 Corinthians 7:8.) Tradition commonly portrayed him as never having been married, but contemporary scholarship suggests that if he (Saul) was a Pharisee, and a member of the Sanhedrin, as many think he was prior to his conversion, social norms would have "nearly required" him to have been married at some point. So, Paul could have been divorced (and not remarried) or widowed. In any case, while the Bible is clear about Paul's status as not married during his ministry, it does not provide us with information about his (Saul's) marital history.
25. Such is, of course, presumed given the biblical witness to Jesus's circumcision. "When eight days were completed for his circumcision, he was named Jesus, the name given him by the angel before he was conceived in the womb" (Luke 2:21).
26. Smit, *Loves Me, Loves Me Not*, 75.
27. Though a feast commemorating this event has been celebrated since the sixth century, even when the exposure of Jesus's genitals became popular during the Renaissance of the fourteenth and fifteenth centuries, they were frequently

portrayed as uncircumcised. I would guess this reflected the anti-Semitism of the era. Graham Ward suggests such politics of embodiment are inevitable. What is assumed to be valuable or to be denigrated in any given time and place—what is associated with the powerful or the marginalized—will shape accounts of Jesus's body. Our task is to be open to correction, critique, and supplementation. See Graham Ward, "Politics of Embodiment and the Mystery of All Flesh," in *The Sexual Theologian: Essays on Sex, God and Politics*, ed. Marcella Althaus-Reid and Lisa Isherwood (New York: T&T Clark International, 2004), 71–85.

28. Lewis Smedes, *Sex for Christians: The Limits and Liberties of Sexual Living*, rev. ed. (Grand Rapids: William B. Eerdmans, 1994), 62.
29. Although it has no parallels in the other gospels, much argues against Matthean authorship of this teaching. Foremost is the fact that it contradicts the clear Jewish moral condemnation of castration as an offense against nature.
30. In his multivolume commentary on Matthew, biblical scholar Ulrich Luz concludes: "In the ancient church Matthew 19:11–12 played only a minor role, and then primarily to justify sexual abstinence. It was not until the Middle Ages that these verses became the cardinal text for the 'evangelical counsel' concerning chastity." Ulrich Luz, *Matthew: A Commentary*, vol. 2, trans. Wilhelm C. Linss (Minneapolis: Augsburg Press, 1989), 497.
31. For a detailed review of the literature in this regard, see J. David Hester, "Eunuchs and the Postgender Jesus: Matthew 19:12 and Transgressive Sexualities," *Journal for the Study of the New Testament* 28/1 (2005): 13–40.
32. The Greek found in 1 Corinthians 7:7 is somewhat ambiguous. Paul is clearly speaking of his own celibacy as a *charisma* and perhaps, given the final phrase "one having one kind and another a different kind," he is suggesting that marriage is also a *charisma*. Or, it could be interpreted as a more general statement that other people have other *charismata*.
33. Amy Jill Levine's answer to this question was that Jesus did not endorse marriage at Cana. She claims that by attending

the wedding feast at Cana, Jesus did not endorse marriage "any more than eating with sinners endorses sin." Perhaps one could reach such a conclusion if in the narrative about Cana Jesus had been reported merely to have accompanied his mother to the event. However, the miracle at Cana contributed to the festivities and surely contributed to the celebration as such of "one flesh" unions. For more details about her perspective, see Amy Jill Levine, "The Word Becomes Flesh: Jesus, Gender and Sexuality," in *Jesus Two Thousand Years Later*, ed. James H. Charlesworth and Walter P. Weaver (Harrisburg: Trinity Press International, 2000), 62–83. See note 29.

34. William Loader, *Sexuality and the Jesus Tradition* (Grand Rapids: William B. Eerdmans, 2005), 251.
35. Leander E. Keck, *The New Interpreter's Bible: Luke-John* (Nashville: Abingdon Press, 1994), 389–390.
36. Many others agree that what Jesus is rejecting here is the reduction of human hope to the sort of immortality aimed at in levirate marriage through the production of heirs. See Wright, *The Resurrection of the Son of God*, 422, and Luke T. Johnson, *Sacra Pagina: The Gospel of Luke* (Collegeville: Liturgical Press, 1991), 318.
37. Joel B. Green, *The Gospel of Luke* (Grand Rapids: W. B. Eerdmans, 1997.)
38. For example, Williamson, *Mark*, 224.
39. Matthew 22:23–33.
40. Consider the stories about the Vineyard (Matthew 21:33–46), the Great Banquet (Matthew 22:1–14), and the joyous Wedding Feast (Matthew 25:1–13). Images of the Messiah as Bridegroom abound in the New Testament. See 2 Corinthians 11:2, John 3:29–30, Revelation 19:6–9 and Ephesians 5.
41. Interestingly, John Milton portrayed the unfallen angels as engaging in a purified and spiritual form of sex in *Paradise Lost* (8.612–629), suggesting that sexual intercourse would be part of life in the age to come.
42. Such a conclusion is already deeply embedded in the Orthodox Christian theology of marriage.
43. In Matthew 22:23–30 (and its parallels Mark 12:18–25 and Luke 20:27–36) the word frequently translated as "marry"

is *gamousin*, the third-person form of *gameó*, which means to enter into the state of marriage, to wed, or to get married. It clearly refers to an action at a point in time, not to a vocational state of being. In English, we would say "he/she/it marries." The second term in the verse, "giving in marriage," is *gamizontai*. This is an alternative way of saying the same thing, with the connotation that one is doing it for one's own benefit. In 1 Corinthians 7:33 we find the phrase that describes a married person: *gamésas*. Jesus Christ is not reported as using this term.

44. Dennis P. Hollinger, *The Meaning of Sex* (Grand Rapids: Baker Academic Books, 2009), 90.
45. Smedes, *Sex for Christians*, 22; interpolation is mine.
46. J. Harold Ellens, *Sex in the Bible: A New Consideration* (Westport: Praeger, 2006), 46. Along these same lines, see Richard McCarty's article on "Eschatological Sex," *Theology and Sexuality* 19/2 (2013): 163–178.
47. Hays, *First Corinthians*, 279. This is reminiscent of the theo-*logical* claim noted earlier in chapter 1 by Ratzinger (see note 9 in chapter 1 in the present volume). Hays brings this same eschatological framework to his consideration of homosexuality in an essay entitled "Awaiting the Redemption of Our Bodies: The Witness of Scripture Concerning Homosexuality," in *Homosexuality in the Church: Both Sides of the Debate*, ed. Jeffrey S. Siker (Louisville: Westminster John Knox Press, 1994), 3–17. While I disagree with Hays's conclusions about homosexuality in that essay, I want here to affirm his recognition of the import of bringing an eschatological framework to the consideration of questions in Christian sexual ethics.
48. Hays, *First Corinthians*, 252–282.
49. Ibid., 277.

CHAPTER 4. AUGUSTINE AND OTHER EARLY CHRISTIANS ABOUT SEX IN HEAVEN

1. The Apostles' Creed may be the oldest of these. It has been variously dated from the second to the fourth century CE. It declares "the resurrection of the flesh." The Nicene Creed

from the fourth century confirms "the resurrection of the dead," while the Athanasian Creed (from the late fifth or early sixth century) reaffirms that "all men [*sic*] shall rise again with their bodies."

2. In her book *Heaven*, journalist Lisa Miller notes that all three Abrahamic traditions envision not merely the immortality of the soul but some sort of "resurrection" in which the righteous are ushered into a paradise with (at least something like) their bodies. In defense of this claim she highlights the explicit promise of heavenly sensual pleasures in Islam. She points out that Moses Maimonides in his twelfth-century *Guide to the Perplexed* made belief in bodily resurrection the last of his thirteen, nonnegotiable tenets of the Jewish faith. She admits, of course, that many Reform Jews today understand such convictions about the resurrection to be only metaphorical rather than ontological. Yet the matter is far from settled for Jews. While noting that in 1824 Reform Judaism substituted the notion of the immortality of the soul for physical resurrection, she points out that in the 2007 revision of its prayer book, the *siddur*, the Reform Movement reinserted the ancient avowal of bodily resurrection as an alternative reading (Miller, *Heaven*, 114). Of course, she cites the centrality of Easter to Christianity as evidence of the import of bodily resurrection to it (ibid., 63). She should also have cited the centrality of Advent with its annual reminder that "Christ will come again!" for Christians as well.
3. For a detailed historical account and constructive Christological analysis of early Christian eschatological perspectives on gender, see Benjamin H. Dunning, *Specters of Paul: Sexual Difference in Early Christian Thought* (Philadelphia: University of Pennsylvania Press, 2011).
4. In his *Letter to the Smyrnaea* (sometimes called *To the Smyrnaeans* and dated around 110 CE), Ignatius of Antioch (50–117 CE) defends the notion of Christ's bodily resurrection against dualistic views. Brian E. Daley has identified several additional texts that contain comparatively unqualified affirmations of the hope for bodily resurrection. See Brian E. Daley, "Eschatology in the Early Church Fathers,"

in *The Oxford Handbook of Eschatology*, ed. Jerry L Walls (New York: Oxford University Press, 2008), 91–109.

5. The Apostles' Creed actually expresses faith in *ressectio carnis* not *mortuorum* or *corporum*. I note this to emphasize the radical nature of this claim. It entails assent to resurrection not just of the dead, or even of the body (*soma* or *corpus*), but of "the flesh" as we know it (*sarx* or *caro*). See Bynum, *The Resurrection of the Body in Western Christianity*, 28.
6. As the interim—the time between the inauguration of the new age in Christ and its full arrival at the end of time—lengthens, this question about what happens to the faithful departed grows in importance. See pages 5–10 in chapter 1 for a discussion of related issues.
7. Earlier translations give the title as "On the Resurrection of the Body" or as "On the Resurrection of the Flesh."
8. Bynum, *The Resurrection of the Body in Western Christianity*, 43ff.
9. Tertullian, *The Resurrection of the Dead*, chapter 40, accessed August 10, 2011, www.newadvent.org/fathers/0316.htm.
10. Ibid., chapters 46, 49, 50.
11. Ibid., chapter 57.
12. Ibid., chapter 36. There was no longer any need (1) for the propagation of a people from whom the Messiah would come, or (2) to build up a sort of immortality based on "an heir and a spare," or even more progeny, if possible. Christians had no need to pursue these ends either on earth or in heaven. Early church fathers apparently could not even imagine other purposes for conceiving and raising children!
13. Ibid., chapter 60.
14. Ibid., chapter 60.
15. Ibid., chapter 61.
16. Even before the later, fully Montanist phase of his life, Tertullian found little to celebrate in the human body. He opposed not only remarriage following divorce but also the remarriage of a widow following the death of a spouse.
17. Tertullian, *The Resurrection of the Dead*, chapter 61; interpolations and emphases mine.

18. Grace Jantzen, "New Creations: Eros, Beauty and the Passion for Transformation," in *Toward a Theology of Eros*, ed. Virginia Burrus and Catherine Keller (New York: Fordham University Press, 2006), 271–287.
19. It was in the *Symposium* (380 BCE) that Plato first introduced us to Diotima's theory of love. In this account, desire for what is good and beautiful "progressed" from the vulgar lust for young bodies to the contemplative appreciation of ideas. In his *Republic* (375–370 BCE) Plato uncoupled "true" love from sexual activity, and in the *Phaedrus* (356 BCE) fleeting sexual pleasures were linked with weakness and drunkenness. For more detail, see Alan Soble, "A History of Erotic Philosophy," *The Journal of Sex Research* 46/2–3 (March–June, 2009): 104–120.
20. Joanne E. McWilliam Dewart, *Death and Resurrection: Message of the Fathers of the Church* (Wilmington: Michael Glazier, 1989), 120; interpolations in original.
21. Segal, *Life after Death*, 571.
22. In general, the church in Alexandria emphasized the unity of the human and divine natures in the person of Christ, while accenting the divine nature of Christ. A bright side of their disdain for the particularities associated with embodiment was that most catechists from the school at Alexandria concluded that women (normally treated poorly because of their association with body) were not only fully human like men but made in the image of God. (They interpreted Genesis 1 in light of Galatians 3:28.)
23. Soble credits Clement of Alexandria with being among the first to declare that sexual acts in marriage were virtuous only if done for procreative purposes, and with recommending spouses minimize their pleasure by keeping their clothes on and proceeding as quickly as possible in the dark. See Soble, "A History of Erotic Philosophy,"109.
24. Clement of Alexandria, *Stromateis*, book 6, chapters 13, 14, accessed August 11, 2011, www.newadvent.org/fathers/0210.htm.
25. Clement is quite clear that among our desires only "a wrongful and insatiable grasping after money" is forbidden by God. Clement of Alexandria, "On Marriage," book

3, chapter 6, paragraph 56 in *Miscellanies* in *Alexandrian Christianity: Selected Translations of Clement and Origin*, ed. Henry Chadwick and J. E. L. Oulton (Philadelphia: Westminster John Knox Press, 1954), 66.

26. Ibid., book 3, chapter 12, paragraph 87, 81.
27. Ibid., book 3, chapter 12, paragraph 79, 76.
28. Ibid., book 3, chapter 6, paragraph 46, 62.
29. Ibid., book 3, chapter 5, paragraph 40, 58.
30. Daley, "Eschatology in the Early Church Fathers," 98.
31. Bynum, *The Resurrection of the Body in Western Christianity*, 66.
32. Bernard McGinn, "The Foundations of Mysticism: Origins to the Fifth Century," *The Presence of God: A History of Western Christian Mysticism* (New York: The Crossroad Publishing Company, 1991), 18.
33. Bernard McGinn, "Mysticism and Sexuality," *The Way Supplement* 77 (1993): 53; my interpolation.
34. See Gregory of Nyssa's dialogue with his sister, Macrina, in *On the Soul and the Resurrection* (written around 380 CE). Kindle edition.
35. Verna E. F. Harrison, "Male and Female in Cappadocian Theology," *Journal of Theological Studies* 41/2 (October 1990): 441–471. Here Harrison establishes that Gregory of Nyssa's views about the place of sexuality in the life of the world to come are shared by his colleagues Basil of Caesarea and Gregory Nazianzen.
36. From a modern perspective one "upside" of Gregory's eschatological speculation is that it grounded an egalitarian (relatively speaking) anthropology before God (if not on earth) and a single system of morality. Men and women within his framework had the same vocational ideals (albeit ascetic, monastic ones). They were to practice the exact same set of virtues. There were no double standards (including no harsher penalties for women, not even for sexual infidelity).
37. Christological controversies formed part of the backdrop to discussions about the resurrection of the body. This is evident in the theology of Dioscorus (d. 454). While he argued vehemently that Christ was truly human, in his view

Christ's humanity was—to put the matter delicately—simply not quite complete in all its parts. In other words, Jesus had no testicles. Dioscorus insisted the Incarnate Christ had no experience of seminal fluid or desire/lust. As he interpreted it, if Jesus was like us, tested in every way, yet without sin (Hebrews 4:15), then he could not really have been sexual. Why? Dioscorus could not imagine an experience of sexual desire that would not prove to be inexorably sinful. He conflated desire with lust. See Harrison, "Male and Female in Cappadocian Theology," 469.

38. Virginia Burrus, "Queer Father: Gregory of Nyssa and the Subversion of Identity," in *Queer Theology: Rethinking the Western Body*, ed. Gerald Loughlin (Oxford, UK: Blackwell, 2007), 162.
39. Harrison, "Male and Female in Cappadocian Theology," 467.
40. Ibid., 469.
41. Elizabeth A. Clark, "The Celibate Bridegroom and His Virginal Brides: Metaphor and the Marriage of Jesus in Early Christian Ascetic Exegesis," *Church History* 77/1 (March 2008): 1–25. See pages 21–22 for her discussion of this matter.
42. Jerome, *Against Jovinianus*, book 1, 36, accessed on June 11, 2015, http://www.newadvent.org/fathers/30091.htm.
43. D. S. Wallace-Hadrill, *Christian Antioch: A Study of Early Christian Thought in the East* (New York: Cambridge University Press, 1982). See especially chapter 7 on "Antiochene Theology and Religious Life."
44. John Chrysostom, "Homily 41 on 1 Corinthian 15: 35–36," in *Nicene and Post-Nicene Fathers: Saint Chrysostom: Homilies on the Epistles of Paul to the Corinthians* (Volume 12), ed. Philip Schaff, trans. Talbot W. Chambers (New York: T&T Clark, 1984), section 250.
45. John Chrysostom, "Homily 31 on 1 Corinthians 12:21," in *Nicene and Post-Nicene Fathers, Saint Chrysostom: Homilies on the Epistles of Paul to the Corinthians*, section 182.
46. Clark notes in her essay "The Celibate Bridegroom and His Virginal Brides" that in his sixth homily on Colossians (2:12) Chrysostom argues that at the moment of death

gender disappears. This is certainly a possible interpretation, but on the basis of the text it may be that only females disappear: "straightway you take into you the Lord Himself, you are mingled with His Body, you are intermixed with that Body that lies above, whither the devil cannot approach. No woman is there, for him to approach, and deceive as the weaker; for it is said, 'There is neither female, nor male.'" Accessed August 11, 2012, http://www.newadvent.org/fathers/230306.htm.

47. David G. Hunter, "Resistance to the Virginal Ideal in Late Fourth Century Rome: Case of Jovinian," *Theological Studies* 48/1 (March 1987): 45–64.
48. Despite his popularity in both Rome and Milan, Jovinian was condemned as a heretic by Pope Siricius as well as Ambrose, the bishop of Milan. Hunter suggests that Jovinian's stance against the supremacy of celibacy was untimely. It challenged Siricius's effort to make celibacy a requirement for priestly ordination. He was also apparently quite undiplomatic, to say the least. He is known to have labeled as Manichean both Ambrose and Siricius.
49. This emphasis found expression in several important creedal formulas. A fifth-century CE creed from Gaul, misnamed *Fides Damasi* (Latin for "Faith of Damasus"), declared that we will be "raised on the Last Day in that flesh in which we now live." The Council of Toledo declared two centuries later that "we will rise again . . . in this self-same flesh in which we live, exist and move." In 1215 CE the Fourth Lateran Council declared that "all will rise with their own bodies, the bodies which they bear here." See Ratzinger, *Eschatology*, 135–136.
50. Augustine, "During the Easter Season on the Resurrection of the Body against the Pagans," (dated 411 CE) sermon 241, *The Works of Saint Augustine: A Translation for the 21st Century*, part 3: sermons/volume 7, trans. and notes by Edmund Hill, O.P. (Hyde Park: New City Press, 1995), 70–77.
51. Augustine, *Of Faith and the Creed*, chapter 10, paragraph 24, accessed August 27, 2011, http://www.newadvent.org/fathers/1304.htm.

52. Augustine, *Confessions*, book 8, accessed August 22, 2011, http://www.ccel.org/ccel/augustine/confessions.xi.html.
53. This interpretation of Augustine's conversion is defended at length by Mark D. Jordan, "Flesh in Confession: Alcibiades beside Augustine," in *Toward a Theology of Eros*, ed. Virginia Burrus and Catherine Keller, 23–37 (New York: Fordham University Press, 2006). Others (in addition to Jordan) have reached similar conclusions about the anti-body nature of Augustine's conversion experience. See Segal, *Life after Death*, 583. For this reason, Segal contends, Augustine purged heaven of all sensuous pleasures.
54. Augustine, *Confessions*, book 3, chapter 1, paragraph 1.
55. Ibid., book 8, chapter 11, paragraph 26.
56. Ibid., book 8, chapter 7, paragraph 17.
57. For a thorough analysis of this polemic, see David G. Hunter, "Helvidius, Jovinian and the Virginity of Mary in Late Fourth-Century Rome," *Journal of Early Christian Studies* 1/1 (Spring 1993): 47–71.
58. See Peter Brown, *The Body and Society: Men, Women, and Sexual Renunciation in Early Christianity* (New York: Columbia University Press, 1988), 350. See as well Augustine, *Confessions*, book 9, chapters 3, 5.
59. Augustine, *Confessions*, book 9, chapter 3.
60. Ibid., chapters 10, 11.
61. David G. Hunter, "Reclaiming Biblical Morality: Sex and Salvation History in Augustine's Treatment of the Hebrew Saints," in *In Dominico Eloquio—In Lordly Eloquence*, ed. Paul M. Blowers, Angela Russell Christman, David G. Hunter, and Robin Darling Young (Grand Rapids: William B. Eerdmans, 2002), 317–335.
62. Augustine, *The Literal Meaning of Genesis*, book 11, chapter 32 in *St. Augustine: The Literal Meaning of Genesis*, trans. John Hammond Taylor (New York: Newman Press, 1982), 165.
63. Augustine, *On Christian Doctrine*, book 3, chapter 10, paragraph 16, accessed August 22, 2011, http://www.ccel.org/ccel/augustine/doctrine.xi_2.html.
64. Though I would not question Augustine's assertion of sufficiency here, it strikes me as an odd quality to ascribe to

life in glory. Trinitarian relations were undoubtedly sufficient yet God's love overflowed into creation, and I find no compelling reason to presume limits to such (pro)creative extravagance in the life of the world to come.

65. Augustine, sermon 362, "On the Resurrection of the Dead," *The Works of Saint Augustine: A Translation for the 21st Century*, part 3: sermons/volume 10, trans. and notes Edmund Hill, O.P. (Hyde Park: New City Press, 1995), 241–265.
66. Augustine, *City of God*, book 14, chapter 3, accessed August 20, 2011, http://www.newadvent.org/fathers/120114.htm.
67. Augustine, *Confessions and Enchiridion*, trans. and ed. Albert C. Outler (Philadelphia: Westminster Press, 1955), 392–393. (Or see any translation of *The Enchiridion*, 23:91.) The parenthetical translation ensouled underscores that the Latin term used here was *animas*, which translates soul.
68. Augustine, *City of God*, book 13, chapter 20.
69. Ibid., book 22, chapters 15, 21.
70. Ibid., book 22, chapter 21.
71. Ibid., book 22, chapter 29.
72. Ibid., book 22, chapters 17, 19, 20.
73. Ibid., book 22, chapter19; interpolation is mine.
74. Ibid., book 14, chapter 23.
75. Kate Cooper and Conrad Leyser, "The Gender of Grace: Impotence, Servitude, and Manliness in the Fifth-Century West," *Gender and History* 12/3 (November 2000): 536–551.
76. John C. Cavadini, "Feeling Right: Augustine on the Passions and Sexual Desire," *Augustinian Studies* 36/1 (2005): 195–217.
77. Augustine, *City of God*, book 14, chapters 10, 16, 26.
78. Ibid., book 22, chapter 17.
79. Ibid., book 22, chapter17. Women will be equal to men according to the virtues they have developed in history.
80. Ibid., book 22, chapter 29.
81. Ibid., book 22, chapter 30.
82. Ibid., book 13, chapter 22.
83. Augustine, *Retractions*, book 1, chapter 16, in *Saint*

Augustine: The Retractions, trans. Mary Inez Bogan, RSM (Washington, DC: Catholic University of America Press, 1968), 74–75.

84. Brown, *The Body and Society*, 424. This letter he notes was not discovered until the late twentieth century.
85. This translation of "Letter 6*" to Atticus of Constantinople is from *St. Augustine on Marriage and Sexuality*, ed. Elizabeth A. Clark (Washington, DC: Catholic University Press of America, 1996), 104; interpolations mine.
86. Augustine, *St. Augustine on Marriage and Sexuality*, 86.
87. Augustine, *Answer to Julian*, volume 1/25 in *Answer to the Pelagians, III: Unfinished Work*, intro., trans., and notes Roland J. Teske, S.J. (Hyde Park: New City Press, 1999), 432. This too was the view espoused by Thomas Aquinas in the *Summa Theologica*. See III. Q. 14, a.4 and Q. 15, a.2.
88. Clark, "The Celibate Bridegroom and His Virginal Brides," 18.
89. John E. Thiel, "Augustine on Eros, Desire and Sexuality," in *The Embrace of Eros: Bodies, Desires, and Sexuality in Christianity*, ed. Margaret D. Kamitsuka (Minneapolis: Fortress Press, 2010), 80.
90. While the sculpture can still be seen inside Santa Maria sopra Minerva in Rome, the church has seen fit to keep Michelangelo's rendition of Christ's glorious genitals covered with a brass loincloth, which ironically, of course, draws even more attention to them.
91. Bynum, *The Resurrection of the Body in Western Christianity*, 94–104.
92. Margaret R. Miles, "Sex and the City (of God): Is Sex Forfeited or Fulfilled in Augustine's Resurrection of Body?" *Journal of the American Academy of Religion* 73/2 (June 2005): 308.

CHAPTER 5. REIMAGINING SEX IN HEAVEN

1. "So then, brothers and sisters, stand firm and hold fast to the teachings we passed on to you, whether by word of mouth or by letter." 2 Thessalonians 2:15.

2. International Theological Commission, "'*Sensus Fidei*' in the Life of the Church," (2014) 62. The publication of this document was authorized by the Vatican's CDF. Accessed August 19, 2015, http://www.vatican.va/roman_curia/congregations/cfaith/cti_documents/rc_cti_20140610_sensus-fidei_en.html.
3. Ibid., 123; interpolation mine. The Vatican also specified in this document several spiritual dispositions that enable believers to enjoy this "*sensus fidelium*" (sense of the faithful). They include: active solidarity with the church, including but not limited to participation in the sacraments; listening to scripture, tradition, and the teachers of the church; openness to reason; peace and joy in the Spirit; and concern that one's reflections serve to edify, rather than divide, the church.
4. Ibid., 80.
5. The relative weight of these criteria and the authority of each of these sources of moral wisdom, along with the exact nature of the interplay among them, are themselves hotly contested matters for Christians. Indeed, suffice it to say, that disagreements about precisely these matters may be at the very root of Christian disunity. Wandering further into this minefield will take us too far from the project at hand.
6. Edward Collins Vacek, S.J., *Love Human and Divine: The Heart of Christian Ethics* (Washington, DC: Georgetown University Press, 1994).
7. Ross, *Extravagant Affections*.
8. James D. Whitehead and Evelyn Eaton Whitehead, *Holy Eros: Recovering the Passion of God* (Maryknoll: Orbis Books, 2009), 30.
9. See Dionysius the Presbyter, "*The Divine Names* in Pseudo-Dionysius," *The Divine Names and The Mystical Theology*, trans. John D. Jones (Milwaukee: Marquette University Press, 1999), 144. I am indebted to Orthodox philosopher Bruce V. Foltz's (unpublished as of now) article entitled "Lessons from the River Oka: Toward an Icon of Marital Chastity" for this reference.
10. Wendy Farley, "Beguiled by Beauty: The Reformation

of Desire for Faith and Theology," in *Saving Desire: The Seduction of Christian Theology*, ed. F. LeRon Shults and Jan-Olav Henriksen (Grand Rapids: William B. Eerdmans, 2011), 128.

11. Jensen, *God, Desire, and a Theology of Human Sexuality*, xi and 1–16.
12. Jan-Olav Henriksen, "Desire: Gift and Giving," in *Saving Desire: The Seduction of Christian Theology*, ed. F. LeRon Shults and Jan-Olav Henriksen (Grand Rapids: William B. Eerdmans, 2011), 21.
13. It is this tendency to conflate erotic desire with lust that makes what Friedrich Nietzsche claimed in *Beyond Good and Evil*—that "Christianity gave Eros poison to drink: he did not die of it, but instead he degenerated into a vice"—a dangerous half-truth. It is easy—if nevertheless mistaken—to conclude that Christianity is "anti-erotic in its intentions." See Kyle Harper, *From Shame to Sin: The Christian Transformation of Sexual Morality in Late Antiquity* (Cambridge: Harvard University Press, 2013), 137ff. The truth about Christianity's evaluation of *eros* is far more complex.
14. Jensen, *God, Desire, and a Theology of Human Sexuality*, 1–17.
15. Ibid., 34.
16. Beguines were members of informal religious communities that developed as part of a Christian revival during the thirteenth century in northern Europe. They were comprised of lay men and women who did not take vows but who lived lives of voluntary poverty, taking care of the poor and sick, in imitation of Christ.
17. For a more thorough review of the literature on this topic, see Joey Gánio Evangelista, M.J., "Mechthild of Magdeburg and Human Sexuality," *East Asian Pastoral Review* 45/4 (2008): 339–361.
18. This is to be distinguished from experiences of desire that stem from suffering lack.
19. Responding to a query from the Pharisees about which was the greatest commandment in the Law, Jesus replied: "You shall love the Lord, your God, with all your heart, with all your soul, and with all your mind. This is the greatest and

the first commandment. The second is like it: You shall love your neighbor as yourself. The whole law and the prophets depend on these two commandments" (Matthew 22:37–40). This was not news to his audience. Such a command is found in the Hebrew Bible as well: "Therefore, you shall love the LORD, your God, with your whole heart, and with your whole being, and with your whole strength" (Deuteronomy 6:5). Love for neighbor and self were linked to this love of God in a similar way as well: "Take no revenge and cherish no grudge against your own people. You shall love your neighbor as yourself. I am the LORD" (Leviticus 19:18). As Vacek reads this command, it is threefold, that is, it is a call to love God, neighbor, and self. This seems right to me as long as the notion of neighbor includes the cosmos. His vision of the interrelationship among these loves emphasizes the unity of these commandments.

20. See for example Ephesians 5:3–5; 2 Timothy 3:2–5; and James 5:5.
21. Philip Sheldrake, *Befriending Our Desires* (Ottawa: Novalis, 2001).
22. Roland A. Delattre, "Desire," in *Encyclopedia of Religion*, 2nd. ed., ed. Lindsay Jones (Detroit: Thomson Gale, 2005), 2303–2309.
23. Henriksen, "Desire: Gift and Giving," 29.
24. Ibid., 6.
25. Sebastian Moore, *Jesus the Liberator of Desire* (New York: Crossroads, 1989), 11.
26. Ibid., 28.
27. I am indebted here to the precision with which James Calvin Davis addressed an analogous question. See his humor-filled essay, "Will There Be Football in Heaven?" *The Presbyterian Outlook* 191/10 (March 23, 2009): 10–11.
28. C. S. Lewis, *Miracles: A Preliminary Study* (New York: MacMillan, 1947), 191.
29. I would not adopt the dichotomous terms employed by either C. S. Lewis or William Blake in their infamous, if entertaining, debate about risen life. For more information about that debate, see William Blake's *The Marriage of Heaven and Hell* and C. S. Lewis's *The Great Divorce*.

30. Dorothy Day, "Aims and Purposes," *Catholic Worker* 7/6 (1940): 7. For a detailed theological account of why this is so, see Henri de Lubac, *Catholicism: Christ and the Common Destiny of Man* (San Francisco: Ignatius Press, 1988).
31. For reviews of these developments, see Germain Grisez, *The Way of the Lord Jesus, Volume 2: Living a Christian Life* (Chicago: Franciscan Herald Press, 1993), 558–569, and John Gallagher, "Magisterial Teaching from 1918 to the Present," in *Readings in Moral Theology No. 8, Dialogue about Catholic Sexual Teaching*, ed. Charles E. Curran and Richard A. McCormick (New York: Paulist Press, 1993), 71–92.
32. Second Vatican Council, "Pastoral Constitution on the Church in the Modern World," 1965: 49, accessed August 19, 2015, http://www.vatican.va/archive/hist_councils/ii_vatican_council/documents/vat-ii_const_19651207_gaudium-et-spes_en.html.
33. Patricia Beattie Jung, "Intersex on Earth as It Is in Heaven," in *Intersex, Theology and the Bible*, ed. Susannah Cornwall (New York: Palgrave Macmillan, 2015), 173–195; Patricia Beattie Jung and Joan Roughgarden, "Gender in Heaven: The Story of the Ethiopian Eunuch in Light of Evolutionary Biology," in *God, Science, Sex, Gender: An Interdisciplinary Approach to Christian Sexual Ethics*, ed. Patricia Beattie Jung and Aana Maria Vigen with John Anderson (Urbana: University of Illinois Press, 2010), 224–240; and Patricia Beattie Jung, "Christianity and Human Sexual Dimorphism: Are They Compatible?" in *Ethics and Intersex*, ed. Sharon E. Sytsma (Dordrecht: Springer, 2006), 259–270.
34. Miroslav Volf, "The Trinity and Gender Identity," in *Gospel and Gender: A Trinitarian Engagement with Being Male and Female in Christ*, ed. Douglas A. Campbell (London: T&T Clark, 2003), 175.
35. This passage is generally accepted by biblical scholars to be a liturgical formula (referenced affirmatively by Paul) commonly used during baptisms in the early church. It has long been searched for insight into how sex (and other variations among the faithful) might be transfigured. In fact, Judith

M. Gundry-Volf has argued that much of 1 Corinthians 7 (arguably the most significant biblical pericope on human sexuality) expresses Paul's response to a debate among the early Christians in Corinth about how best to interpret Galatians 3:28c. See Judith M. Gundry-Volf, "Male and Female in Creation and New Creation: Interpretations of Galatians 3:28C in 1 Corinthians 7," in *To Tell the Mystery: Essays on New Testament Eschatology in Honor of Robert H. Gundry*, ed. Thomas E. Schmidt and Moisés Silva (Sheffield, England: Sheffield Academic Press, 1994), 95–121.

36. Todd A. Salzman and Michael G. Lawler, *The Sexual Person: Toward a Renewed Catholic Anthropology* (Washington, DC: Georgetown University Press, 2008).
37. Herbert McCabe, *What Is Ethics All About?* (Washington, DC: Corpus Books, 1968), 68.
38. Patricia Beattie Jung, "A Case for Sexual Fidelity," *Word and World* 14/2 (Spring 1994): 115–124.
39. Even those who carefully consider omnigamy note that "polyamorists have found ways to include additional relationships into their lives without lying to one another and destroying their *primary* relationship" (emphasis mine). Christopher Ryan and Cacilda Jetha, *Sex at Dawn: How We Mate, Why We Stray and What It Means for Modern Relationships* (New York: Harper Books, 2010), 310.
40. John E. Thiel, "For What May We Hope? Thoughts on the Eschatological Imagination," *Theological Studies* 67/3 (September, 2006): 517–541.

CHAPTER 6.TRANSFORMING SEX ON EARTH

1. Much of tremendous value has already been said about how principles associated with justice—like nonmaleficence and rules of consent, mutuality, equality, commitment, fruitfulness, and social justice, to name those articulated by Margaret A. Farley in her masterwork, *Just Love: A Framework for Christian Sexual Ethics* (New York: Continuum International, 2006)—must serve as norms for sexual desires.

2. The story of King David's ruinous attraction to Bathsheba can be found in 2 Samuel 11. The story of the sexual harassment of Susanna by much-revered judges is found in Daniel 13.
3. Deanna A. Thompson, "Hoping for More: How Eschatology Matters for Lutheran Feminist Theologies," in *Transformative Lutheran Theologies: Feminist, Womanist and Mujerista Perspectives*, ed. Mary J. Streufert (Minneapolis: Fortress Press, 2010), 228.
4. Immanuel Kant, *Lectures on Ethics*, ed. Peter Heath and J. B. Schneewind (Cambridge: Cambridge University Press, 1997), 156.
5. Jo Ind, *Memories of Bliss: God, Sex, and Us* (London: SCM Press, 2003).
6. Diarmuid O'Murchu, M.S.C., *The Transformation of Desire: How Desire Became Corrupted—and How We Can Reclaim It* (Maryknoll: Orbis Books, 2007), 118.
7. Given its misuse, even "the pill" has a contraceptive failure rate over a five-year period of 35 percent.
8. Given human bipedalism and the lengthy time human infants remain helpless and require being carried, human mothers had to form bonds with some adults if they and their infants were to survive. See especially chapter 7 in Helen E. Fisher's *Anatomy of Love: The Natural History of Monogamy, Adultery and Divorce* (New York: W. W. Norton, 1992).
9. Despite common myths to the contrary, sexual arousal and desire onsets long before puberty.
10. Traina explores the moral implications of the connection between good touch and human flourishing in the fifth chapter of her text entitled "The Right to Be Touched." (See Traina, *Erotic Attunement*, 115–140.) Traina uses a Thomistic notion of flourishing in relationship to touch. See Thomas Aquinas, *Summa Theologica*, II–II. Q.141 a.6.
11. Many texts by Joan Roughgarden might be of interest in this regard. I would recommend *Evolution's Rainbow: Diversity, Sexuality and Gender in Nature and People* (Berkeley: University of California Press, 2004) and the chapter

on "Gender and Sexuality," in *Evolution and Christian Faith: Reflections of an Evolutionary Biologist* (Washington, DC: Island Press, 2006), 102–124. See also Jaak Panksepp, *Affective Neuroscience: The Foundations of Human and Animal Emotions* (Oxford, England: Oxford University Press, 1998), 228.

12. David A. Hogue, "The Desiring Brain: Contemporary Neuroscientific Insights into Pleasure and Longing," in *City of Desires—A Place for God? Practical Theological Perspectives*, ed. R. Ruard Ganzevoort, Rein Brouwer, and Bonnie Miller-McLemore (Zurich: Lit Verlag GmbH, 2013), 51–61.
13. Ibid., 57.
14. For more detail, see James G. Pfaus, "Pathways of Sexual Desire," *Journal of Sex Medicine* 6 (2009): 1506–1533.
15. John J. Medina, *The Genetic Inferno: Inside the Seven Deadly Sins* (Cambridge, England: Cambridge University Press, 2000), 26.
16. For an extended discussion of various theories about how bodily sexual responses take social forms, see Judy Root Aulette, Judith Wittner, and Kristin Blakely, *Gendered Worlds*, 1st ed. (New York: Oxford University Press, 2008), 16–47.
17. According to the analyses of Ind, Sigmund Freud suggested that our libido can be traced back to the "memories of bliss" we experienced as suckling infants. For more information about this and related hypotheses, see Ind, *Memories of Bliss*.
18. Martha C. Nussbaum, "Constructing Love, Desire, and Care," in *Sex, Preference, and Family: Essays on Law and Nature*, ed. David M. Estlund and Martha C. Nussbaum (New York: Oxford University Press, 1997), 17–43.
19. This typology entered popular culture with the publication of the results of Alfred Kinsey's studies beginning in the 1930s.
20. It is important to distinguish between descriptive and normative forms of relativism. It is absolutely right to avoid treating deviations from statistically "normal" experiences of desire as if they are automatically immoral. There is no

fixed, "normal" experience of what is "sexy" for human beings. Every experience of sexual desire is "queer," from one viewpoint or another. Indeed, one aim of "queer theory" is to encourage us to question the "normality" of all we take for granted.

And yet, despite evidence of the cultural and historical relativity in the experience of human sexuality, we can and ought to continue to make normative moral judgments about sexual desire and practices. Nussbaum argues rightly that we can still determine which experiences of sexual desire contribute to human flourishing in given contexts and, hence, determine which are morally good. We can identify what sorts of sexual desires and practices are (in)compatible with other values we hold dear, like equality and fairness among persons, economic productivity, friendship, and other types of love (filial, parental, and so on). But, she argues, when we recognize the cultural relativity of all erotic feelings, we are less likely to be ethically derailed by hegemonic, or excessively romantic, responses to what is familiar, or by phobic responses to what is strange. Furthermore, we are likely to regard even our best moral judgments as tentative and open to revision, should new information suggest their reconsideration.

21. This led many—most infamously perhaps Immanuel Kant—to conclude erroneously that we have no control whatsoever over our feelings.
22. For another text that takes a similar approach to emotion, see Robert C. Roberts, *Spiritual Emotions: A Psychology of Christian Virtue* (Grand Rapids: William B. Eerdmans, 2007).
23. Beverly Wildung Harrison, "The Power of Anger in the Work of Love," *Union Seminary Quarterly Review* 36 (1981): 41–57.
24. In contrast, Nussbaum notes that the ancient Greeks and their eastern Indian neighbors viewed erotic desires as dangerous, that is, as having a terrible potential to entrap people. See Nussbaum, "Constructing Love, Desire and Care."
25. This is not an altogether modern idea. Though they did not understand desire to be socially constructed over time across generations as we now do, the Stoics of the late first

century of the Common Era understood desire to be within a person's power at least to moderate.

26. So, though it may be true that some feelings can be encouraged by acting in conformity with them, this strategy most likely will not work in regard to altering one's fundamental experience of sexual desire.
27. Diana Fritz Cates, *Aquinas on the Emotions: A Religious Ethical Inquiry* (Washington, DC: Georgetown University Press, 2009), 5.
28. On October 24, 2009, a fifteen-year-old Richmond High School girl was gang-raped by several males in the presence of twenty or more bystanders at her homecoming dance in northern California. These bystanders did nothing but look on for more than two hours.
29. For an interesting psychological account of our capacity to learn to delay the gratification of spontaneous desires, see Walter Mischel's *The Marshmallow Test: Mastering Self-Control* (New York: Little, Brown, 2014).
30. The particular sexual obligations of any individual will vary in accord with the culture in which their experience of sexuality has been shaped and with their personal sexual histories. To state the obvious, the capacity of a fifteen-year-old who has been gang-raped to (re)educate his or her sexual affections might well be so gravely inhibited by that trauma that healing might well find its first expression in a "healthy" absence of desire.
31. This unresponsiveness to command may well have been what convinced Augustine that all sexual feelings and pleasures were morally problematic and led him to conflate all experiences of sexual desire with lust.
32. Traina, *Erotic Attunement.*
33. Nussbaum, "Constructing Love, Desire and Care."
34. Marie M. Fortune, *Love Does No Harm: Sexual Ethics for the Rest of Us* (New York: Continuum, 1995).

CHAPTER 7. CULTIVATING SEXUAL DESIRE

1. Joan H. Timmerman, *The Mardi Gras Syndrome: Rethinking Christian Sexuality* (New York: Crossroads, 1984).

2. Christine E. Gudorf, "Why Sex Is So Good for Your Marriage," *U.S. Catholic* 57/11 (November 1992): 6.
3. Harrison, "The Power of Anger in the Work of Love." Also see Andre D. Lester's *The Angry Christian: A Theology for Care and Counseling* (Louisville: Westminster John Knox Press, 2003).
4. It is mistaken, of course, to conclude that because it will be left behind in our life to come, there is no need to cultivate now on earth that which has no future. For some who find themselves numbed by various expressions of what Walter Brueggemann has labeled "Royal Consciousness" the energizing force of prophetic anger is life giving. See Walter Brueggemann, *The Prophetic Imagination*, 2nd ed. (Minneapolis: Fortress Press, 2001).
5. This blessing was clearly not designed to be a bond that closes couples off from either God, neighbor, or the rest of creation. It is important to note here that this "clinging" is not equivalent to seeking control over or an unhealthy dependence on each other. In the life to come, we will have to "let go" of any idolatrous sexual relationships and have these partnerships healed of any aspects that do not strengthen us for communion with all that is.
6. "If a man has recently married, he must not be sent to war or have any other duty laid on him. For one year he is to be free to stay at home and bring happiness to the wife he has married" (Deuteronomy 24:5).
7. It is interesting to note that the tradition was quite clear early on about the need for the practice of sexual abstinence within marriage to be mutual. In contrast, only relatively recently has the church taught clearly that sexual activity within marriage likewise requires mutual consent.
8. Thomas Aquinas, *Summa Theologica*, II–II. Q.153 a.3.3, accessed October 12, 2014, http://www.newadvent.org/summa/3153.htm#article3.
9. Christine E. Gudorf, "Sexual Pleasure as Grace and Gift," *The Other Side* 34 (May/June 1998): 13. For an extended analysis of this, see also Christine E. Gudorf, *Body, Sex and Pleasure: Reconstructing Christian Sexual Ethics* (Cleveland: Pilgrim Press, 1994), 81–138.

10. Edward Collins Vacek, S.J., "Orthodoxy Requires Orthopathy: Emotions in Theology," *Horizons* 40/2 (December 2013): 219.
11. Though I will argue strongly for the cultivation of sexual desire, I am inclined to challenge the idea that penetrative sex is requisite for sharing pleasure, whether one is male or female, heterosexual or homosexual. While I would not rule out the treatment of erectile dysfunction with drugs like Viagra, Cialis, and Levitra, among others, I do not think my argument sanctifies their widespread adoption.
12. Howard L. Harrod, "An Essay on Desire," *Journal of the American Medical Association* 289/7 (February19, 2003): 813–814.
13. All, not just females, who are trafficked routinely do this because their "johns" (like all of us) find it exciting to be perceived as attractive and adept lovers. This is part of the "illusion" for which they are paying.
14. Breanne Fahs, *Performing Sex: The Making and Unmaking of Women's Erotic Lives* (Albany: State University of New York Press, 2011).
15. Ibid., 25.
16. We have discussed the social construction of sexuality extensively in the previous chapter, so here I would only draw your attention to other key contributors to our understanding that nothing about sexuality exists outside of its social interpretation. For historical perspectives on this argument against biological essentialism, see Simone de Beauvoir, *The Second Sex* (New York: Knopf Books, 1953) and Judith Butler, *Gender Trouble: Feminism and the Subversion of Identity* (New York: Routledge Press, 1990).
17. Instead of being a consequence of socialization, some evolutionary biologists want to argue that males have an innately stronger sex drive, but this is highly contested. Many scientists believe women are not innately less interested in making sexual contact. They are just socialized to be so. Primate studies for example show females to initiate sexual activity on a par with males.
18. E. O. Laumann, A. Nicolosi, D. B. Glasser, A. Paik, C. Gingell, E. Moreira, T. Wang for the GSSAB Investigators

Group, "Sexual Problems among Women and Men Aged 40–80: Prevalence and Correlates Identified in the Global Study of Sexual Attitudes and Behaviors," *International Journal of Impotence Research* 17/1 (February 1, 2005): 39–57.

19. E. O. Laumann, A. Paik, and R. C. Rosen, "Sexual Dysfunction in the United States: Prevalence and Predictors," *Journal of the American Medical Association* 281/6 (February 10, 1999): 537–544.
20. Fahs, *Performing Sex*, 119.
21. A. Nicolosi, E. O. Laumann, D. B. Glasser, E. D. Moreira, Jr., A. Paik, C. Gingell (Global Study of Sexual Attitudes and Behaviors Investigators Group), "Sexual Behavior and Sexual Dysfunctions after Age 40: The Global Study of Sexual Attitudes and Behaviors," *Urology* 64/5 (November 2004): 991–997. These statistics include the growing rate of erectile dysfunction with real (as distinct from virtual) sexual partners among younger men, which is skyrocketing in correlation with their use of internet porn, a problem that will be examined in the next chapter.
22. Daniel Bergner, "Unexcited? There May Be a Pill for That," *New York Times Magazine* (May 26, 2013): MM22. For more information, see his *What Do Women Want? Adventures in the Science of Female Desire* (New York: Harper Collins, 2013).
23. Nancy E. Avis, Sarah Brockwell, John F. Randolph, Jr., Shunhua Shen, Virginia S. Cain, Marcia Ory, and Gail A. Greendale, "Longitudinal Changes in Sexual Functioning as Women Transition through Menopause: Results from the Study of Women's Health across the Nation (SWAN)," *Menopause* 16/3 (2009): 442.
24. Stuart N. Seidman and Steven P. Roose, "The Sexual Effects of Testosterone Replacement in Depressed Men: Randomized, Placebo-controlled Clinical Trials," *Journal of Sexual Marital Therapy* 32/3 (May–June, 2006): 267–273.
25. Kornrich Sabino, Julie Brines, and Katrina Leupp, "Egalitarianism, Housework, and Sexual Frequency in Marriage," *American Sociological Review* 78/1 (2013): 26–50.

26. Marie M. Fortune, *Love Does No Harm: Sexual Ethics for the Rest of Us* (New York: Continuum, 1995), 128–138.
27. Marvin M. Ellison, *Erotic Justice: A Liberating Ethic of Sexuality* (Louisville: Westminster John Knox Press, 1996), 76–93.
28. J. Bancroft, J. Loftus, and S. J. Long, "Distress about Sex: A National Survey of Women in Heterosexual Relationships," *Archives of Sexual Behavior* 13/3 (2004): 193–208.
29. J. L. Shifren, B. U. Monz, P. A. Russo, A. Segretti, and C. B. Johannes, "Sexual Problems and Distress in U.S. Women: Prevalence and Correlates," *Obstetrics and Gynecology* 122/5 (2008): 970–978.
30. John Bancroft, "The Medicalization of Female Sexual Dysfunction: The Need for Caution," *Archives of Sexual Behavior* 31/5 (2002): 451–455.
31. Leonore Tiefer, *Sex Is Not a Natural Act* (Boulder: Westview, 2004).
32. Fahs, *Performing Sex*, 132.
33. Of course, living chastely requires that a person sometime practice some degree of sexual restraint. Depending upon whether the person is married, single, or living in community as a vowed religious, the Christian may practice temporary or perpetual abstinence from genital activity with all or some people. For example, traditionally chastity fosters fidelity among Christian spouses, inviting them to order their sexual desires in genitally exclusive as well as steadfast ways.
34. Gudorf, "Sexual Pleasure as Grace and Gift," 12.
35. Keith Graber Miller, "Sex without Shame," *Sojourners* 38/9 (September–October, 2009): 23.

CHAPTER 8. PORNOGRAPHY AND THE EDUCATION OF SEXUAL DESIRE

1. Robert Jensen, *Getting Off: Pornography and the End of Masculinity* (Cambridge: South End Press, 2007), 184.
2. Farley, "Beguiled by Beauty: The Reformation of Desire for Faith and Theology," 129.

3. Christine Roy Yoder, "The Shaping of Desire in Proverbs 1–9," in *City of Desires—A Place for God? Practical Theological Perspectives*, ed. R. Ruard Ganzevoort, Rein Brouwer, and Bonnie Miller-McLemore (Zurich: Lit Verlag GmbH, 2013), 148–163.
4. Jensen, *Getting Off*, 162.
5. I really don't want to plunge into this debate and spend the rest of this chapter arguing about this issue. In many ways I believe this particular topic has been worked to death by theologians of my generation from North Atlantic countries. Additionally, it would appear to be an understatement to suggest that this horse has already left the barn in many contexts. For example, most Christians in North Atlantic countries not only practice contraception but do so in good conscience. For a good overview of this, see Peter Steinfels, "Contraception and Honesty: A Proposal for the Next Synod," *Commonweal* 142/10 (June 1, 2015): 12–19.

   But I do feel obliged to lay my cards on the table about this matter. I don't believe a scriptural case can be made for this particular cluster of teachings. Furthermore, I do not believe it can be established as a matter of natural law. I believe the nature of the link between sexual and reproductive activities varies considerably between men and women. When this variation is taken seriously, the claim that there is an "inseparable connection" between love making and baby making does not appear to be normatively human, but merely normatively male.

   What do I mean when I assert that this claim is androcentric? Consider the connection between sexual desire and reproduction for men. Among the many human sexual activities, vaginal/penile intercourse alone is potentially reproductive. Let me be frank: coitus requires an erect penis. Desire and pleasure are prerequisite for male erection. In men, orgasm and ejaculation are simultaneous. So, reproduction requires that men sexually enjoy the activity. This is not the case for women. Furthermore, though sperm count and motility decline with age, if they do not suffer from ED, most men have the potential to procreate through coital activity until death.

In contrast, female desire, pleasure, and orgasm have no necessary connection to coital activity at all. Neither ovulation nor fertilization are linked to female orgasm. For women, the natural connection between sexual pleasure and reproduction appears to be far more tenuous. It is at most periodic, and then, only for a season of a woman's sexual life. It is noteworthy as well that the clitoris is not anatomically located in a manner that particularly commends coital over other sexual activities. Furthermore, healthy women from developed countries expect to enjoy sexual desire and pleasure for some thirty years on average after they have completely lost the potential to procreate. When we consider women's bodies and women's experience when thinking about what might be normatively human, it is clear (to me at any rate) that it is perfectly natural for sexual activity to not even be potentially procreative.

6. Farley, *Just Love*, 204.
7. Ibid., 196.
8. Ibid., 215ff.
9. Sharing pleasure does not require multiple, simultaneous, mutual and/or even one orgasm, though these all could be included. When I talk about sharing pleasure, I am talking about attending to whether sexual activity is mutually joyful and erotically sensuous.
10. Farley, *Just Love*, 204–232.
11. For example, consider mid-twentieth-century Roman Catholic Church teachings in this regard. They broach the subject of sexual pleasure in marriage only very briefly. Pope Pius XI in his 1930 encyclical "On Christian Marriage" (*Casti connubii*) did note that spouses have the right to use the marital act to procreate and that it may cultivate marital love (59). Accessed August 19, 2015, http://w2.vatican.va/content/pius-xi/en/encyclicals/documents/hf_p-xi_enc_31121930_casti-connubii.html.

    Two decades later, Pope Pius XII confirmed that spouses do no wrong when they seek and enjoy pleasure as long as this is subordinated to the generation and education of children (70). He dismissed as unduly hedonistic and unnecessary any need for spousal education in this regard however.

See Pius XII, "Address to the Italian Catholic Society of Midwives," *Acta Apostolicae Sedis* 43 (October 29, 1951): 845–846, accessed December 6, 2015, http://www.vatican.va/archive/aas/documents/AAS-43-1951-ocr.pdf.

12. Verlee A. Copeland and Dale B. Rosenberger, *Sex and the Spirit: The Romance of Heaven and Earth* (Cleveland: Pilgrim Press, 2014).
13. For an in-depth analysis of this evangelical literature, wonderful for its attention to the different nuances expressed across various evangelical subcultures, see Amy DeRogatis's *Saving Sex: Sexuality and Salvation in American Evangelicalism* (New York: Oxford University Press, 2014).
14. Christiane Northrup, *Women's Bodies, Women's Wisdom: Creating Physical and Emotional Health and Healing* (New York: Random House, 2010), 246.
15. It goes without saying that domestic forms of sexual violence will not be unitive. And yet, in many cultures—including North America—rape at the hands of one's current or former intimate partner remains epidemic. Still, there is little explicit church teaching or preaching about unwanted, coerced sex within marriage or other forms of committed partnerships. For an analysis of the social construction of (heterosexual) rape, see Nicola Gavey, *Just Sex? The Cultural Scaffolding of Rape* (New York: Routledge, 2005).
16. Rowan Williams, "The Body's Grace," was originally delivered as the 10th Michael Harding Memorial Address in London to the Lesbian and Gay Christian Movement in 1989, accessed August 20, 2015, http://www.igreens.org.uk/bodys_grace.htm.
17. James A. Baldwin, "Interview," first published in *The Advocate* and excerpted in the *Utne Reader* (July/August 2002): 100.
18. Ola Sigurdson, "The Passion of Christ: On the Social Production of Desire," in *Saving Desire: The Seduction of Christian Theology*, edited by F. LeRon Shults and Jan-Olav Henriksen (Grand Rapids: William B. Eerdmans, 2011), 31–54.
19. Though she does not address the issue of sexual desire, Tina Rosenberg discusses analogous kinds of issues in her

book *Join the Club: How Peer Pressure Can Transform the World* (New York: W.W. Norton, 2011).

20. Farley, *Just Love*, 225.
21. Ibid.
22. One concern I have about my focus on *internet* pornography is its emphasis on videos and what materials it leaves "off the table." It is I believe important to ask whether some popular "romance" (or as they are sometimes called "beach") novels might not also be pornographic. On the one hand, they often challenge rigid sexist stereotypes and treat domestic and sexual violence as negative, in the spirit of their literary archetype, *Jane Eyre*. On the other hand, they are infused with themes of eroticized bondage, control, and coercion. Admittedly, the degree to which these narratives are explicitly sexual varies considerably. But as the recent blockbuster book series *Shades of Grey* makes clear, they may increasingly share both the narratives and explicitly sexual features characteristic of pornography.
23. I first read of this in a short, editors' "Century Marks" paragraph entitled "Repressed Desires?" *Christian Century* 131/23 (November 12, 2014): 9. It referenced the following study: Cara C. Macinnis and Gordon Hodson, "Do American States with More Religious or Conservative Populations Search More for Sexual Content on Google?" *Archives of Sexual Behavior* 44/1 (January 2015): 137–147.
24. Amy Frykholm, "Pastors and Pornography: Addictive Behavior," *Christian Century* 124/18 (September 4, 2007): 20–22.
25. Jane M. Ussher, *Fantasies of Femininity: Reframing the Boundaries of Sex* (New Brunswick: Rutgers University Press, 1997), 165.
26. Chiara Sabina, Janis Wolak, and David Finkelhor, "The Nature and Dynamics of Internet Pornography Exposure for Youth," *CyberPsychology and Behavior* 11/6 (December 2008): 691.
27. Regrettably, social scientists appear reluctant to make the sort of normative judgment between erotica and porn I have been commending. In the studies cited later all sexually explicit materials are labeled porn.

28. Gary Wilson, "The Great Porn Experiment," accessed November 24, 2014, http://www.singjupost.com/gary-wilson-discusses-great-porn-experiment-transcript/2/.
29. Simon Louis Lajeunesse and J-M. Deslauriers, "Point de vue Masculin sur la Pornographie: des Fantasmes à la Réalité," *Sexologies* 22/1 (2013): 32–41.
30. I am indebted to a graduate student of mine who taught me that for most men neither masturbation nor pornography can be evaluated apart from each other. There are, of course, individuals (including recovering sex addicts) who do masturbate without porn.
31. Ussher, *Fantasies of Femininity*, 147. Ussher notes that the first use of the term pornography emerges in English with the discovery of the artifacts at Pompeii and the decision to hide these materials away in a secret museum in Naples when they were first uncovered.
32. Jensen, *Getting Off*, 53ff.
33. A brief word needs to be said about the many moral problems surrounding the production and regulation of porn. In addition to the blatant evils linked to the creation of child pornography and snuff films, there are a myriad of questions that arise about the validity of the consent offered by the men and women who "star" in the production of adult porn. There is the interaction between this industry and other forms of sex trafficking (such as prostitution and sexual slavery). There is a question about whether there is something inherently immoral about all forms "sex work," that is, about the commodification and marketing of human sexuality (just as some have argued there is something morally problematic about buying and selling other aspects of human embodiment like the use of one's womb, organs for transplant as well as the sale of infants and slave labor). There are also questions about whether the production of certain forms of pornography involve so much abuse of the adults involved that adult productions (like child porn and snuff films) should simply be declared illegal. As Marie Fortune notes, it may be "possible to imagine non-exploitative erotica in which women (and men) are not humiliated and victimized for the entertainment of others," but the burden

of proof in this regard rests with those involved in such productions if one is committed minimally to doing no harm. See Fortune, *Loves Does No Harm*, 125.

There are also questions about whether additional legal forms of censorship could be effectively enforced. There is some evidence that broader forms of prohibition would simply drive more products and people into the "deep web." To give you a sense of the spectacular growth of the cybersex industry so you can consider the economic forces at play here, note that in 1998, N2H2 (a global internet filtering company) reported approximately fourteen million pages of porn on the internet. In 2010 it identified over four hundred million pages. These are just of few of the many important ethical issues linked to the production and public regulation of the porn industry that warrant careful consideration.

34. Ellison, *Erotic Justice*, 76.
35. Jane Caputi, "Everyday Pornography," in *Gender, Race and Class in Media: A Text Reader*, ed. Gail Dines and Jean McMahon Humez (Thousand Oaks: Sage, 2006), 434.
36. Ussher, *Fantasies of Femininity*, 153.
37. Ibid. Here Ussher was quoting from the introduction to Lynne Segal and Mary McIntosh's *Sex Exposed: Sexuality and the Pornography Debate* (London: Virago, 1992), 6.
38. Ussher, *Fantasies of Femininity*, 171. Here Ussher references the Meese Report. See Henry E. Hudson, Diane D. Cusack, Park Elliot Dietz, James Dobson, Bruce Ritter, Frederick Schauer, Deanne Tilton-Durfee, Judith V. Becker, Ellen Levine, Edward J. Garcia, Tex Lezar, and Alan E. Sears, *Attorney General's Commission on Pornography: Final Report*, July, 1985: 901–1033, http://catalog.hathitrust.org/Record/000824987.
39. Ussher, *Fantasies of Femininity*. Here Ussher references the work of psychologists Dennis Howitt and Guy Cumberbatch in *Pornography: Impact and Influences* (London: Home Office Research and Planning Unit, 1990).
40. Ussher, *Fantasies of Femininity*, 168.
41. Ellison, *Erotic Justice*, 129. For more discussion of this point, see Sylvia Thorson Smith, *Pornography: Far from*

the Song of Songs (Louisville: Office of the General Assembly, Presbyterian Church USA, 1988).

42. Howitt and Cumberbatch, *Pornography: Impact and Influences*, 30–40.
43. Paul J. Wright, "A Longitudinal Analysis of U.S. Adults' Pornography Exposure: Sexual Socialization, Selective Exposure, and the Moderating Role of Unhappiness," *Journal of Media Psychology: Theories, Methods, and Applications* 24/2 (2012): 67.
44. Ussher, *Fantasies of Femininity*, 180.
45. Dylan Stein, Richard Silvera, Robert Hagerty, and Michael Marmor, "Viewing Pornography Depicting Unprotected Anal Intercourse: Are There Implications for HIV Prevention among Men Who Have Sex with Men?" *Archives of Sexual Behavior* 41/2 (2012): 411–419.
46. Clearly, in the past porn did not eroticize sexual encounters in which condoms were employed, though this may be changing at least for "above ground" productions. In California, recent law now requires the use of a condom during video takes.
47. Jensen, *Getting Off*, 178.
48. Andreas G. Philaretou, Ahmed Y. Mahfouz, and Katherine R. Allen, "Use of Internet Pornography and Men's Wellbeing," *International Journal of Men's Health* 4/2 (2005): 149–169.
49. J. Michael Bostwick and Jeffrey A. Bucci, "Internet Sex Addiction Treated with Naltrexone," *Mayo Clinic Proceedings* 83/2(2008): 226–230.
50. Joyce Ann Mercer, "Virtual Sex, Actual Infidelity? A Practical Theological Inquiry into (Dis)Embodied Desire and Cybersex," in *City of Desires—A Place for God? Practical Theological Perspectives*, ed. R. Ruard Ganzevoort, Rein Brouwer, and Bonnie Miller-McLemore (Zurich: Lit Verlag GmbH, 2013), 73.
51. Hogue, "The Desiring Brain," 58. Hogue cites the work of neuroscientist David J. Linden, *The Compass of Pleasure: How Our Brains Make Fatty Foods, Orgasm, Exercise, Marijuana, Generosity, Vodka, Learning and Gambling Feel So Good* (New York: Viking, 2011).

52. Fahs, *Performing Sex*, 273.
53. Lori Gottlieb, "Sexless but Equal," *New York Times Magazine* (February 9, 2014): 32.
54. Sigurdson, "The Passion of Christ: On the Social Production of Desire," 44.
55. Sigurdson suggests those seeking more information about this "visual" turn in the West should see Nicholas Mirzoeff, *An Introduction to Visual Culture* (New York: Routledge, 1999).
56. Richard Kearney, "Losing Our Touch," Sunday Review *New York Times*, August 31, 2014, 4. See as well Richard Kearney and Brian Treanor, eds., *Carnal Hermeneutics* (New York: Fordham University Press, 2015).
57. According to their study of over 1,500 eighteen- to thirty-five-year-old men, Michael Malcolm and George Sami Naufal found not only a strong correlation between pornography use and a decline in their marriage rates but what appears to be a causal relationship, which suggests the sexual gratification associated with internet porn use functions as an alternative to marriage. See Michael Malcolm and George Sami Naufal, "Are Pornography and Marriage Substitutes for Young Men?" IZA Discussion Paper No. 8679, posted December 6, 2014, available at SSRN: http://ssrn.com/abstract=2534707.
58. Farley, *Just Love*, 225.
59. I was privileged to hear Father Ted Curtis make such a suggestion from the pulpit while serving as the rector at Grace Episcopal Church Chicago.

Bibliography

Alison, James. "The Gay Thing: Following the Still Small Voice." In *Queer Theology: Rethinking the Western Body*, edited by Gerald Loughlin, 50–62. Oxford: Blackwell, 2007.

Allison, Dale C. *Jesus of Nazareth: Millenarian Prophet*. Minneapolis: Augsburg Fortress Press, 1998.

Althaus, Paul. *The Theology of Martin Luther*. Philadelphia: Fortress Press, 1966.

Anderson, Raymond Kemp. "Corporate Selfhood and *Meditatio Vitae Futurae:* How Necessary Is Eschatology for Christian Ethics?" *Journal of the Society of Christian Ethics* 23/1 (Spring–Summer 2003): 39–40.

Aquinas, Thomas. *Summa Theologica*. Accessed October 12, 2014. http://www.newadvent.org/summa.

Aristotle. *Nicomachean Ethics*. Translated by W. D. Ross. Book 10, chapter 4. Accessed November 20, 2015. http://classics.mit.edu/Aristotle/nicomachaen.10.x.html.

Augustine. *Answer to Julian*. In *Answer to the Pelagians, III: Unfinished* Work, introduction, translation, and notes by Roland J. Teske, S.J. Hyde Park: New City Press, 1999.

———. *City of God*. Accessed August 20, 2011. http://www.newadvent.org/fathers/120114.htm.

———. *Confessions*, book 8. Accessed August 22, 2011. http://www.ccel.org/ccel/augustine/confessions.xi.html.

———. *Confessions and Enchiridion*. Translated and edited by Albert C. Outler. Philadelphia: The Westminster Press, 1955.

———. "During the Easter Season on the Resurrection of the Body against the Pagans." In *The Works of Saint Augustine: A Translation for the 21st Century*, translation and notes by Edmund Hill, O.P., 70–77. Hyde Park: New City Press, 1995.

———. "Letter 6*." In *St. Augustine on Marriage and Sexuality*, edited by Elizabeth A. Clark. Washington, DC: Catholic University Press of America, 1996.

———. *St. Augustine's The Literal Meaning of Genesis*. Translated by John Hammond Taylor. New York: Newman Press, 1982.

———. *Of Faith and the Creed*. Accessed August 27, 2011. http://www.newadvent.org/fathers/1304.htm.

———. *On Christian Doctrine*. Accessed August 22, 2011. http://www.ccel.org/ccel/augustine/doctrine.xi_2.html.

———. "On the Resurrection of the Dead." In *The Works of Saint Augustine: A Translation for the 21st Century*, translation and notes by Edmund Hill, O.P., 241–265. Hyde Park: New City Press, 1995.

———. *Retractions*. In *Saint Augustine: The* Retractions, translated by Mary Inez Bogan, RSM. Washington, DC: Catholic University of America Press, 1968.

———. *St. Augustine on Marriage and Sexuality*. Edited by Elizabeth A. Clark. Washington, DC: Catholic University Press of America, 1996.

Aulette, Judy Root, Judith Wittner, and Kristin Blakely. *Gendered Worlds*, 1st ed. New York: Oxford University Press, 2008.

Avis, Nancy E., Sarah Brockwell, John F. Randolph, Jr., Shunhua Shen, Virginia S. Cain, Marcia Ory, and Gail A. Greendale. "Longitudinal Changes in Sexual Functioning as Women Transition through Menopause: Results from the Study of Women's Health across the Nation (SWAN)." *Menopause* 16/3 (2009): 442–452.

Baldwin, James A. "Interview." *Utne Reader* (July/August 2002): 100.

Bancroft, John. "The Medicalization of Female Sexual Dysfunction: The Need for Caution." *Archives of Sexual Behavior* 31/5 (2002): 451–455.

Bancroft, J., J. Loftus, and S. J. Long. "Distress about Sex: A National Survey of Women in Heterosexual Relationships." *Archives of Sexual Behavior* 13/3 (2004): 193–208.

Barclay, William. *The Letters to the Corinthians*, rev. ed. Philadelphia: Westminster Press, 1975.

Bergner, Daniel. "Unexcited? There May Be a Pill for That." *New York Times Magazine* (May 26, 2013): MM22.

———. *What Do Women Want? Adventures in the Science of Female Desire*. New York: Harper Collins, 2013.

Bieler, Andrea, and Luise Schottroff. *The Eucharist: Bodies, Bread and Resurrection*. Minneapolis: Fortress Press, 2007.

Blodgett, Barbara. *Constructing the Erotic: Sexual Ethics and Adolescent Girls*. Cleveland: Pilgrim Press, 2002.

Bonhoeffer, Dietrich. "A Wedding Sermon from a Prison Cell, May, 1943." In *Letters and Papers from Prison*, translated by Reginald Fuller, Frank Clark, and others, 41–55. New York: Touchstone, 1997.

Boring, M. Eugene. *Mark: A Commentary*. Louisville: Westminster John Knox Press, 2006.

Bostwick, J. Michael, and Jeffrey A. Bucci. "Internet Sex Addiction Treated with Naltrexone." *Mayo Clinic Proceedings* 83/2 (2008): 226–230.

Boulton, Elizabeth Myer, and Matthew Boulton. "Sacramental Sex: Divine Love and Human Intimacy." *Christian Century* 128/6 (March 22, 2011): 28–31.

Brock, Rita Nakashima. *Journeys by Heart: A Christology of Erotic Power*. New York: Crossroads, 1988.

Brown, Peter. *The Body and Society: Men, Women, and Sexual Renunciation in Early Christianity*. New York: Columbia University Press, 1988.

Brueggemann, Walter. *The Prophetic Imagination*, 2nd ed. Minneapolis: Fortress Press, 2001.

Burrus, Virginia. "Queer Father: Gregory of Nyssa and the Subversion of Identity." In *Queer Theology: Rethinking the Western Body*, edited by Gerald Loughlin, 147–162. Oxford, UK: Blackwell, 2007.

Butler, Judith. *Gender Trouble: Feminism and the Subversion of Identity.* New York: Routledge Press, 1990.

Bynum, Caroline Walker. *The Resurrection of the Body in Western Christianity, 200–1336*. New York: Columbia University Press, 1995.

Caputi, Jane. "Everyday Pornography." In *Gender, Race and Class in Media: A Text Reader*, edited by Gail Dines and Jean McMahon Humez, 434–450. Thousand Oaks: Sage, 2006.

Catechism of the Catholic Church. New York: Doubleday, 1995.

Cates, Diana Fritz *Aquinas on the Emotions: A Religious Ethical Inquiry*. Washington, D.C.: Georgetown University Press, 2009.

Cavadini, John C. "Feeling Right: Augustine on the Passions and Sexual Desire." *Augustinian Studies* 36/1 (2005): 195–217.

Chivers, Meredith L. "A Brief Review and Discussion of Sex Differences in the Specificity of Sexual Arousal." *Sexual and Relationship Therapy* 20/4 (2005): 377–390.

Chrysostom, John. "Homily 31 on 1 Corinthians 12:21." In *Nicene and Post-Nicene Fathers: Saint Chrysostom: Homilies on the Epistles of Paul to the Corinthians* (volume 12), edited by Philip Schaff and translated by Talbot W. Chambers. New York: T&T Clark, 1984.

———. "Homily 41 on 1 Corinthian 15: 35–36." In *Nicene and Post-Nicene Fathers: Saint Chrysostom: Homilies on the Epistles of Paul to the Corinthians* (volume 12), edited by Philip Schaff and translated by Talbot W. Chambers. New York: T&T Clark, 1984.

Clark, Elizabeth A. "The Celibate Bridegroom and His Virginal Brides: Metaphor and the Marriage of Jesus in Early Christian Ascetic Exegesis." *Church History* 77/1 (March 2008): 1–25.

Clement of Alexandria. "On Marriage." In *Miscellanies* in *Alexandrian Christianity: Selected Translations of Clement and Origin*, edited by Henry Chadwick and J. E. L. Oulton. Philadelphia: Westminster John Knox Press, 1954.

———. *Stromateis*. Accessed August 11, 2011. www.newadvent.org/fathers/0210.htm.

Cloutier, David. "Composing Love Songs for the Kingdom of God? Creation and Eschatology in Catholic Sexual Ethics." *Journal of the Society of Christian Ethics* 24/2 (2004): 71–88.

Code of Canon Law. *Libreria Editrica Vaticana*, 1983. Accessed December 2, 2015. http://www.vatican.va/archive/ENG1104/_INDEX.HTM#fonte.

Collins, John J. *Daniel: A Commentary on the Book of Daniel*. Minneapolis: Fortress Press, 1993.

Collins, Raymond F. *First Corinthians*. Collegeville: Liturgical Press, 1999.

Cooper, Kate, and Conrad Leyser. "The Gender of Grace: Impotence, Servitude, and Manliness in the Fifth-Century West." *Gender and History* 12/3 (November 2000): 536–551.

Copeland, Verlee A., and Dale B. Rosenberger. *Sex and the Spirit: The Romance of Heaven and Earth*. Cleveland: Pilgrim Press, 2014.

Cullman, Oscar. *Christ and Time: The Primitive Christian Conception of Time and History*, 3rd ed. Translated by F. Filson. London: SCM, 1962.

Daley, Brian E. "Eschatology in the Early Church Fathers." In *The Oxford Handbook of Eschatology*, edited by Jerry L. Walls, 91–109. New York: Oxford University Press, 2008.

Davis, James Calvin. "Will There Be Football in Heaven?" *The Presbyterian Outlook* 191/10 (March 23, 2009): 10–11.

Day, Dorothy. "Aims and Purposes." *Catholic Worker* 7/6 (1940): 7.

de Beauvoir, Simone. *The Second Sex*. New York: Knopf Books, 1953.

de Lubac, Henri. *Catholicism: Christ and the Common Destiny of Man*. San Francisco: Ignatius Press, 1988.

Delattre, Roland A. "Desire." In *Encyclopedia of Religion*, 2nd ed., edited by Lindsay Jones, 2303–2309. Detroit: Thomson Gale, 2005.

DeRogatis, Amy. *Saving Sex: Sexuality and Salvation in American Evangelicalism*. New York: Oxford University Press, 2014.

Dewart, Joanne E. McWilliam. *Death and Resurrection: Message of the Fathers of the Church*. Wilmington: Michael Glazier, 1989.

Diamond, Lisa. *Sexual Fluidity: Women's Love and Desire*. Cambridge: Harvard University Press, 2008.

Dionysius the Presbyter. *The Divine Names and The Mystical Theology*. Translated by John D. Jones. Milwaukee: Marquette University Press, 1999.

Donahue, John R., S.J., and Daniel J. Harrington, S.J. *The Gospel of Mark*. Collegeville: Liturgical Press, 2002.

Driver, Thomas Faw. "Sexuality and Jesus." *Union Seminary Quarterly Review* 20/3 (March 1965): 235–246.

Dunning, Benjamin H. *Specters of Paul: Sexual Difference in Early Christian Thought*. Philadelphia: University of Pennsylvania Press, 2011.

Ellens, J. Harold. *Sex in the Bible: A New Consideration*. Westport: Praeger, 2006.

Ellison, Marvin M. *Erotic Justice: A Liberating Ethic of Sexuality*. Louisville: Westminster John Knox Press, 1996.

Endsjø, Dag Ølstein. *Greek Resurrection Beliefs and the Success of Christianity*. New York: Palgrave Macmillan, 2009.

Evangelista, Joey Gánio, M.J. "Mechthild of Magdeburg and Human Sexuality." *East Asian Pastoral Review* 45/4 (2008): 339–361.

Fahs, Breanne. *Performing Sex: The Making and Unmaking of Women's Erotic Lives*. Albany: State University of New York Press, 2011.

Farley, Margaret A. *Just Love: A Framework for Christian Sexual Ethics*. New York: Continuum International, 2006.

Farley, Wendy. "Beguiled by Beauty: The Reformation of Desire for Faith and Theology." In *Saving Desire: The Seduction of Christian Theology*, edited by F. LeRon Shults and Jan-Olav Henriksen, 128–147. Grand Rapids: William B. Eerdmans, 2011.

———. *The Wounding and Healing of Desire: Weaving Heaven and Earth*. Louisville: Westminster John Knox Press, 2005.

Fisher, Helen E. *Anatomy of Love: The Natural History of Monogamy, Adultery and Divorce*. New York: W. W. Norton, 1992.

Fitzmeyer, Joseph A., S.J. *First Corinthians: A New Translation with Introduction and Commentary*. New Haven: Yale University Press, 2008.

Fortune, Marie M. *Love Does No Harm: Sexual Ethics for the Rest of Us*. New York: Continuum, 1995.

Frykholm, Amy. "Pastors and Pornography: Addictive Behavior." *Christian Century* 124/18 (September 4, 2007): 20–22.

Gallagher, John. "Magisterial Teaching from 1918 to the Present." In *Readings in Moral Theology No. 8, Dialogue about Catholic Sexual Teaching*, edited by Charles E. Curran and Richard A. McCormick, 71–92. New York: Paulist Press, 1993.

Gavey, Nicola. *Just Sex? The Cultural Scaffolding of Rape*. New York: Routledge, 2005.

Gottlieb, Lori. "Sexless but Equal." *New York Times Magazine* (February 9, 2014): 32.

Green, Joel B. *The Gospel of Luke*. Grand Rapids: W. B. Eerdmans, 1997.

Gregory of Nazianzus. "Gregory of Nazianzus on Apollinarianism." In *Christian Theology Reader*, 3rd ed, edited by Alister E. McGrath, 229. Malden: Blackwell, 2006.

Gregory of Nyssa. *On the Soul and the Resurrection*. Kindle ed.

Grenz, Stanley J. *Sexual Ethics: An Evangelical Perspective*. Louisville: Westminster John Knox Press, 1997.

Grisez, Germain. *The Way of the Lord Jesus, Volume 2: Living a Christian Life*. Chicago: Franciscan Herald Press, 1993.

Gudorf, Christine E. *Body, Sex and Pleasure: Reconstructing Christian Sexual Ethics*. Cleveland: Pilgrim Press, 1994.

———. "Sexual Pleasure as Grace and Gift." *The Other Side* 34 (May/June 1998):10–13.

———. "Why Sex Is So Good for Your Marriage." *U.S. Catholic* 57/11 (November 1992): 6–13.

Gundry-Volf, Judith M. "Male and Female in Creation and New Creation: Interpretations of Galatians 3:28C in 1 Corinthians 7." In *To Tell the Mystery: Essays on New*

Testament Eschatology in Honor of Robert H. Gundry, edited by Thomas E. Schmidt and Moisés Silva, 95–121. Sheffield, England: Sheffield Academic Press, 1994.

Harper, Kyle. *From Shame to Sin: The Christian Transformation of Sexual Morality in Late Antiquity*. Cambridge: Harvard University Press, 2013.

Harrison, Beverly Wildung. "The Power of Anger in the Work of Love." *Union Seminary Quarterly Review* 36 (1981): 41–57.

Harrison, Verna E. F. "Male and Female in Cappadocian Theology." *Journal of Theological Studies* 41/2 (October 1990): 441–471.

Harrod, Howard L. "An Essay on Desire." *Journal of the American Medical Association* 289/7 (February 19, 2003): 813–814.

Hays, Richard B. "Awaiting the Redemption of Our Bodies: The Witness of Scripture Concerning Homosexuality." In *Homosexuality in the Church: Both Sides of the Debate*, edited by Jeffrey S. Siker, 3–17. Louisville: Westminster John Knox Press, 1994.

———. *First Corinthians*. Louisville: John Knox Press, 1997.

Henriksen, Jan-Olav. "Desire: Gift and Giving." In *Saving Desire: The Seduction of Christian Theology*, edited by F. LeRon Shults and Jan-Olav Henriksen, 1–30. Grand Rapids: William B. Eerdmans, 2011.

Hester, J. David. "Eunuchs and the Postgender Jesus: Matthew 19:12 and Transgressive Sexualities." *Journal for the Study of the New Testament* 28/1 (2005): 13–40.

Heyward, Carter. *The Erotic as Power and the Love of God*. San Francisco: HarperCollins, 1989.

Hilkert, Mary Catherine, O.P. "Grace-Optimism." *America* 202/2 (January 18, 2010): 4.

Hogue, David A. "The Desiring Brain: Contemporary Neuroscientific Insights into Pleasure and Longing." In *City of Desires—A Place for God? Practical Theological Perspectives*, edited by R. Ruard Ganzevoort, Rein Brouwer, and Bonnie Miller-McLemore, 51–61. Zurich: Lit Verlag GmbH, 2013.

Hollinger, Dennis P. *The Meaning of Sex*. Grand Rapids: Baker Academic Books, 2009.

Howitt, Dennis, and Guy Cumberbatch. *Pornography: Impact and Influences*. London: Home Office Research and Planning Unit, 1990.

Hudson, Henry E., Diane D. Cusack, Park Elliot Dietz, James Dobson, Bruce Ritter, Frederick Schauer, Deanne Tilton-Durfee, Judith V. Becker, Ellen Levine, Edward J. Garcia, Tex Lezar, and Alan E. Sears. *Attorney General's Commission on Pornography: Final Report*, July, 1985: 901–1033. Accessed December 6, 2014. http://catalog.hathitrust.org/Record/000824987.

Hunter, David G. "Helvidius, Jovinian and the Virginity of Mary in Late Fourth-Century Rome." *Journal of Early Christian Studies* 1/1 (Spring 1993): 47–71.

———. "Reclaiming Biblical Morality: Sex and Salvation History in Augustine's Treatment of the Hebrew Saints." In *In Dominico Eloquio—In Lordly Eloquence*, edited by Paul M. Blowers, Angela Russell Christman, David G. Hunter, and Robin Darling Young, 317–335. Grand Rapids: William B. Eerdmans, 2002.

———. "Resistance to the Virginal Ideal in Late Fourth-Century Rome: Case of Jovinian." *Theological Studies* 48/1 (March 1987): 45–64.

Ind, Jo. *Memories of Bliss: God, Sex, and Us*. London: SCM Press, 2003.

International Commission on English in the Liturgy. *Order of Christian Funerals*. Chicago: Liturgy Training Publications, 1989.

International Theological Commission. "'*Sensus Fidei*' in the Life of the Church," 2014. Accessed August 19, 2015. http://www.vatican.va/roman_curia/congregations/cfaith/cti_documents/rc_cti_20140610_sensus-fidei_en.html.

Jacobson, Arland Dean. "Jesus against the Family: The Dissolution of Family Ties in the Gospel Tradition." In *From Quest to Q: Festschrift James M. Robinson*, edited by J. Ma Asgeirsson, Kristin De Troyer, and Marvin W. Meyers, 189–218. Leuven: Leuven University Press, 2000.

Jantzen, Grace. "New Creations: Eros, Beauty and the Passion for Transformation." In *Toward a Theology of Eros*, edited by Virginia Burrus and Catherine Keller, 271–287. New York: Fordham University Press, 2006.

Jensen, David H. *God, Desire, and a Theology of Human Sexuality*. Louisville: Westminster John Knox Press, 2013.

Jensen, Robert. *Getting Off: Pornography and the End of Masculinity*. Cambridge: South End Press, 2007.

Jerome. *Against Jovinianus*. Accessed on June 11, 2015. http://www.newadvent.org/fathers/30091.htm.

John Paul II. *The Theology of the Body: Human Love in the Divine Plan*. Boston: Pauline Books, 1997.

———. *The Theology of Marriage and Celibacy*. Boston: St. Paul Editions, 1984.

Johnson, Luke T. *Sacra Pagina: The Gospel of Luke*. Collegeville: Liturgical Press, 1991.

Johnson, William Stacey. *A Time to Embrace: Same-Gender Relationships in Religion, Law and Politics*. Grand Rapids: William B. Eerdmans, 2006.

Jordan, Mark D. "Flesh in Confession: Alcibiades beside Augustine." In *Toward a Theology of Eros*, edited by Virginia Burrus and Catherine Keller, 23–37. New York: Fordham University Press, 2006.

Jung, L. Shannon. *Sharing Food: Christian Practices for Enjoyment*. Minneapolis: Fortress Press, 2006.

———. "Spatiality, Relativism and Authority." *Journal of the American Academy of Religion* 50/2 (June 1982): 215–235.

Jung, Patricia Beattie. "A Case for Sexual Fidelity." *Word and World* 14/2 (Spring 1994): 115–124.

———. "Christianity and Human Sexual Dimorphism: Are They Compatible?" In *Ethics and Intersex*, edited by Sharon E. Sytsma, 259–270. Dordrecht: Springer, 2006.

———. "Intersex on Earth as It Is in Heaven." In *Intersex, Theology and the Bible*, edited by Susannah Cornwall, 173–195. New York: Palgrave Macmillan, 2015.

Jung, Patricia Beattie, and Joan Roughgarden. "Gender in Heaven: The Story of the Ethiopian Eunuch in Light of Evolutionary Biology." In *God, Science, Sex, Gender: An Interdisciplinary Approach to Christian Sexual Ethics*, edited by Patricia Beattie Jung and Aana Maria Vigen with John Anderson, 224–240. Urbana: University of Illinois Press, 2010.

Kamitsuka, Margaret D. "Sex in Heaven? Eschatological Eros and the Resurrection of the Body." In *The Embrace of Eros: Bodies, Desires, and Sexuality in Christianity*, edited by Margaret D. Kamitsuka, 261–276. Minneapolis: Fortress Press, 2010.

Kant, Immanuel. *Lectures on Ethics*. Edited by Peter Heath and J. B. Schneewind. Cambridge: Cambridge University Press, 1997.

Kearney, Richard. "Losing Our Touch." Sunday Review *New York Times* (August 31, 2014): 4.

Kearney, Richard, and Brian Treanor, editors. *Carnal Hermeneutics*. New York: Fordham University Press, 2015.

Keck, Leander E. *The New Interpreter's Bible: Luke–John*. Nashville: Abingdon Press, 1994.

———. The New Interpreter's Bible: Matthew–Mark. Nashville: Abingdon Press, 1994.

Keller, Catherine. "Eschatology." In *Dictionary of Feminist Theologies*, edited by Letty M. Russell and J. Shannon Clarkson, 87. Louisville: Westminster John Knox Press, 1996.

Knight, Henry H., III. *Anticipating Heaven Below: Optimism of Grace from Wesley to the Pentecostals*. Eugene: Cascade Books, 2014.

Lajeunesse, Simon Louis, and J-M. Deslauriers. "Point de vue Masculin sur la Pornographie: des Fantasmes à la Réalité." *Sexologies* 22/1 (2013): 32–41.

Laumann, E. O., A. Nicolosi, D. B. Glasser, A. Paik, C. Gingell, E. Moreira, T. Wang for the GSSAB Investigators Group. "Sexual Problems among Women and Men Aged 40–80: Prevalence and Correlates Identified in the Global Study of Sexual Attitudes and Behaviors." *International Journal of Impotence Research* 17/1 (February 1, 2005): 39–57.

Laumann, E. O., A. Paik, and R. C. Rosen. "Sexual Dysfunction in the United States: Prevalence and Predictors." *Journal of the American Medical Association* 281/6 (February 10, 1999): 537–544.

Laytham, D. Brent. "'The Membership Includes the Dead': Wendell Berry's Port William Membership as *Communio Sanctorum*." In *Wendell Berry and Religion: Heaven's Earthly Life*, edited by Joel James Schuman and L. Roger Owens, 173–189. Lexington: University Press of Kentucky, 2009.

Lester, Andre D. *The Angry Christian: A Theology for Care and Counseling*. Louisville: Westminster John Knox Press, 2003.

Levine, Amy Jill. "The Word Becomes Flesh: Jesus, Gender and Sexuality." In *Jesus Two Thousand Years Later*, edited by James H. Charlesworth and Walter P. Weaver, 62–83. Harrisburg: Trinity Press International, 2000.

Levinson, Jon D. *Resurrection and the Restoration of Israel: The Ultimate Victory of the God of Life*. New Haven: Yale University Press, 2006.

Lewis, C. S. *Miracles: A Preliminary Study*. New York: MacMillan, 1947.

Lincoln, Timothy D. "Sacramental Marriage: A Possibility for Protestant Theology." *ATLAS Proceedings* (1995): 205–216.

Loader, William. *Sexuality and the Jesus Tradition*. Grand Rapids: William B. Eerdmans, 2005.

Lorde, Audre. *Sister Outsider: Essays and Speeches*. Freedom: Crossing Press, 1984.

Louw, Daniel J. *Cura Vita: Illness and the Healing of Life*. Wellington: Lux Verbi, 2008.

Luther, Martin. "Assertion of All the Articles of M. Luther Condemned by the Newest Bull of Leo X," November 29, 1520, Art. 27. In *Works of Martin Luther*, vol. 7. Weimar: Hermann Bohlhaus Nachfolger, 1897.

Luz, Ulrich. *Matthew: A Commentary*, vol. 2. Translated by Wilhelm C. Linss. Minneapolis: Augsburg Press, 1989.

MacDannell, Colleen, and Bernhard Lang. *Heaven: A History*. New Haven: Yale University Press, 1988.

Macinnis, Cara C., and Gordon Hodson. "Do American States with More Religious or Conservative Populations Search More for Sexual Content on Google?" *Archives of Sexual Behavior* 44/1 (January 2015): 137–147.

Mackin, Theodore, S.J. *The Marital Sacrament*. Mahwah: Paulist Press, 1989.

MacMullen, Ramsey. *Paganism in the Roman Empire*. New Haven: Yale University Press, 1981.

Malcolm, Michael, and George Sami Naufal. "Are Pornography and Marriage Substitutes for Young Men?" IZA Discussion Paper No. 8679. Posted December 6, 2014. Accessed December 1, 2015. http://ssrn.com/abstract=2534707.

Marcus, Joel. *Mark 8–16: A New Translation with Introduction and Commentary*. New Haven, CT: Yale University Press, 2009.

Martin, James Alfred, Jr. *Beauty and Holiness: The Dialogue between Aesthetics and Religion*. Princeton, NJ: Princeton University Press, 1991.

Mays, Melanie A. *A Body Knows: A Theopoetics of Death and Resurrection*. New York: Continuum, 1995.

McCabe, Herbert. *What Is Ethics All About?* Washington, DC: Corpus Books, 1968.

McCarty, Richard. "Eschatological Sex." *Theology and Sexuality* 19/2 (2013): 163–178.

McCormick, Patrick A. *God's Beauty: A Call to Justice*. Collegeville: Liturgical Press, 2012.

McGinn, Bernard. "Mysticism and Sexuality." *The Way Supplement* 77 (1993): 53.

———. *The Presence of God: A History of Western Christian Mysticism*. New York: Crossroad, 1991.

McGuckin, John Anthony. *The Orthodox Church: An Introduction to Its History, Doctrine and Spiritual Culture*. Oxford: Wiley Blackwell, 2011.

Medina, John J. *The Genetic Inferno: Inside the Seven Deadly Sins*. Cambridge, England: Cambridge University Press, 2000.

Mercer, Joyce Ann. "Virtual Sex, Actual Infidelity? A Practical Theological Inquiry into (Dis)Embodied Desire and Cybersex." In *City of Desires—A Place for God? Practical Theological Perspectives*, edited by R. Ruard Ganzevoort, Rein Brouwer, and Bonnie Miller-McLemore, 65–86. Zurich: Lit Verlag GmbH, 2013.

Middleton, J. Richard. *A New Heaven and Earth: Reclaiming*

Biblical Eschatology. Grand Rapids: Baker Academic, 2014.

Miles, Margaret R. "Sex and the City (of God): Is Sex Forfeited or Fulfilled in Augustine's Resurrection of Body?" *Journal of the American Academy of Religion* 73/2 (June 2005): 307–327.

———. *The Word Made Flesh: A History of Christian Thought*. Malden: Blackwell, 2005.

Miller, Keith Graber. "Sex without Shame." *Sojourners* 38/9 (September–October, 2009): 20–21, 23–25, 27.

Miller, Lisa. *Heaven: Our Enduring Fascination with the Afterlife*. New York: HarperCollins, 2010.

Milton, John. *Paradise Lost*. Introduction and notes by John A. Himes. New York: Dover, 2005.

Mirzoeff, Nicholas. *An Introduction to Visual Culture*. New York: Routledge, 1999.

Mischel, Walter. *The Marshmallow Test: Mastering Self-Control*. New York: Little, Brown, 2014.

Moore, Sebastian. *Jesus the Liberator of Desire*. New York: Crossroads, 1989.

Morse, Christopher. *The Difference Heaven Makes: Rehearing the Gospel as News*. New York: T&T Clark, 2010.

Nelson, James B. *Body Theology*. Louisville: Westminster John Knox Press, 1992.

The New American Bible, Revised Edition (*NABRE*). Translation approved by the United States Conference of Catholic Bishops. Washington, DC: United States Conference of Catholic Bishops, 2010.

Nicolosi, A., E. O. Laumann, D. B. Glasser, E. D. Moreira, Jr., A. Paik, C. Gingell (Global Study of Sexual Attitudes and Behaviors Investigators Group). "Sexual Behavior and Sexual Dysfunctions after Age 40: The Global Study of Sexual Attitudes and Behaviors." *Urology* 64/5 (November 2004): 991–997.

Northrup, Christiane. *Women's Bodies, Women's Wisdom: Creating Physical and Emotional Health and Healing*. New York: Random House, 2010.

Nussbaum, Martha C. "Constructing Love, Desire, and Care." In *Sex, Preference, and Family: Essays on Law and Nature*, edited by David M. Estlund and Martha C. Nussbaum, 17–43. New York: Oxford University Press, 1997.

O'Murchu, Diarmuid, M.S.C. *The Transformation of Desire: How Desire Became Corrupted—and How We Can Reclaim It.* Maryknoll: Orbis Books, 2007.

Panksepp, Jaak. *Affective Neuroscience: The Foundations of Human and Animal Emotions.* Oxford, England: Oxford University Press, 1998.

Paulsell, Stephanie. *Honoring the Body: Meditations on a Christian Practice.* San Francisco: Jossey-Bass, 2002.

Pfaus, James G. "Pathways of Sexual Desire." *Journal of Sex Medicine* 6 (2009): 1506–1533.

Philaretou, Andreas G., Ahmed Y. Mahfouz, and Katherine R. Allen. "Use of Internet Pornography and Men's Well-being." *International Journal of Men's Health* 4/2 (2005): 149–169.

Pius XI. "On Christian Marriage" (*Casti connubii*). Accessed August 19, 2015. http://w2.vatican.va/content/pius-xi/en/encyclicals/documents/hf_p-xi_enc_31121930_casti-connubii.html.

Pius XII. "Address to the Italian Catholic Society of Midwives." *Acta Apostolicae Sedis* 43 (October 29, 1951): 845–846. Accessed December 6, 2015. http://www.vatican.va/archive/aas/documents/AAS-43-1951-ocr.pdf.

Prusak, Bernard P. "Bodily Resurrection in Catholic Perspectives." *Theological Studies* 61/1 (February 2000): 64–105.

Rabinowicz, Harry. "Death." In *Encyclopedia Judaica*, 2nd ed., vol. 5, edited by Fred Skolnik, 510–513. New York: Thomson and Gale, 2007.

Ratzinger, Joseph. *Eschatology: Death and Eternal Life*, 2nd ed. Washington, DC: Catholic University of America Press, 1988.

Rees, Geoffrey. *The Romance of Innocent Sexuality.* Eugene: Cascade Books, 2011.

Reuther, Rosemary Radford. "Eschatology and Feminism." In *Lift Every Voice: Constructive Christian Theologies from the Underside*, edited by Susan Brooks Thistlethwaite and Mary Potter Engel, 129–142. San Francisco: HarperSanFrancisco, 1990.

Rhee, Helen. "Wealth, Poverty and Eschatology: Pre-Constantine Christian Social Thought and the Hope for the World to Come." In *Reading Patristic Texts on Social Ethics: Issues and Challenges for Twenty-First-Century Christian Social Thought*, edited by Johan Leemans, Brian J. Matz, and Johan Verstraeten, 64–84. Washington, DC: Catholic University Press of America, 2011.

Roberts, Robert C. *Spiritual Emotions: A Psychology of Christian Virtue*. Grand Rapids: William B. Eerdmans, 2007.

Rosenberg, Tina. *Join the Club: How Peer Pressure Can Transform the World*. New York: W.W. Norton, 2011.

Ross, Susan A. *Extravagant Affections: A Feminist Sacramental Theology*. New York: Continuum Books, 1998.

———. "Women, Beauty and Justice: Moving beyond von Balthasar." *Journal of the Society of Christian Ethics* 25/1 (Spring/Summer 2005): 79–98.

Roughgarden, Joan. *Evolution and Christian Faith: Reflections of an Evolutionary Biologist*. Washington, DC: Island Press, 2006.

———. *Evolution's Rainbow: Diversity, Sexuality and Gender in Nature and People*. Berkeley: University of California Press, 2004.

Ruddy, Christopher. "In Defense of Desire: The Theology of James Alison." *Commonweal* 136/2 (January 30, 2009): 12–15.

Ryan, Christopher, and Cacilda Jetha. *Sex at Dawn: How We Mate, Why We Stray and What It Means for Modern Relationships*. New York: Harper Books, 2010.

Sabina, Chiara, Janis Wolak, and David Finkelhor. "The Nature and Dynamics of Internet Pornography Exposure for Youth." *CyberPsychology and Behavior* 11/6 (December 2008): 691–693.

Sabino, Kornrich, Julie Brines, and Katrina Leupp. "Egalitarianism, Housework, and Sexual Frequency in Marriage." *American Sociological Review* 78/1 (2013): 26–50.

Sacred Congregation for Divine Worship. *Pastoral Care of the Dead (Ordo Exsequiarum)*. 1969.

Sacred Congregation for the Doctrine of the Faith. "Letter on Certain Questions concerning Eschatology." 1979. Accessed

November 20, 2015. http://www.vatican.va/roman_curia/congregations/cfaith/documents/rc_con_cfaith_doc_19790517_escatologia_en.html.

Salzman, Todd A., and Michael G. Lawler. *The Sexual Person: Toward a Renewed Catholic Anthropology*. Washington, DC: Georgetown University Press, 2008.

Scroggs, Robin. "Paul and the Eschatological Woman." *Journal of the American Academy of Religion* 40/3 (Spring 1972): 283–303.

Second Vatican Council. *Pastoral Constitution on the Church in the Modern World* (*Gaudium et spes*). 1965. Accessed December 3, 2015. http://www.vatican.va/archive/hist_councils/ii_vatican_council/documents/vat-ii_cons_19651207_gaudium-et-spes_en.html.

Segal, Alan F. *Life after Death: A History of the Afterlife in Western Religion*. New York: Doubleday, 2004.

Segal, Lynne, and Mary McIntosh. *Sex Exposed: Sexuality and the Pornography Debate*. London: Virago, 1992.

Seidman, Stuart N., and Steven P. Roose. "The Sexual Effects of Testosterone Replacement in Depressed Men: Randomized, Placebo-controlled Clinical Trials." *Journal of Sexual Marital Therapy* 32/3 (May–June, 2006): 267–273.

Sheldrake, Philip. *Befriending Our Desires*. Ottawa: Novalis, 2001.

Shifren, J. L., B. U. Monz, P. A. Russo, A. Segretti, and C. B. Johannes. "Sexual Problems and Distress in U.S. Women: Prevalence and Correlates." *Obstetrics and Gynecology* 122/5 (2008): 970–978.

Sigurdson, Ola. "The Passion of Christ: On the Social Production of Desire." In *Saving Desire: The Seduction of Christian Theology*, edited by F. LeRon Shults and Jan-Olav Henriksen, 31–54. Grand Rapids: William B. Eerdmans, 2011.

Smedes, Lewis B. *Sex for Christians: The Limits and Liberties of Sexual Living*, rev. ed. Grand Rapids: William B. Eerdmans, 1994.

Smit, Laura A. *Loves Me, Loves Me Not: The Ethics of Unrequited Love*. Grand Rapids: Baker Academic Press, 2005.

Smith, Daniel A. *Revisiting the Empty Tomb: The Early History of Easter*. Minneapolis: Fortress Press, 2010.

Smith, Sylvia Thorson. *Pornography: Far from the Song of Songs*. Louisville: Office of the General Assembly, Presbyterian Church USA, 1988.

Soble, Alan. "A History of Erotic Philosophy." *The Journal of Sex Research* 46/2–3 (March–June 2009): 104–120.

Stein, Dylan, Richard Silvera, Robert Hagerty, and Michael Marmor. "Viewing Pornography Depicting Unprotected Anal Intercourse: Are There Implications for HIV Prevention among Men Who Have Sex with Men?" *Archives of Sexual Behavior* 41/2 (2012): 411–419.

Steinfels, Peter. "Contraception and Honesty: A Proposal for the Next Synod." *Commonweal* 142/10 (June 1, 2015): 12–19.

Stuart, Elizabeth. "Queering Death." In *The Sexual Theologian: Essays on Sex, God and Politics*, edited by Marcella Althaus-Reid and Lisa Isherwood, 58–70. London: Continuum, 2005.

Taylor, Barbara Brown. "Our Bodies, Our Faith." *Christian Century* 126/2 (January 27, 2009): 24–29.

Tertullian. *The Resurrection of the Dead*, chapter 40. Accessed August 10, 2011. www.newadvent.org/fathers/0316.htm.

Thiel, John E. "Augustine on Eros, Desire, and Sexuality." In *The Embrace of Eros: Bodies, Desires, and Sexuality in Christianity*, edited by Margaret D. Kamitsuka, 67–81. Minneapolis: Fortress Press, 2010.

———. "For What May We Hope? Thoughts on the Eschatological Imagination." *Theological Studies* 67/3 (September 2006): 517–541.

Thompson, Deanna A. "Hoping for More: How Eschatology Matters for Lutheran Feminist Theologies." In *Transformative Lutheran Theologies: Feminist, Womanist and Mujerista Perspectives*, edited by Mary J. Streufert, 225–236. Minneapolis: Fortress Press, 2010.

Tiefer, Leonore. *Sex Is Not a Natural Act*. Boulder: Westview, 2004.

Timmerman, Joan H. *The Mardi Gras Syndrome: Rethinking Christian Sexuality*. New York: Crossroads, 1984.

Traina, Cristina H. L. *Erotic Attunement: Parenthood and the Ethics of Sensuality between Unequals*. Chicago: University of Chicago Press, 2011.

Twain, Mark. *Letters from the Earth*. Edited by Bernard Devoto. New York: Harper and Row, 1938.

Ussher, Jane M. *Fantasies of Femininity: Reframing the Boundaries of Sex*. New Brunswick: Rutgers University Press, 1997.

Vacek, Edward Collins, S.J. *Love Human and Divine: The Heart of Christian Ethics*. Washington, DC: Georgetown University Press, 1994.

———. "Orthodoxy Requires Orthopathy: Emotions in Theology." *Horizons* 40/2 (December 2013): 218–241.

Volf, Miroslav. "The Trinity and Gender Identity." In *Gospel and Gender: A Trinitarian Engagement with Being Male and Female in Christ*, edited by Douglas A. Campbell, 213–237. London: T&T Clark, 2003.

Wall, Robert W., J. Paul Sampley, and N. T. Wright. *The New Interpreter's Bible: Acts–First Corinthians*. Nashville: Abingdon Press, 1994.

Wallace-Hadrill, D. S. *Christian Antioch: A Study of Early Christian Thought in the East*. New York: Cambridge University Press, 1982.

Ward, Graham. "Politics of Embodiment and the Mystery of All Flesh." In *The Sexual Theologian: Essays on Sex, God and Politics*, edited by Marcella Althaus-Reid and Lisa Isherwood, 71–85. New York: T&T Clark International, 2004.

Warren, Rick, Daniel Amen, and Mark Hyman. *The Daniel Plan: 40 Days to a Healthier Life*. Grand Rapids: Zondervan, 2013.

Whitehead, James D., and Evelyn Eaton Whitehead. *Holy Eros: Recovering the Passion of God*. Maryknoll: Orbis Books, 2009.

Wiesner-Hanks, Merry E. *Christianity and Sexuality in the Early Modern World: Regulating Desire, Reforming Practice*. New York: Routledge, 2000.

Williams, Rowan. "The Body's Grace." Accessed August 20, 2015. http://www.igreens.org.uk/bodys_grace.htm.

Williamson, Lamar, Jr. *Mark: Interpretation: A Bible Commentary for Teaching and Preaching*. Atlanta: John Knox Press, 1983.

Wilson, Gary. "The Great Porn Experiment." Accessed November 24, 2014. http://www.singjupost.com/gary-wilson-discusses-great-porn-experiment-transcript/2/.

Witherington, Ben, III. *The Rest of Life: Rest, Play, Eating, Studying, Sex from a Kingdom Perspective*. Grand Rapids: William B. Eerdmans, 2012.

Wright, Nicholas Thomas (aka N. T.). *The Resurrection of the Son of God*. Minneapolis: Fortress Press, 2003.

———. *Surprised by Hope: Rethinking Heaven, the Resurrection, and the Mission of the Church*. New York: HarperCollins Books, 2008.

Wright, Paul J. "A Longitudinal Analysis of U.S. Adults' Pornography Exposure: Sexual Socialization, Selective Exposure, and the Moderating Role of Unhappiness." *Journal of Media Psychology: Theories, Methods, and Applications* 24/2 (2012): 67–76.

Yoder, Christine Roy. "The Shaping of Desire in Proverbs 1–9." In *City of Desires—A Place for God? Practical Theological Perspectives*, edited by R. Ruard Ganzevoort, Rein Brouwer, and Bonnie Miller-McLemore, 148–163. Zurich: Lit Verlag GmbH, 2013.

INDEX